Midway

MAGIC

BY SCOTT MCGAUGH

C·S

CDS BOOKS

CDS
425 Madison Avenue
New York, NY 10017
(212) 223-2696, Fax (212) 223-1504

or to

Scott McGaugh
scott@midwaymagic.com
www.midwaymagic.com

Book design and typeformatting by Bernard Schleifer
Printed in the United States of America
10 9 8 7 6 5 4 3 2

To Jerrold D. McGaugh
and fellow WWII veterans
who silently sacrificed
to make today possible

CONTENTS

AN ENDURING MAGIC

by Wally Schirra
Astronaut,
USS Midway naval aviator

As the nuclear dust over Hiroshima and Nagasaki settled, a ship slipped out of its berth to embark on what became a 47-year odyssey. Coming out of the Naval Academy, I had no idea I might become part of an adventure that crossed every ocean on the globe—one that began a week after Japan surrendered World War II in 1945 and ended only after the liberation of Kuwait in 1991. More than 200,000 American men and—by extension, their families—shared this pioneering odyssey, one that cost lives, took lives, and saved lives. The ship was the United States aircraft carrier USS Midway.

It was a voyage like no other. Midway CV-41 (the designation means Midway was the 41st "carrier version" ship in the Navy) stood at the heart of nearly every international crisis, conflict, disaster, and threat that defined our world in the second half of the twentieth century. Launched in 1945, Midway was as much a microcosm of American society and politics at the end of WWII as it was in 1992 when it passed the Old Point Loma Lighthouse and turned into San Diego Bay for decommissioning at NAS North Island, a cradle of naval aviation nearly 80 years earlier.

In her time, she was an engineering marvel. For the first 10 years of her active duty, she was the largest ship in the world—the first that was too large to sail through the Panama Canal. Her design was drawn from the lessons of WWII. Modifications to the ship over the ensuing

47 years reflected each new generation of naval aviation, technology, and warfare.

Literally a "city at sea" with a combined ship's company and air wing crew of 4,500, Midway was a floating isle of sovereignty, built to protect, enforce, and enhance American interests. She projected power and purpose independent of nations' borders and ground-based interference. When the only captured German V-2 rocket to be tested at sea was launched from her stern near Bermuda, the Midway proved the potential of naval missile warfare. Missions ranged from a show of nuclear deterrent force in the early days of the Cold War to evacuating refugees fleeing a volcanic eruption in Southeast Asia 40 years later. CV-41, the namesake of the Midway class of aircraft carrier, became the prototype for the role the aircraft carrier plays today in foreign policy. When President Clinton was aboard the carrier Theodore Roosevelt in 1997, he summed up more than 75 years of American aircraft carrier experience: "When word of a crisis breaks out in Washington, it's no accident the first question that comes to everyone's lips is where is the nearest carrier?"

Midway's extraordinary odyssey tracked the unprecedented and sometimes cataclysmic changes the world has experienced over the past 50 years. Launched only a few months before Winston Churchill proclaimed an Iron Curtain was descending across Europe, she was decommissioned the year former President Bush and Boris Yeltsin formally proclaimed an end to the same Cold War. When her keel first touched the water, the first all-electronic computer was unveiled, a contraption spanning 800 square feet with 18,000 vacuum tubes. By the time Midway was decommissioned, personal digital assistants had made their debut. In 1945, the United Nations was created. Almost 47 years later, Midway was being decommissioned as Yugoslavia and Czechoslovakia were disintegrating into a handful of warring republics. As the Navy's "Tip of the Sword" of American military foreign policy, Midway's first commander in chief was President Harry S. Truman. In her career, she and her men answered the call from seven subsequent presidents, a feat unmatched in carrier history.

Over that time, Midway developed a reputation throughout the armed services called "Midway Magic," a name that expressed the extraordinary track record of accomplishment and active-duty stamina of the carrier and her men. Midway's reputation was built over five decades by hundreds of thousands of men, a total greater than the population of most state capitals.

Most served aboard for two years or less. They were young men, many still teenagers, asked to assume unimagined responsibility and perform mission-critical tasks on a daily basis. Some chose to make the Navy a career. For others it was two years of force-fed maturity through intensive training and an opportunity to see the world, often in the vortex of international crisis. Through "Midway Magic," the nation's call was always answered. For me, it led elsewhere.

I was one of those fresh-faced kids aboard Midway in 1950, learning to be a hot-shot aviator at the dawn of the jet age. We were patrolling the Mediterranean, the backyard of the Cold War as it blanketed Europe in a postwar world that had been turned upside down. Long-standing alliances were crumbling as new international relationships tentatively emerged. Half a world away, a war broke out in Korea.

Air support was critically needed and the aircraft carrier Philippine Sea was one of those that got the call. Only a month before, she had transferred from Norfolk to San Diego, in part because she could get through the Panama Canal and thereby get to San Diego relatively quickly. Meanwhile, Midway—too large for the Panama Canal—remained on duty in the Med and homeported in Norfolk. I knew that several Navy aviators aboard the Philippine Sea were slated for an Air Force exchange program. But with the outbreak of the Korean War, they likely had to remain aboard the Philippine Sea. (The carrier ultimately played a long and distinguished role in the Korean War, launching as many as 145 sorties a day.) So I did some checking, applied for one of those anticipated vacancies in the Air Force exchange program, and was accepted. Coupled with my jet experience aboard Midway, the transfer put me into a career trajectory that 12 years later led to piloting a Mercury spacecraft and splashing down only 275 miles northeast of an island called Midway. One of the original seven astronauts at NASA, my training as a young pup of 27 aboard Midway ultimately led to nearly 300 flight hours in space and to becoming the only astronaut to fly missions aboard Mercury, Gemini, and Apollo spacecraft.

For men and nations alike, Midway did more than influence our world. Midway dictated the course of world events, sometimes by her mere presence as a beat cop stepping into the middle of a heated dispute, at other times as the fireman rushing into harm's way to save lives. For me and thousands of other young men over the expanse of nearly 50 years,

Midway Magic showed each of us our backbone, inspired us to never cut our dreams to fit, and taught us values and ideals that served as guideposts for the rest of our lives. And in the hearts and souls of the men who served aboard her, the magic continues to this day.

CHAPTER 1

FROSTBITE

B UDDY HERRMANN'S HANDS ACHED as he held on to the ship's wheel in
the darkened pilothouse. Night blanketed the USS Midway as
60-knot winds drove rolling mountains of waves into the world's most
sophisticated aircraft carrier on its first mission. Each wave's attack spun
the wheel free from his grip, throwing Herrmann against nearby equipment. Bruised and battered, he fought one thundering wave after another
through the night. Below on the hangar deck, each roll pitched men off
their feet and bounced them across the nonskid surface. Some broke
fingers when they tried to grab a recessed padeye as they scraped along the
tarred surface. Back and forth every few seconds, all night across the
square steel cavern. The Labrador Sea threatened to pound the life out
of Midway.

The enemy had learned to fear America's warm-water carriers in
World War II. Now war planners contemplated a new enemy, Russia, with
sub-Arctic navy bases. What were the physical and natural limits of aircraft
carrier deployment and effectiveness in the far reaches of the north
Atlantic? The Navy knew what humidity could do to a dive-bomber. But
what about frost? The effects of rain could be managed, but what of snow?
To find out, the Navy ordered the largest and most sophisticated aircraft

carrier in the world to steam outside the known limits of naval aviation.

Operation Frostbite might provide answers. The monthlong exercise in March 1946 would be conducted in the Labrador Sea and Davis Strait, a triangle of turbulent and uncertain ocean bordered by Labrador, Newfoundland, and Greenland. An unusual confluence of land, wind, and current created demanding and brutal naval aviation conditions. Low-pressure systems moving through the Labrador Sea often rode on 40- to 60-knot gales. Cold, dry northerly winds danced on the churning sea and produced instant snow showers. When the northerly winds blew hard enough, secondary cold fronts formed, resembling squall lines that could extend as much as 200 miles in a northeast-southwest line across the Labrador Sea.

It was there that Navy planners decided to test the hardened steel of Midway. On March 1, Midway left berth ZEBRA at NAS Norfolk. As it passed through the mouth of Chesapeake Bay bracketed by Cape Charles and Cape Henry, the flight deck and hangar bays echoed with the sounds of an air wing complement that represented the best of naval aviation at the time. But in the postwar era of massive demobilization, Midway's crew was not as proven as the carrier's aircraft inventory. Of the 82 pilots on board for Operation Frostbite, 35 were new to aircraft carriers and only 16 had seen combat. They were all led by the commander of the air group (CAG), Tommy Blackburn, one of the Navy's most famous war aces.

Only three years earlier Blackburn had created the famed VF-17 Jolly Rogers squadron. The VF-17 Jolly Rogers became known as one of the deadliest squadrons of WWII. In one day alone during the Battle of the Solomon Sea, Blackburn's squadron was credited with 18.5 confirmed kills and seven damaged enemy aircraft. In only five months of action in the Solomons, 12 Jolly Roger pilots became aces, the most of any Navy unit. Shorter than every man in his command, Blackburn's pencil-thin mustache and piercing eyes radiated a bravado that appealed even to the men who towered over him. Attitude was all-important to Blackburn. It was a cocky, battle-hardened CAG Tommy Blackburn who led Midway pilots in Operation Frostbite as the nation watched.

Harry Brumbaugh and his crewman William Anton Conrad Jr. were worried. Flying near the Arctic Circle was largely unknown territory. Not even their CAG had flown in blowing snow before. They had never launched from an icy flight deck. And they weren't anxious to test a new flight suit—called a "poopy" suit—that the Navy claimed would minimize hypothermia in water that froze a man to death in minutes.

But it would be at least a week before Brumbaugh and Conrad had to confront their fears in a brutally cold headwind as Midway headed north. Until then, they could take comfort in the routine of daily flight operations in more benign conditions. About 100 miles from Norfolk, that routine unraveled.

One morning, after a successful launch, they settled into their final approach astern of Midway. Swaying in the wind, Conrad's plane homed in on the middle of the 12 arresting wires stretched across the deck. His engine briefly sputtered, caught, and then died. Quickly losing speed against the headwind, the plane nosed up, then settled, and slammed into the sea. The plane split in half when it spun into the water, throwing Brumbaugh free. In the choking, churning wake of Midway, Brumbaugh climbed into a life raft as another plane dropped a smoke bomb to mark the crash site. Red-, white-, and blue-helmeted flight deck crews scanned the ocean, hoping to spot Conrad among the floating wreckage as Midway steamed away. He was never found. After 3,000 successful landings and takeoffs, Midway had lost its first man. In a somber mood, Midway's task group resumed its course toward the sub-Arctic.

On the third day out of Norfolk, Midway left the Gulf Stream and within a few days the sea temperature plummeted from 68 to 38 degrees. Midway sailors were issued standard foul-weather gear: windbreakers over several layers of clothing that included wool socks, long johns, and jackets. Standard issue also included a dark blue face mask, a must for those who regularly worked in 20- to 30-knot icy winds. Midway's crew would discover the Navy had a long way to go in perfecting foul-weather gear.

As the days rolled by and Midway and its escorts steamed north, the calm weather and flat water were precisely what the task group's commander, Rear Admiral John H. Cassady, didn't want. The task group soon reached the Grand Banks and passed not far from where an iceberg had sunk the Titanic. It steamed almost due north toward Newfoundland and then turned northwest in search of foul weather. The armada continued past the mouth of the St. Lawrence Seaway, and then on past Labrador, still heading northwest through the Davis Strait, which began to narrow as Greenland loomed to the northeast. Still, only good weather.

Good weather meant CAG Blackburn could turn up the heat on his collection of greenhorn pilots. As Corsairs and Helldivers were put through their paces, pilots came to count on a flight deck officer as grizzled and hoarse-voiced as any man in the Navy. Vern Prather was responsible for the 187 men who toiled as plane handlers, chockers, and the others who made launch and recovery on a floating steel platform possible.

A veteran of four carriers and 17 years' Navy experience, Prather told stories dating back to his assignment aboard the Langley, a converted coal ship that was the Navy's first aircraft carrier a lifetime ago. "Hell, I remember how we ran after those damn biplanes after they hit the deck. If we didn't catch 'em, they sure as hell kept on goin' over the side," he'd tell anyone who would listen. "'Course, we didn't have to run far. Shee-it, Langley was so small a man could spit from one side of the deck to the other."

To the youngsters on the Navy's 41st carrier, it seemed Prather had survived every major World War II battle in the Pacific. He was an unforgettable man as quick to encourage as he was to lecture. His slow Southern drawl belied an intensity gilded with experience that everyone on Midway came to respect. Prather was near legendary in the eyes of young men at sea for the first time in their lives.

After almost a week of fruitlessly searching for sub-Arctic weather, Midway had steamed more than 3,500 miles and was only 210 miles south of the Arctic Circle. The carrier's accompanying task force comprised of destroyers and supply ships kept pace. Rear Admiral Cassady paced back and forth on the flag bridge. Midway's captain, H. S. Duckworth, stood nearby and out of Cassady's path.

"To tell the truth, I'm disappointed," said Cassady. "All we've had is mild weather so we'll quit steaming north. Turn south and west. Head for the Labrador ice fields. We'll find what we're looking for—cold, dirty weather." Cassady was rolling late-winter dice, betting the fierce winds blowing to the east out onto the ice fields would produce the hellish weather he sought for Midway's armada.

Admiral Cassady's bet paid off. It wasn't long before the weather roughened as the wind picked up to 35 miles per hour as Midway's guns crusted with ice. The next day, March 8, howling winds and gray, heavy clouds shrouded the task group. Usually 50 feet above the water in calm seas, Midway's flight deck dug into the oncoming waves and green roiling seas raced down the deck, reaching the superstructure before spilling over the side.

As blowing wave crests and snow attacked the bridge, one of Midway's earliest legends began to take shape. Midway leaned sideways into each rolling crest as the seas strengthened. Sailors' eyes widened as the carrier's momentum grew from one roll to the next. Rumors shot through a terrified crew about just how far Midway was rolling between crests. The crew didn't know that the day Midway had been launched the carrier was top-heavy. It had been built on a Montana-class battleship hull because early-war carrier losses prompted an emergency change in Navy ship construction plans. It made Midway one of the most unstable carriers in the fleet.

Midway officially recorded a 19-degree roll in Operation Frostbite. It was the first of many rolls that served as legendary memory makers for the 200,000 sailors who served on the carrier. Yet it was dwarfed by the rolls suffered by the crews of the accompanying destroyers on Operation Frostbite. On March 8, they recorded 42-degree rolls, foul-weather pitching so severe that their crews joked that white caps rolled across their coffee cups. The next day the seas rose even higher as the sky fell. It began to snow, testing the crew's ability to clear two and a half acres of flight deck. It snowed the next day and the day after that. Midway had found the weather it wanted: cold, blustery winds driving seas boiling with white caps as ice fields and icebergs appeared on the horizon. Flight deck crews leaned into a stinging wind, feet wide apart, soles always flat on the deck to keep from soaring over the side. For the next two weeks angry storms that merged with the ocean would test pilots and ship's company alike. It was perfect.

Dick Parker couldn't wait to face those tests in what many pilots called a "flying shithouse." One of the few Naval Academy graduates aboard Midway, at six feet four inches Parker towered over his fellow pilots and shipmates. His warm, engaging handshake reflected a man who flew hard, a man whose every gesture was gauged at full throttle. A long patrician nose divided his blue-gray eyes and an analytical mind powered his rise to commanding officer of squadron VB-74. He first flew aboard Midway on Halloween Day, 1945.

Parker flew an SB2C Helldiver. "It was too goddamn slow, didn't maneuver at all and once you put it into a dive, that was it," one pilot groused. Parker and others in his squadron had to figure out how to land a lumbering World War II dive-bomber with a mind of its own in a sub-Arctic storm. And they had to do it on an aircraft carrier so long and top-heavy its keel arched upward in heavy seas, forcing the bow down into the oncoming waves. Many Midway pilots swore they could see the carrier bend in heavy seas as they approached.

If Parker missed all 12 arresting wires in those conditions it could cost his life and the lives of dozens of other men. He prayed the engine would respond when he "firewalled" the throttle, dropped a wing, and turned toward open ocean. Parker had less than two seconds to maneuver his plane up and off the flight deck. If man or motor were a split second slow, he'd plow into sailors tending aircraft parked on the bow.

Every landing in the thick Arctic air was an adventure during Operation Frostbite. "Punch" Knox became famous when, for some unknown reason, he didn't take a wave-off command and instead chose to land. He promptly slid off the side of the deck. Parker and others watched it in slow motion, the plane slowly toppling over the side, taking out deck-edge antennas before hanging up on the sponson deck that ran along most of both sides and below the flight deck. Knox was a lucky pilot that day in the north Atlantic. With his plane hanging by its tail 35 feet above the water, he gingerly eased out of his cockpit, climbed back up the fuselage and onto the deck to windswept safety.

In the sub-Arctic, the water was the enemy. A man's life in the ocean was measured in minutes. Operation Frostbite tested Midway pilots both in the air and the sea. Pilots were given very specific instructions in how to wear the new rubberized nylon poopy suit. First, avoid overheating and sweating by dressing too quickly. Sweat becomes ice in the sub-Arctic. Wear long underwear, two pairs of socks, two pairs of gloves, and a scarf. Keep everything bone dry. Walk—don't run—to the plane. And don't touch metal with bare hands.

The pilots discovered the key to the poopy suit was putting it on correctly. If a pilot failed to tie the bottoms of the trousers tightly or neglected to cinch the scarf around his neck, 35-degree water seeped inside the suit and not only threatened the pilot with hypothermia, but could pull him under the surface before a destroyer or helicopter reached him.

W. F. Paris was among the first to find out if the poopy suit was up to sub-Arctic conditions. One day Paris sat scanning the controls in his Helldiver as it sat on the catapult. He looked up, then over and down at the flight deck crew. He thought he saw the signal to go to full throttle. He was wrong. The catapult wasn't ready. Paris left the catapult behind as he rumbled toward the bow at only 60 miles an hour. He had barely raised the landing gear before he pancaked into the water.

Gasping for breath, Paris clambered out onto the wing of his aircraft seconds before Midway's bow wave washed him into the icy water. He and his crewman, John Thomas, scrambled into a life raft and rode it in high waves, their hands turning a creamy white before Midway's plane guard destroyer came alongside. The ship's crane dropped a rescue basket together with a swimmer into the water, a technique that had not been used before to rescue downed pilots. It saved the two pilots' lives.

A few days later, Ensign Thomas Dixon Keller and his gunner approached Midway in another Helldiver. When they were waved off Keller went to full throttle, raised his flaps, and felt a severe drag on the right wing. It wasn't a good sign. Keller did everything he could to close the flap that forced a 10-degree bank to the right. It remained "full open." The north Atlantic was no place to be flying in circles, low on fuel, and with no landing strip other than Midway for hundreds of miles. Keller opened and closed the bomb doors to bleed any air that might have seeped into the hydraulic system. The flap remained frozen. Keller watched his engine temperature gauge redline, a dangerous sign that prompted CAG Blackburn to order him to land in the water in front of one of the destroyers.

Keller had never ditched in the ocean. He had been warned the water would feel like concrete and could pound a man into unconsciousness. Keller fought to steady his shaking hands as he lined up and then stalled a few feet above the frigid water. He hit hard. He couldn't tell whether seconds or minutes passed before his senses cleared enough to scramble into a life raft and join his gunner. They were far from being out of danger, though. Water had seeped inside the gunner's poopy suit and he had lost his gloves in the crash. He soon began to shiver uncontrollably as his hands turned fish-belly white. His joints stiffened. He tried to climb into the rescue basket hanging from the destroyer, only to roll out of it and drop into the roiling sea. The rescue diver repeatedly grabbed his collar and yanked him back into the life raft. Finally, a second line stabilized the rescue basket so that Keller and his crewman could be hauled to safety.

Small islands of ice pounded Midway's hull as planes flew and lookouts watched for icebergs. One night 25-foot waves crashed into Midway's hull, hurling tons of ice at one of Midway's weakest points, the roller curtain on the hangar deck. The roller curtain was a giant door that could be raised to allow the exhaust fumes from planes on the hangar deck to escape. In the southern latitudes during heavy seas, the roller curtain was lifted six feet to allow the tops of waves to harmlessly wash in and out of the carrier. But in sub-Arctic conditions, the roller curtains were closed to keep tons of ice from flooding Midway. The relentless pounding of the ice crumpled Midway's massive roller curtain as seawater seeped into the carrier.

Like many young men, seaman Donald Frye thought he was invincible as he climbed into his bunk three decks below the hangar deck and deep inside Midway. Frye, a restless teenager who hailed from York, Pennsylvania, had enlisted less than a year earlier. He manned a gun tub station on Midway and had just finished standing another watch that night in the middle of a sub-Arctic winter.

A sparkle of light caught Frye's eye as he was about to go to sleep. He reached up and touched the bulkhead. It was cold. It was wet. It was seawater. The north Atlantic had seeped down through dimly light passages and into the darkened berths and spaces of Midway. Several levels below the flight deck, Frye could smell the salt water. He suddenly felt anything but invincible.

Each day's storm was another round in the prizefight that became Operation Frostbite. Freshly forged steel buckled under the onslaught. Brand-new, 15-man life rafts were ripped from their lashings just under the flight deck and disappeared in the green-black sea. Frye knew it was even worse for the men on the destroyers that accompanied Midway. Driven by 60-mile-an-hour winds, waves avalanched onto destroyers that now seemed no sturdier than tin cans, burying the deck and most of the superstructure while plunging much of the ship underwater for several terrifying seconds. The rolling destroyers were so unstable their cooks couldn't get bread dough to rise in the relentless high seas. Midway's bakers supplied the task group with baked bread, transferring loaves to other ships when they came alongside to refuel.

While sailors on destroyers feared being swamped, for Frye and others, the most terrifying moments came when the carrier's bow pierced a monster wave. Like a porpoise arching a return to the water, Midway's bow sometimes bit hard into the wave, thrusting the fantail free of the ocean. When all four of Midway's 18-foot screws lifted into the air and raced at an unnerving speed, the chilling vibration reached into every crevice of the ship.

Storms raged day after day. The pitching, the rolling, the seasickness were unrelenting. Herrmann, Frye, and others who could stand up looked forward to movie night on the hangar deck for distraction. As others played basketball or sparred in a makeshift boxing ring nearby, they sat in metal folding chairs and leaned into each wave as they watched two-year-old movies. Sometimes the screech from the sliding chairs drowned out the movies' soundtracks as Midway rolled through the night.

When plane captain Bill Larkin stood on the flight deck and leaned into the stinging black wind, memories of the hot, humid Caribbean nights of his previous assignment seemed a fairy tale. The West Virginia native had enlisted in 1944 and spent most of the last year of the war based in Puerto Rico, tending patrol aircraft that guarded the Panama Canal. He was one of the few veterans on Midway who could explain the real meaning of sailing in harm's way.

Larkin had been on a transport heading south along the eastern seaboard as he marveled at "the strings of convoys as far as a man could see, all headed east toward Europe." That sense of wonder melted into horror one day when a German torpedo turned a tanker off Savannah, Georgia, into a searing ball of flame that sank in minutes. Horror turned to worry when Larkin's transport left the convoy and plodded south at only 10 knots, straight into the path of a German submarine that had surfaced. Larkin and 500 men froze, willing themselves invisible. Minutes passed while his eyes swept the ocean for the wake of an inbound torpedo. None came as the submarine disappeared into the Atlantic. Perhaps Larkin's troop transport had been mistaken for a minor supply ship. Perhaps the submarine was out of torpedoes.

Larkin's job on the flight deck was to make sure his squadron's aircraft crew were ready to fly while avoiding frostbite. Left unprotected, both man and machine would freeze within minutes. It took three pairs of gloves to keep the blood moving through a man's hands, but that left him with almost no manual dexterity. Oil, the lifeblood of the aircraft, had to be protected from the coagulating cold. Larkin found the solution: add gasoline to the oil as an antifreeze. A special blanket was designed to cover the motor of each aircraft and customized to accommodate a hot air tube so that a gasoline-powered blower could keep the motors warm. Sometimes plane crews used their bodies as a windbreak to protect the small fires they built under the engines of their aircraft. Ingenuity triumphed over the bitter cold.

As plane captain, Larkin made sure his assigned aircraft was operating properly before a pilot took control. He checked to see that fueling was completed. Although he couldn't fly, Larkin climbed up into the plane and warmed it up, checking the magnetos, and conducting last-minute systems checks before handing it over to the pilot and escorting the aircraft to the catapult.

It was one of the most dangerous jobs on Midway. At times during flight operations, 20 planes rumbled as their motors loosened, their blurred propellers only a few feet apart. Larkin hung on to the wheel well under his plane to keep from being blown off his feet as his pilot waited for his turn on the catapult. Crouching low, Larkin leap-frogged the wheel chocks from back to front as the plane taxied toward its turn on the catapult. Once his pilot got set up on the catapult, he went to full throttle. Larkin hung on tighter to keep from getting blown into the planes behind him. It was even more treacherous when Larkin manually pulled down some aircrafts' folded wings into their locked position as they approached the catapult. When there was work to do, hanging on for safety became a luxury.

The nation followed Operation Frostbite. Nearly a dozen reporters and photographers sailed with the crew. The Associated Press, United Press International, *Boston Globe, Washington Star*, International News Service, and others filed daily dispatches. The presence of civilians made the flight deck even more dangerous. One day as Larkin walked away from a plane, a *Time* magazine photographer came out, knocking Larkin off his feet and under the blurred propeller of a Corsair. Another plane captain screamed at the pilot to cut his engine as Larkin froze on the cold steel deck, the whine of the prop only three feet above his head. It was nearly a minute before the propeller slowed to a stop. For the remainder of Operation Frostbite civilians were not allowed on the flight deck without an escort.

While the flight deck crew moved across the slick deck, others stood stock still in the howling wind for hours. Likely the coldest job went to the sailors who stood "smoke watch." Perched on the highest platform on the mast, they reported any fouled smoke rising from any of Midway's 12 smokestacks to engineering. As Midway plowed through brutal wind and plummeting temperatures, the ship's doctor found the men's body temperature dropped to 96 degrees during a four-hour watch. Orders immediately were issued to limit outside watches to two hours.

Midway entered ice fields as it approached Greenland in the second week of Operation Frostbite. The width of the ice fields along the Labrador coast averaged 150 miles. As Midway approached, the sea's temperature dropped another five degrees to near freezing. Out on deck, the air temperature plummeted six degrees more. When the ice fields dampened the seas and wind, pure cold became the enemy of the crew of Midway as they watched for icebergs, flew, and learned.

Finally on March 26, Midway turned south, destined for New York City. When the carrier reached its 92nd Street berth just before 1200 on March 28, Midway had become the first aircraft carrier to operate for an extended period among sub-Arctic winds, ice fields, and icebergs. Its pilots had crashed into paralyzing waters and all but one had survived. Flight deck crews had learned how to launch and recover planes in weather that froze men and water in minutes. The Navy now understood how to fly among the icebergs. A green, largely untested crew developed a sense of unity that grew from overcoming adversity. They came home armed with self-confidence, proud in knowing they had blazed a new naval aviation trail.

A YEAR EARLIER, stars had surrounded the giant silhouette of Midway towering into the night on the last day of winter in March 1945. At river's edge it rose more than 150 feet into the blackened sky. Night sounds drifted across the shipyard. The granular grind of an outboard motor pushed a skiff downstream toward Chesapeake Bay. Off in the distance, a dog yapped in an unlit backyard. Red, white, and blue bunting along the flight deck gently wobbled high in the night breeze that drifted across the James River. Guarded and silent, the hulk soon would be the largest and most powerful ship in the world.

Half a world away British troops slogged toward Mandalay, Burma. A squadron of B-29 bombers lined up to drop mines into Japanese waters. Iwo Jima raged for a 30th day. Tens of thousands of young men were preparing to invade an island called Okinawa. And teenagers fresh out of high school would soon join exhausted Navy veterans who had survived horrors in the Coral Sea and on Guadalcanal aboard the most potent warship ever built.

In the months following Pearl Harbor, America's military and political leaders had conceived the "maximum war-effort program" to funnel massive amounts of the nation's resources into developing an American war machine as quickly as possible. Open to debate had been whether part of the program should be allocated to developing a new class of aircraft carrier or whether the maximum war effort should focus on existing, interim designs that could be produced sooner and less expensively. The Navy could have as many as 16 smaller escort carriers in the time it might take to build one massive carrier. However, the slow escort carriers were of limited tactical value. Was it better to invest in larger, more capable carriers that might not be ready by war's end, or build smaller, slower, and less useful carriers in a short amount of time?

President Franklin D. Roosevelt favored construction of escort carriers and asked Admiral Ernest King to canvass his fleet officers. Admiral Chester Nimitz spoke frankly, saying a 45,000-ton aircraft carrier concentrated too many resources in a single hull while an alternative 11,000-ton carrier was too small to meet combat needs. Many Navy officers favored a new carrier in the 20,000- to 30,000-ton range, largely because carriers of that size could be built fairly quickly following the devastating Navy losses suffered early in the war.

The Navy needed carriers and believed it needed them quickly. But when Rear Admiral Edward Cochrane found a way to begin simultaneous construction on two of what would become known as the Midway class of carriers—possibly having both ready before war's end—the debate was settled. On December 29, 1942, the president reluctantly approved construction of Midway as the lead ship of the new class of carrier. America was now committed to a new generation of aircraft carrier so large it merited a new designation, CVB.

To many in the Navy, the "B" stood for "battle wagon," a reflection of the massive firepower that the new carriers would possess. Midway and two additional carriers would be built on the hulls of the cancelled Montana-class battleship leading others to suggest that "B" stood for "battleship."

The new aircraft carrier class needed armored protection from new enemy tactics and from more powerful bombs. The possibility of enemy fighters catching fueled and armed American planes on the Navy's wooden-deck carriers posed another concern. Even in war conditions, air wings were grounded about seven-eighths of the time. The odds of the enemy finding an American carrier with highly explosive aircraft on deck were quite good. Thus Midway would be the first American Navy carrier with an armored flight deck.

Although an armored deck would reduce internal damage from a catastrophic bomb hit, a stiff price would be paid for deck armor. The steel deck was so heavy that the aircraft carrier tended to sit lower in the water and plunge into heavy seas. That would make it difficult to park aircraft on the flight deck in rough weather because high waves more frequently washed over the deck (called "green water" by many sailors). The number of aircraft had to be reduced to keep an armor-decked carrier from becoming even more top-heavy and unstable. Strengthened elevators would be slower, adversely impacting flight operations. One American Navy observer aboard an armored British carrier concluded that the armor of the Midway class would reduce the operational efficiency of the air wing by 50 percent, calling the armored-deck concept a defensive approach to naval aviation.

Early war experience had shown ship designers that traditional American aircraft carrier design was vulnerable to catastrophic torpedo damage. To remedy this, Midway would be diced into a honeycomb of more than 1,750 watertight compartments, many of them offset above and below one another. The standard eight engineering compartments were subdivided into 26. In addition, a seven-inch belt of hull armor at the waterline, tapering to two inches upward to the hangar deck, was strategically placed outside the engineering spaces and magazines. The four engine rooms were widely separated and the 12 boilers feeding them were cross-connected for backup operability to minimize the chances of an enemy attack rendering Midway dead in the water. The power plant was increased to 212,000 horsepower (the most powerful available at the time) so that Midway could steam at 33 knots with an endurance radius of 20,000 miles at 15 knots.

The vision that would become Midway was complete. It required 90 tons of blueprints for the thousands of workers at Newport News Shipbuilding & Dry Dock Company waiting to get to work.

Construction of Midway began on October 27, 1943. The design posed monumental engineering and construction challenges. Some became evident in the early stages as the hull began to take shape. The hull alone weighed 29,000 tons, nearly two-thirds of Midway's weight. The world's largest jigsaw puzzle, more than 196,000 pieces of steel, some weighing as little as a pound and others weighing several tons, was assembled by a relatively new method called electric welding that reduced the potential weight of the carrier by 10 percent.

As Midway took shape, a small town was erected on its flight deck. Eight, 650-square-foot wooden houses were built on the deck to protect the welders in the 24-hour-a-day operation, regardless of the winter weather that typically was in the 30s and 40s much of the time, with winds of 12 to 14 knots coming off the James River. A small city of thousands of shipyard workers worked almost around the clock for 18 months in the race to get Midway into the war.

Roy Allen and Jerome Evans were among the hundreds of men who walked through the Newport News Shipyard gate earlier than usual on the morning of March 20, 1945. From the start they had helped shape Midway, bending metal and snaking wires. They had worked through bitter winters, taking breaks to warm their hands in a makeshift city of huts on the flight deck. When the weather turned sharp as the war raged, the push had been on to add Midway to the fleet. Allen and Evans were anxious to stake out a good spot to watch Midway slide into the water seconds after a champagne bottle exploded across its bow. Like many others, both had developed a sense of personal ownership in Midway. Proud of their work, they weren't quite ready to turn Midway over to the Navy and the Japanese.

Allen and Evans joined more than 1,000 ship workers, most in overalls and many wearing white woolen caps, who gathered close together on the pier near Midway's bow as they waited for the christening ceremony. They watched battleship-gray cranes move along the pier on Midway's starboard side, hoisting boxes, crates, and cartons onto the flight deck. Hundreds of cords, wires, and tubes hung down from the deck to the pier below, like vines descending from a jungle canopy. Antiaircraft guns that soon would ring Midway on the sponson deck were not yet installed. At the base of a crane nearby, a sign proclaimed Midway "Queen of the Seven Seas" (a nickname for Midway that never caught on) and encouraged visitors to buy commemorative war bonds. As the river breeze lifted the giant bunting draped across the carrier's open bow, a Navy band awaited its cue below on the pier.

Tidal flows would determine the precise moment when Midway would be launched. The tide in the James River had to be just right when Midway slid into the black water. A miscalculation and Midway could run aground within minutes of being christened. When the tide rose to cover a measuring rod planted in the river, huge mallets slammed against selected shores making Midway's bracing less sound. A-frame supports were knocked aside as the James River flooded the shipway. The river's current running downstream would help seven tugs nudge the 38,000-ton unfinished aircraft carrier out into the channel so it could be moved to its outfitting berth. It was a complicated process made less risky through repetition. Newport News Shipbuilding had built all but one U.S. Navy aircraft carrier.

As Midway began to float, everyone's attention turned to a small platform tucked under the bow. Two chin-high microphone stands stood in the center. Six feet away, three motion picture cameras sat on shoulder-high tripods, their operators milling about, waiting like everyone else. Three uniformed Navy photographers stood next to them.

Standing behind one microphone was a freckle-faced young woman who looked more like a college coed than the widow of a Navy pilot. Mrs. Bradford William Ripley Jr. was both a war widow and the "sponsor" of Midway. By Navy tradition, a sponsor was given the honor of breaking a bottle of champagne across the bow of a ship at christening. The Secretary of the Navy selected the sponsor, usually the wife of a public official or senior Navy officer. Midway's sponsor was the daughter of James M. Cox.

Cox had made a name for himself beginning in 1909 when as an Ohio congressman he introduced workmen's compensation and minimum wage legislation. Later he was elected governor and in 1920 became the Democratic nominee for president. His running mate was a 38-year-old Assistant Secretary of the Navy named Franklin Delano Roosevelt. After losing in a landslide, Cox retired from public life to build a massive media conglomerate. Nearly 25 years later, his erstwhile running mate was in the White House and his daughter was given the honor of christening Midway.

The young widow smiled nervously. Her hair was loose at the shoulders, and bounced in the river breeze that wrapped around Midway's bow. A white jacket covered most of a floral print dress that fluttered at the hem. She wore two strings of pearls and a cattelya orchid pinned to one side of her chest, balanced by a flower tucked behind an opposite ear. She glanced at the awkward-looking man standing next to her and made small talk.

He was clearly uncomfortable. Ensign George Gay was the sole survivor of Torpedo Squadron Eight that had been decimated in the Battle of Midway three years earlier. He had recovered from relatively minor injuries and had become a poster boy, drumming up support on the home front through appearances at ships' christenings. His smile was forced. His cheeks were pockmarked and a thin scar sliced through his left eyebrow. Standing erect in his dress blues, his eyes held a sad, faraway look as he shifted from one foot to the other on the podium. In the six years since he had left Texas A&M, he had aged considerably. He had turned 28 just 12 days before.

As cigarette smoke drifted up from the crowd of onlookers, oversized bunting on the bow riffled under several formations of Navy Corsairs ceremonially passing overhead. Mrs. Ripley (few women owned first names in the formal events of 1945) took three practice swings with a tethered champagne bottle wrapped in red, white, and blue streamers. Like a golfer addressing her ball, she paused, reared back, and flung the bottle into the bow. White foam exploded across the hull and quickly drained into the flooded shipway. As the applause of off-duty shipyard workers, men in uniform, and civilians in suits died away, the world's largest, most powerful warship—nearly five years in the making, 1,000 feet long, more than 250 feet wide, and weighing 45,000 tons—embarked on an unparalleled journey.

On Midway's first day afloat, an early spring warmed the South. In three months Ray Shirley would graduate from high school and spend another northern Georgia summer behind two mules and a plow, waiting for his draft notice. In Massachusetts, a high school senior wasn't getting along with his divorced family and thought about leaving home when he graduated in a few months. A farm boy in Wisconsin couldn't wait for graduation day so he could enlist and fight. The three lived very separate lives in early 1945, unaware of their shared future on Midway.

They would become residents of a city at sea along with more than 3,000 other young men assigned to Midway's "ship's company," responsible for the operation and safety of the ship. Fifteen hundred pilots and specialists who were needed to keep as many as 144 aircraft aboard Midway armed and in the air, composed the air wing. Crew plans had been finalized when many of those young men were still in high school and making plans for their prom.

Their Midway experience began in boot camp in the summer of 1945 as Midway was outfitted for war. Candidates were screened for natural aptitude and talent. Some were tapped to become plane handlers and sent to Naval Air Station Glenview, a massive training facility 20 miles north of Chicago built in less than a year after Pearl Harbor. Hangar One was so large an aircraft carrier's deck was painted on the floor so future flight deck crews could practice with actual aircraft.

Throughout the summer, some graduated to practicing on the Wolverine, a 30-year-old converted side-wheel steamer, on Lake Michigan. Others trained on the Sable, another ship converted into a training carrier that plied the Great Lakes. Pilots qualified aboard the same ships. The two old paddle wheelers logged more than 125,000 landings by pilot trainees.

Meanwhile, some boot camp graduates who were assigned to damage control traveled to Philadelphia for four weeks of intense training. Not far away, other young men learned how to operate and maintain the carrier's catapult system at a Philadelphia airfield. Teenagers assigned to gunnery reported to Newport, Rhode Island, to learn how to operate guns on what would become the world's most fortified aircraft carrier. Regardless of the primary assignment, one of the final stages of training for everyone was a weeklong firefighting school, even though Midway would be the Navy's first steel-decked aircraft carrier.

Then the world changed. In the span of four days in August, two nuclear bombs decimated Japan's will to wage war. In the time it took to split an atom, plans for Midway and, as a result, the fate of its crew mutated. They would not fight the Japanese as most expected. Midway's mission became one of preserving the hard-won peace rather than fighting in the war.

Mostly by rail, thousands of young men destined for Midway began arriving at Newport, Rhode Island, on Labor Day 1945 after completing six months of frenetic advanced training. On Sunday, September 9, four transports carried nearly 3,000 men—a few of them battle-tested veterans, but mostly farm boys and city sons of machinists and school teachers—to Newport News Shipbuilding and Dry Dock Company, Pier No. 9, where Midway awaited them.

More than 2,500 miles of copper conductors had been connected to 12,000 electrical lamps and over 2,000 motors. Nearly 300 ventilation and heating systems had been installed. Almost 550 electrical tests evaluated the six radio rooms, motion picture room, fire control, search lighting, radar circuits, and communications systems. Hospital spaces, a dentist's office, ordnance magazines, a cobbler's shop, a print shop, an engine repair shop, a tailor shop, an ice cream plant, and a laboratory had been outfitted. A massive sprinkler system on the cavernous hangar deck, capable of spraying 40,000 gallons of water per minute, had been installed, as well as more than 225 hydraulically operated valves. Everything had to work perfectly throughout more than 1,750 compartments as 4,500 men came aboard.

When sailors reported, each was given a pocket-sized book, "This is the U.S.S. Midway, Largest, Fastest, Toughest Carrier Ever Built." "Restricted" was stamped on the cover and it included a host of instructions and room for a sailor to record his berthing space and commanding officer. It gave the location of the suggestion box for improving the food, and described how to find each of six chow lines that together served 10,000 meals a day. It instructed the crew how to tie their socks together before sending them to the laundry and reminded them, "When in Doubt, SALUTE."

They were told "filthy language . . . stinks up the Navy just as much as it does at home" and encouraged to buy National Service Insurance to protect their dependents. The proper uniform was a must and sailors were instructed never to wear white socks with a uniform. No beards, no earrings.

Instructions further read, "Flowing locks are all right on gigolos, movie actors, violinists and small town hicks. Get yours cut to look like you are—a sailorman. You can grow all the hair you want on your chest. You can wear a zoot suit later if you want to. So long as you are in the Navy, try to look like a blue-water sailor—round hat and square jaw."

As the crew settled in and began to explore, movies started on the hangar deck. By 2200, Midway was quiet and mostly dark.

America had known only eight days of peace as the nation's attention turned to commissioning Midway. Her first commanding officer, Captain Joseph F. Bolger, was a short and stocky man whose paternal manner hid the tender scars from one of the most ferocious sea battles that had been fought in the Pacific theater.

A mere 10 months earlier, Bolger had led another carrier into battle. On November 25, 1944, dozens of Japanese kamikazes had targeted his carrier, the Intrepid, and sister ships in the Philippine Sea. One kamikaze snaked through Intrepid's defensive fire, crashing into the pilots' ready room before exploding. Bolger ordered the carrier to make hard turns to starboard, forcing flaming gasoline and planes over the port side, away from critical systems in the ship's island. Not long after, a second Japanese Zero ripped into Intrepid's heart. It reached the hangar deck before exploding, killing dozens more Americans. Captain Bolger kept his ship afloat as his crew braved exploding ammunition to fight the fires. The sight of the Intrepid limping into Pearl Harbor, a brutally twisted mangle of steel, became one of the more memorable sights of the war in the Pacific. Captain Bolger received two Navy Crosses for his bravery, cool wit, and command skill that day.

On Monday, September 10 at 0830, massive lines crashed onto the pier as four Navy assist tugs cozied up to the massive hull of Midway. "Two-thirds astern" was followed by several long whistle blasts that echoed across the James River through the early morning mist as Midway was positioned to make the short run to Pier No. 2 in the Norfolk Navy Yard for commissioning a few miles away.

Construction workers in overalls on the carrier Leyte nearby stopped to watch. Many had worked for years on Midway. As Midway moved out into the river a British ship saluted by lowering its colors in respect. Midway answered the same as a handful of men walked its flight deck, avoiding the fenced-off square aircraft elevator shaft on the centerline near the bow. Sailors filled the gallery deck, a small ledge at the bow just under the flight deck. Bolger stood silent on the bridge, taking stock of his new crew.

Two hours later, Midway passed Hospital Point. Wounded men in slippers and bathrobes, gleaming white in the brightening morning sun, walked, hobbled, and wheeled to outside vantage points to see their nation's newest warship at the dawn of peace.

Midway arrived at Norfolk Navy Yard at 1150, just as the Navy had requested. The day grew hot and sticky as the breeze died. Thousands of sailors assembled on deck in rows that stretched from bow to stern, facing the island as they waited for the commissioning ceremony.

The sailors snapped to attention at 1500 sharp. Invocations followed the raising of the colors, and the national anthem played as the crew raised the National Ensign, Union Jack, and Commissioning Pennant in unison. Homer Ferguson, president of Newport News Shipbuilding, formally presented Midway to the Navy.

The Undersecretary of the Navy, Artemus L. Gates, delivered a principal address that reflected the times faced by the Navy. As Midway was going to sea, the Navy was beginning a postwar demobilization program that would release three million men from active duty in 12 months. Gates talked of Navy plans that called for aircraft carrier–based planes capable of carrying nuclear weapons and characterized Midway as "evidence of our will to maintain peace."

Captain Bolger acknowledged that while most veterans welcomed peace, many of his young sailors lamented the final surrender when he said, "[Our] regret naturally arising from our disappointment in not testing this ship in combat is [offset by] the realization that we shall render a greater service in preserving the peace." A benediction followed and with an order to "pipe down," Midway took its place at the forefront of the United States Navy fleet. That afternoon Midway sat in the crosscurrents of a changing world whose future was as volatile as it was unpredictable.

Midway had been under way for the first time when exercises off Virginia were cut short after only one month. The carrier was ordered to New York City to be the centerpiece of the nation's first Navy Day celebration in four years—a celebration that combined a ships' review with a parade and the commissioning of the second Midway-class carrier, the Franklin D. Roosevelt, by President Truman.

Rain pelted Midway's windows on the bridge when the carrier turned into the Hudson River on October 27, 1945. As Midway plowed upriver along the eastern side of Manhattan, thousands of civilians lined both sides of the river, peering through the mist and spray at the much heralded ship. Overhead, dozens of Navy fighters streaked down the river, rattling windows in New York and New Jersey, drowning out the "Palisades" being broadcast from Midway's massive loudspeakers on deck. As the clouds parted at midafternoon, Midway and dozens of other ships weighed anchor while ferries delivered thousands of soaked spectators for onboard tours.

The day was one of celebration as countless numbers of New Yorkers celebrated the two-month-old peace. It began with the commissioning of the Roosevelt at the Navy Yard in Brooklyn, followed by a parade of celebrities, dignitaries, elected officials, and crew contingents from the ships at anchor on the Hudson River. It ended at Central Park nearly two hours later where one million New Yorkers watched President Truman address the nation on radio.

After Truman's speech, 1,200 Navy planes rose into the air from 23 airfields from Maine to South Carolina. Dive bombers, torpedo planes, fighters, and fighter-bombers piloted by war-toughened veterans converged on the sky over Long Branch, New Jersey, for a flyby over the Hudson River armada. They approached the staging area from three different directions to give as many New Englanders as possible a chance to see them. Forming up into three massive air groups, they flew a 12-mile oval around the line of ships on the Hudson, streaking over the crowds at 155 knots at an elevation of only 3,000 feet.

Midway sat in the middle of the Hudson. The carrier Enterprise and then the battleship Missouri were off the bow. After his speech, Truman boarded the Navy destroyer Renshaw for a bow-to-stern review of seven miles of warships at anchor. It was an unprecedented concentration of Navy firepower. As Truman passed each ship, its guns fired in salute. Every ship manned and loaded standby guns in the event the primary guns malfunctioned as he passed. The continuous barrage of almost 1,000 blasts slowly moving upriver lasted nearly two hours.

The international celebration of the Navy's birthday reached as far as Tokyo Bay where several American ships rested. In Honolulu, the Pearl Harbor Navy Yard was opened to the public for the first time since December 7, 1941. In Los Angeles, a reenactment of the Japanese signing the surrender agreement aboard the battleship Missouri was held in the Memorial Coliseum. San Franciscans thrilled to a flyby of 200 Navy planes, streaking over the battleships Alabama, Wisconsin, South Dakota, and Indiana as the famed Yorktown aircraft carrier idled nearby. City namesake ships such as the San Diego, Savannah, and Portland were open to the public in their hometown ports.

The 170th birthday of the United States Navy prompted people to reflect on the dead of WWII. Senior Navy officials made speeches honoring the 54,000 Navy, Marine, and Coast Guard men and women killed, and sounded the call to remain battle-ready in an era of international uncertainty. "The seven seas have never borne a mightier fleet, proven in war . . .

it is incumbent upon us as a nation that this sea power not be squandered or bartered away or allowed to fall into disuse. We will never permit this, I am sure, if we understand what it might mean in terms of America's future in the world of tomorrow," said Admiral Ernest King.

Midway was ready to put to sea, testing both ship and crew. On November 7, the carrier and a mostly green crew left Norfolk for a 57-day shakedown cruise to the Caribbean. Every component, compartment, and complement of young men was tested, both for operational efficiency as well as for battle readiness. Finely tuned coordination within and between divisions was still a goal rather than a reality as Midway and its escorts steamed south.

A severe shortage of new recruits in some areas posed a major challenge to developing a tightly operating unit of strangers. A paucity of men qualified for engineering almost prevented Midway from departing for its shakedown cruise. Once under way, many veterans earned enough points to be discharged after Midway got under way. Nearly 500 men transferred off the carrier to head home. Other war-scarred veterans short of the service points necessary for discharge found the adjustment to a peacetime navy difficult.

Ray Shirley saw what war could do to a man's nerves. One day a sullen sailor in front of Shirley in the chow line took offense to something. He reached across the food, grabbed a mess cook, and started punching him before they could be separated. Captain Bolger held a "captain's mast," an onboard hearing to determine guilt and punishment for an infraction. Shirley testified in front of Captain Bolger. After listening to everyone, Bolger peered into the eyes of the short-fused veteran. Bolger's face softened. He told the offender he understood "where you're coming from, but things are different now." After a long pause he let the sailor off with a warning. Peacetime sailors learned to give seagoing veterans from the Pacific war a wide berth.

Days passed with drills that tested individual crews as well as the coordination and communication between divisions. Officers supervised 17 bombing, strafing, and torpedo exercises, plus "routine" landings and takeoffs on 50 of the cruise's 57 days at sea. The flight deck crew was constantly on duty. For some, getting blown off their feet and tumbling

50 yards in the wash of a Corsair at full throttle provided their first lesson in concentration, alertness and communication. As Midway recorded its 1,000th landing a few weeks into the shakedown, the flight deck crew was able to cut landing intervals from 35 seconds early in the cruise to 25 seconds. Meanwhile, the red-jerseyed ordnance crews practiced arming and rearming aircraft with 500- and 1,000-pound bombs, napalm bombs, rockets, and machine gun ammunition.

Of all the units on board, the 240 pilots were perhaps most impressed with Midway. The relocation of the preceding Essex-class island and anti-aircraft guns off the flight deck made it gargantuan by combat standards. The joke among the plane crews was that the flight deck looked as large as LaGuardia Field so pilots should ask which runway to use when landing aboard Midway.

Carrier losses early in the war had placed a high priority on survivability. Midway was the most armored carrier ever built. It also was an unprecedented floating maze of compartments that could be sealed to minimize flooding. Damage control was paramount. A damage control drill conducted every morning at precisely 0815 tested the knowledge and reaction of the crew. Weekly quizzes stretched the crew's recall. The intricacies of using the ship's extensive telephone system became rote from practice.

The core strength of Midway was its power. Boilers fed huge turbines that generated the horsepower necessary for the 45,000-ton carrier to make 33 knots. The "crash back" exercise stretched the power system and sailors' nerves to the breaking point. With Midway steaming nearly full speed the order would go out "full-speed astern." The shudder down the spine of the ship spread into the bones of every man on board, including Ed Cherenson, a bright college graduate with a chemical engineering degree who moonlighted as the ship's assistant movie officer. It "had guys jumping as it took an awfully long time for it to come to a stop."

The shakedown exercises also tested the habitability of the world's most advanced aircraft carrier. Massive evaporators had been installed to provide fresh water. The evaporators' capacity was enough to steadily supply fresh water to 1,400 homes. This had been a major priority of the carrier's designers, as veteran sailors complained of early carriers' chronic shortage of fresh water. It wasn't long, though, before Midway found itself on "water hours," the equivalent of fresh-water rationing as the evaporators struggled to keep up with demand.

Although designed as a ship of war with minimal crew comfort, designers nonetheless had to meet all the needs of daily life within the confines of a warship. The challenges were immense, considering an aircraft carrier never rested when at sea. Food preparation, laundry, and even medical services operated on a 24-hour-a-day basis. Midway's coffeemakers brewed 10,000 cups at a time. Six massive roasting ovens cooked more than a half-ton of meat at once. It took two barrels of dough to fill a single dough mixer. Midway was known for good Navy food in the early days. (The official *Navy Cook Book* of 1945 contained more than 200 recipes, all in increments of 100 servings.)

Nonetheless Midway was a warship. Crew comfort was relatively low on the list of priorities. Early on its shakedown cruise, the crew discovered that some sleeping quarters were nearly uninhabitable. In many areas bunks were stacked four high with the top bunk having so little clearance below the bulkhead that a man could not turn over once he climbed into it.

Only a few areas aboard Midway had air conditioning, an almost unheard of amenity during World War II. The vast majority of the carrier's interior only had forced-air ventilation through more than six miles of vent trunks powered by 291 blowers. Most men aboard Midway were lucky if they had a fan attached to the bulkhead where they worked or slept.

Midway also tested its war-waging capability. The "enemy" was Culebra Island about 25 miles east of Puerto Rico's main island. Under Navy control since 1901, it was a favorite for Navy and Marine training exercises. War veteran Captain Bolger saw to it that Midway's shakedown attack had all the earmarks of war. Well ahead of the two-day exercise, pilots flew photographic reconnaissance missions according to preestablished schedules. The night before the live-ammunition strikes, plane captains checked out their aircraft on the hangar deck. Crews fueled some of the 95 planes that would fly the following day. At last the ship grew quiet, just before General Quarters sounded at 0430. The crew of Midway scrambled to their assigned stations. Within 30 minutes the first airplanes launched into the pink dawn, streaking toward a two-mile patch of Culebra Island, replete with pillboxes and other replica targets. Virtually every department on board took part, even the galley. To add realism to the exercise, the crew only ate battle-station fare: sandwiches, coffee, and K rations. Battle-station rations haunted war veterans. For others new to the Navy, it was as close battle as they might ever get.

Not everyone aboard Midway was in uniform. Civilians abounded, mostly representatives of the ship's builder and the legions of subcontractors. They watched, recorded, and later reported. One of them, John Hospers of United Aircraft Service Corporation, filed a detailed report on the shakedown.

He found Midway's steel deck much more slippery than the wooden decks of predecessors. A coating of nonskid material called monk cloth had limited value once oil, grease, and dirt saturated the material. When a film of sea spray covered the flight deck, crews sometimes found themselves sliding and lurching, often within a few feet of the spinning props of Helldivers and Corsairs.

Hospers also witnessed how human error, skill, and judgment sometimes overrode equipment functionality. One day a Corsair pilot was waved off but reacted slowly and still caught an arresting cable as he was going to full throttle. Caught by the wire, the Corsair slid diagonally across the deck of Midway as flight deck crews dashed for safety. Almost in slow motion as it dragged its left wing across the deck, the plane went over the port side, taking the arresting cable with it. At some point, the Corsair's tailhook gave way, snapping the cable back into place as the plane dropped 50 feet into the ocean. With only the plane's tail sticking up out of the water as Midway passed, spotters saw the pilot's head bobbing in the waves nearby. An escort destroyer retrieved him and returned the aviator to Midway unhurt.

On New Year's Day, 1946 Midway turned toward Norfolk. It had become evident that repairs and modifications were necessary to get into fighting trim. Over the next 19 months they would be made, interspersed with training exercises off the coast of Virginia to keep the crew seaworthy. While routine, not all went as planned.

One day as Midway was conducting flight operations Ensign James Russell Williams drew a bead on Midway in his final approach in a Corsair. Seconds later, he slammed onto the deck and the aircraft disintegrated before it disappeared over the side. Shards of aircraft speckled the deck.

The flight deck crew was shocked by the suddenness and finality of the crash. Later as they cleared the wreckage from the flight deck, Buddy Herrmann picked up a two-inch square piece of the Corsair's wing. On it he scratched a memorial.

Piece of wing from F4U Corsair which crashed into fantail May 18, 1946, as it came in for a landing. It was waved off but as it went to gain altitude the wing caught the edge of the flight deck hurtling the plane down and over the port side. In memoriame [sic] of James Russell Williams, Ensign, UNSR, lost at sea, May 18, 1946.

Even in a new era of peace, young men found themselves powerless as they watched other young men die. Death in service to country continued in an era when Cold War had replaced overt war. It cast an uncertain light on the future of Midway. Christened in war and commissioned in peace, the carrier and its crew sailed in a confused sea. After operating among icebergs to explore the limits of naval aviation, Midway would be ordered off the coast of Virginia to secretly test a piece of Adolph Hitler's legacy.

CHAPTER 3

SANDY

BLACK SMOKE BILLOWED across Chesapeake Bay as three nondescript boxcars arrived on the pier after traveling by rail under armed guard from White Sands, New Mexico. Midway towered above as sailors leaned over the flight deck's edge to look down on the train after the engine detached and pulled away. Each boxcar held a rocket nestled in a cradle, ready to be pulled out and hoisted aboard Midway.

Tractors straddled the tracks as the front end of each boxcar was opened. Before the rockets were extracted, the enlisted men were hustled below while officers gathered for a closer look at the 28,000-pound rockets.

Their imminent arrival and purpose had not been a secret to Midway's crew in the summer of 1947, nearly two years after the carrier had been commissioned. The rumors were confirmed as each rocket was eased out into the morning sun. "German V-2 Rocket, U.S. Army Ordnance Dept., White Sands Proving Grounds, New Mex." was painted in simple block letters on each side. Nearly a ton of explosives had been removed from each of the nose cones.

Two of the rockets were gently lifted onto the hangar deck. To even a casual observer, one looked slightly different from the other. That led to new rumors that the mismatched V-2 had been used as some kind of decoy on the train trip from New Mexico. A Marine assigned to Midway was ordered to guard both the V-2 rockets and their fuel supply. He had been told the rockets were a secret but then was ordered to rope them off in full view of the crew, dress in his blues, and stand guard. Eight hours a day during the upcoming deployment he would pace 26 steps in one direction, then 26 steps back in front of the rope. Over and over for everyone to see.

After the two V-2s had been secured in a hangar bay, the remaining rocket was lifted up to the flight deck. Its trailer was pushed down to the fantail, just to the port side of the centerline. A crane on a barge was brought up against Midway's stern which lifted the rocket by its nose upright, onto its four fins, and free of its trailer. White scaffolding—called a "gantry"—gripped the rocket, holding it upright. Perfectly symmetrical on each side of the V-2, the gantry was 40 feet forward from the stern of the ship. Attached to one side, a U.S. flag drifted in the Hampton Roads breeze. Not far away, also on portable trailers, sat two ominous bulbous metal containers. Twice the height of a man, they held the extremely volatile liquid propellant required by the V-2s.

This particular V-2 stood as white as the Atlas and Saturn rockets of future generations that would follow. Alternating tail fins were painted black so observers could more easily determine whether the rocket rolled during flight. The Germans had experimented with a number of black-and-white patterns on V-2s to maximize visual acuity during and immediately after launch. Soon this V-2 would be launched from the deck of Midway.

The rockets' arrival on Midway marked the close of a two-year journey that had begun deep inside a German mountain. As the war had drawn to a close in April 1945, American troops neared Nordhausen, only hours ahead of Russian soldiers approaching from the east. Intelligence officers had alerted commanders of the two American task forces, "Welborn" and "Lovelady," that they might find something unusual in the Nordhausen region.

The discovery of 5,000 decaying corpses in a concentration camp had become grim routine. The surprise came when troops found a tunnel at the base of a mountain. As the men on point entered, caution gave way to amazement. Precision machine-tooling equipment, parts, and supplies for 100 V-2 rockets sat neatly arranged and in perfect working order. American soldiers had discovered the heart of Adolph Hitler's dreaded V-2 war-making machine. The underground factory had been abandoned only the day before when scientists and specialists fled to nearby villages after herding slave laborers back to the region's concentration camp.

The Americans' discovery led to Operation Paperclip, a daring mission to spirit the treasure trove of rocketry out of Germany before the Russians arrived. Major James Hamill was assigned the task of removing the missiles out of the German mountains and transporting them to White Sands Proving Grounds in the New Mexico desert. The mission required more than 340 railroad carloads and included more than 120 German scientists— many of whom had been captured after being part of Hitler's machine. Ultimately many of them accepted five-year employment contracts with the U.S. Army.

A testing program began almost immediately. The notion of whether V-2s could be successfully launched from the deck of a ship at sea without causing catastrophic hull damage intrigued war planners. Also, could missile launches and aircraft operations be compatible? The mobility implications of ballistic missiles being fired from multiple seagoing platforms were enormous.

To find out, at least one of the V-2s would be launched from the deck of Midway on September 6, 1947. It was the first time a ballistic missile would be fired at sea. Whether that date marked the first generation of naval missile warfare depended on whether Midway survived Operation Sandy.

Midway was quiet on Labor Day, September 1, 1947. Captain Albert K. Morehouse walked onto a nearly deserted bridge and settled into his elevated captain's chair overlooking the flight deck. Thin lips pinched together, forcing his captain's worry wrinkles spreading from the corners of his eyes to deepen. Balding and heavy-lidded, he squinted into the sun across Chesapeake Bay. Morehouse wore his officer's hat low over his eyes, a long black leather jacket tightly cinched at the waist.

He knew the following day Midway would leave port and steam toward the unknown. The Battle of Midway, the Pacific war's turning point, had been won by heroic pilots flying into the teeth of withering enemy machine gun fire. Now the namesake stood ready to test warfare across unimagined distances with massive, ballistic firepower. Only two years earlier, Morehouse had sat on another carrier's bridge and barely survived naval warfare's most intimate and horrifying attack tactic.

The American Navy was driving toward Japan at the time. As commanding officer of the escort carrier Natoma Bay, Morehouse sailed in the middle of the American juggernaut. One day's air strikes in support of island invasions blended with the next. When Natoma Bay reached Okinawa in June 1945, the Japanese turned the table on Morehouse. Early on the morning of June 7, Natoma Bay spotters saw a Japanese Zero racing over the wave tops, bank hard, and head low and fast for the escort carrier. It approached from the stern and sprayed the bridge with incendiary fire. Windows exploded and sparks erupted from ricocheting shrapnel that burrowed into the arms, faces, and chests of those aboard. Morehouse's gunnery crews held steady, filling the Zero's canopy with fire before it nosed over and crashed onto the wooden deck. The Zero's prop tore a 240-square-foot hole in the flight deck before the plane exploded.

Within minutes, Moorehouse's crew extinguished the fire and began hauling timbers up onto the flight deck as more enemy aircraft raked the carrier with machine gun fire. Some sailors shoved smoldering pieces of hot wreckage over the side while others patched the deck wound. The war raged overhead, but only four hours later Natoma Bay resumed flight operations and then disengaged. When Natoma Bay reached San Diego on August 19, the war was over.

Kamikaze visions were still fresh as Morehouse prepared to lead the Navy's first armored carrier in Operation Sandy. If Midway was successful, naval warfare someday might be waged across time zones.

As Captain Morehouse looked down on the flight deck, among the handful of men working below was Ray Dall. A member of the flight deck crew, the color of Dall's jersey designated him part of the team responsible for fueling aircraft and maintaining the carrier's massive aviation fuel systems. Color followed function. Yellow shirts directed aircraft on deck. White shirts enforced safety procedures. It was a blend and sometimes a blur of colors in a ballet of more than 60 men that took place with the launch and recovery of each aircraft. It was choreographed to the last move, to the last wave of a hand, on one of the most dangerous places on earth.

After enlistment and the training that followed, Dall had been assigned to Midway and promptly received a full dose of life aboard a spit-and-polish United States Navy aircraft carrier. He was taken to the

"Lucky Bag" and shown a pile of dress blues confiscated from sailors who had violated the prohibition against wearing them on board. Dall was shocked at the story of the ship's carpenter who, even with 16 years' service, lost his "tailor mades" because they were prohibited as well. Dall learned wearing white socks violated Navy regulations. "Captain A. K. Moorehouse's Midway goes by the book, Mr. Dall. Remember that."

Not far below the flight deck, Tom Murphy, a Marine assigned to Midway, sat oiling a weapon. He welcomed the break from pacing back in forth in front of the V-2s on the hangar deck. Midway was a waystop on his path to college. Two years earlier, Murphy was about to lose his job at an ice plant as the winter of 1945 approached. There wasn't much demand for ice during winters in Indiana. College was beyond the means of a youngster who always had a basketball in his hands. With the G.I. Bill about to expire, Murphy decided maybe a few years in the service would be his ticket to college. Within a year he had been assigned to Midway and had found himself in the middle of a Navy public relations battle in the months leading up to Operation Sandy.

For several years the Navy and Air Force had been locked in a nasty and public battle over which should be named the lead service in developing fighter and bomber aircraft in the nuclear era. Whenever Midway was in Norfolk, Navy leaders used the carrier to showcase the glory and potential of the latest in naval aviation technology to Washington power brokers. Murphy had devised a different definition for U.S.S. It came to mean "Underway Saturday and Sunday." Weekend outings off Virginia became the norm, intended to impress the politicos routinely ferried aboard to watch the drills, exercises, launches, and traps. To much of the crew, it seemed a waste of time. Then President Truman came on board. The former World War I officer won over Midway's Marines when he arrived at their compartment to inspect their weapons and to exchange a kind word. Growing up in Indiana, Murphy never dreamed he might meet the president aboard an aircraft carrier.

The unending stream of weekend VIPs often clashed with ship's operations. On occasion Murphy and others met dignitaries at the most inopportune times. One day Murphy was on steam-ironing detail for his Marine detachment. If a Marine got in trouble aboard Midway, he often was assigned the ironing detail. Murphy was standing in his compartment with steaming iron in hand, wearing only underwear and shoes. A woman walked in and stopped short when she saw the mortified Murphy. It was Congresswoman Clare Booth Luce. Neither said a word as she turned and left.

Only 20 at the time, Murphy didn't know he had seen one of the mid–twentieth century's most influential women. Before being elected to Congress for most of the war years, Luce had been an award-winning playwright. She became an advocate of the men of Midway as a member of the Military Affairs Committee, and ended her political career an outspoken critic of communism. She played a key role in creating the Atomic Energy Commission.

Popeye and Olive Oyl were aboard Midway for Operation Sandy. A detailed booklet full of Popeye and Olive Oyl cartoons, puns, and admonitions had been distributed to the crew, visiting scientists, and the security detail as they boarded. It provided a layman's overview of the V-2 and noted that once 19,000 pounds of its fuel was consumed, the rocket would be traveling 3,500 miles per hour. The booklet devoted far more space to navigating the maze that was Midway. If a scientist wished to see Captain Morehouse, he was advised to start on the hangar deck and *"descend hatch at frame 189 starboard. Turn right through passageway C-218-L to door at frame 181, then through passageway C-211-T and through door at frame 179."* The route to the barbershop was even more cryptic.

Booklets didn't stop rumors from racing through the crew ranks. While there was no question about the German origin or mission of the rockets under guard on the hangar deck and at the stern, intrigue abounded. The day before Midway left port, a mess cook with what some crewmen called "a Russian-sounding name" had taken a break and sat down at the stern, a few yards away from the gantry. In times of quiet, sailors often sat there, hanging their legs over the deck's edge, smoking and gazing over and beyond Midway's wake. Apparently he was too close to the V-2. Plainclothed civilians handcuffed the wayward sailor and escorted him off the ship. The crew never knew what happened to the shipmate with the strange-sounding last name. They only knew to stay clear of the contraption at the stern on the flight deck.

On September 2, a nervous energy spread through Midway as the sun rose. Morehouse's bridge was now a hive of activity as the carrier prepared to go to sea. Morehouse glanced at his watch: 0630. "Light the fires." Four hours later four assist tugs separated from Midway as the carrier turned toward Bermuda and a patch of water that usually was among the smoothest found anywhere in the Atlantic in September. That was crucial because the scientists aboard didn't want a lot of pitching and rolling if an unpredictable rocket powered by ethyl alcohol and liquid oxygen was to be launched. The launch would be especially risky because Midway would be under way and aircraft would be in the air, ready to be recovered.

Soon the carrier and crew fell into the natural rhythm of sailing in blue water. As Midway headed south, the sea flattened and its blue deepened. The sun shot darts of light deep into the ocean, disappearing in the swarms of jellyfish suspended under the dead-flat calm. Tom Murphy marveled the neon blue of the sea. One day the ocean's serenity disappeared in an explosion of chop. Thousands of flying fish fled into the air with legions of dolphins in pursuit. As far as Murphy could see, golden-green dolphins leaped after flying fish gliding less than a foot above the ocean's surface on outstretched pink-blue fins. He grabbed an expensive camera he had just bought and climbed out the fo'c'sle onto the anchor chain. He gingerly took as many pictures as he could while dolphins danced on the surface, right up to the moment he dropped the camera into the water. The event produced in Murphy a lifelong aversion to buying expensive cameras. But it didn't stop him from sneaking another camera onto the sponson deck for the V-2 takeoff a few days later.

September 6 dawned gray and flat with an uneven cloud cover at 5,000 feet. By early afternoon Midway's aircraft were in the air. The flight deck had been cleared of all but a handful of scientists and officers, most of whom stood on deck-edge catwalks where they could duck for cover if necessary. Some stood at the base of the island, close to an unlocked hatch. Men from each department of the ship selected as observers moved to their assigned locations along the rails on the hangar deck and up on the island in case the Navy needed additional witnesses to the launch. As Midway's planes circled overhead, all eyes on the escort destroyers turned to the upright rocket on Midway's stern.

As the clock crept past 1500, Gordon Vandiver stood at the helm. Minutes before the scheduled launch a quartermaster relieved him. Since he hadn't been dismissed from the bridge, Vandiver retreated to a corner. He had left the farmland of Ohio to become a Navy printer assigned to

Midway. He was an unnoticed young man about to see history from the shadows as the others on the bridge rushed to the outside walkway to see it for themselves.

Off-duty sailors sneaked to unguarded vantage points on the sponson deck, staying low to keep out of the line of sight of the bridge, and yet remain in a spot where they might glimpse the historic launch and trajectory. Tom Murphy joined them with what he called his "spy camera." Designed to look like a pack of cigarettes, he thought it would take good photos of the launch. Not far away stood Gerald Bazinet on a catwalk, clad in firefighting gear. Assigned to the hull department, the history buff from the Bronx had volunteered for emergency firefighting duty aboard Midway.

One of the crewmen ordered to track the launch was a 17-year-old who had escaped from Oklahoma by joining the Navy. Neal Casey was a fire control man, third class. Assigned to "Sky One" just above the bridge, he tracked airborne enemy for his fellow battery mates. His assignment that day was to follow the V-2 and call its range down to the plotting room. He could see the movie camera tripods down on the flight deck, up toward the bow, 400 feet away from the rocket. Even though the crew had been told the launch of the V-2 was secret, within weeks millions of Americans might see its launch on newsreel film.

Meanwhile Dall and nearly 4,500 other young men stood, sat, or paced below deck. They couldn't be sure the three inches of armored deck above their heads was enough to withstand the 56,000 pounds of thrust necessary to hurl 14 tons of rocket straight into the air and reach a speed of 5,000 feet per second. Helmsman Vandiver held his breath on the bridge. Murphy stayed low on the sponson deck. Bazinet, in his fire suit, crouched under a platform.

When a civilian scientist hit the launch button, the gantry wobbled as a deep growl erupted from the base of the V-2, a rumble that spread through the steel deck, down through the bulkheads, and into the souls of the ship and those aboard. A whitish orange flame spread sideways from between the rocket's fins. The rocket seemed to wobble in place for a moment, as if trying to make up its mind whether to leave Midway. Grayish black smoke billowed up both sides of the gantry. Just before the rocket would have disappeared in the expanding bloom, the gantry fell away and the rocket inched upward. Then things began to go wrong.

The V-2 rose slightly and then leaned almost over on its side. Spotter

Casey tracked the rocket as it headed toward the carrier's island. It passed to the outside of Midway's superstructure by about 100 yards with about a 20-degree up-angle. From his vantage point on the bridge, Vandiver thought at one point, "The thing was headed straight for us. You never saw so many scrambled-egg officers dive for cover in all your life. A lot of brass turned green in an instant" as the rocket narrowly missed the island.

Right after it passed Casey's post, it started tumbling end over end toward an escort destroyer. Fearing the rocket might veer toward Bermuda, launch officials detonated the V-2 just before it reached the mottled cloud cover. When it exploded a few moments later, the elapsed time of flight totaled only 12 seconds.

The few scientists allowed topside for the launch had frantically looked for nonexistent cover when the V-2 wobbled on deck. One was Leo D. "Pappy" White, an employee of General Electric, the company that ran the testing program. A 31-year Navy veteran, pilot, researcher, and pioneer in rocketry, he was in charge of firing the rocket. Afterward, Navy personnel jokingly honored Pappy for "digging a three-foot fox hole on the deck of an aircraft carrier in 15 seconds."

For most of the crew, the V-2's launch was either disappointing or anticlimactic. Would-be Marine photographer Murphy squeezed off as many pictures with his spy camera as the few seconds of flight allowed. Volunteer firefighter Bazinet had nothing to do. The portion of the flight deck where the V-2 was launched had been scraped clean of the deck coating designed to give men and planes traction. Had the rocket exploded on the flight deck, Bazinet would have been powerless to stop it.

After traveling a scant 10 kilometers and reaching an altitude of almost 5,000 feet, its detonation had split the V-2 into three large pieces that fell into the Atlantic. For many it was a fitting end to the launch. They had expected it to leave the deck "in a flash." Rather, it took a second or two to build vertical momentum as its exhaust splayed across the deck, slowing lifting into the air and seemingly in search of a flight path.

While most observers were mesmerized by the short flight, Vandiver was one of the few who turned his attention to the gantry once the rocket was away. Within a few seconds of launch, flight deck crews raced to dismantle the gantry and take it below on an aircraft elevator. When the elevator came back up, it was clean. Within minutes flight deck crews rerigged Midway's arresting wires. Recovery of planes began almost immediately and went off without a hitch.

Midway's V-2 was another in a long line of German rogue rockets. It added to the lore of the V-2's reputation as a weapon of terror that was as unpredictable as it was deadly. For many scientists aboard Midway that day, the V-2's wayward journey was hardly a surprise. A few months earlier in May, a V-2 launched from White Sands headed south instead of north. A cloud of dust marked the spot where it nosed into a cemetery near Juarez, Mexico. One of the breakthroughs in the Allied pursuit of German rocket technology during the war came when a V-2 aimed at England somehow flew into Sweden. Its remains ultimately reached British Intelligence.

The government claimed on its newsreels the test of the wayward V-2 aboard Midway was a resounding success, much to the surprise and delight of the crew. Most thought the flight was far from successful as it tumbled end over end before it was blown up. Despite the V-2's unnerving trajectory off the deck of Midway, it was, in fact, a qualified success. Midway had survived. Properly fortified warships could withstand the thrust of missiles and missile warfare could be integrated with carrier air operations.

Still, the scientists were worried about the damage that might be caused if a liquid-fueled V-2 exploded prematurely on deck. That led to Operation Pushover the following year when the Navy assessed the risk of at-sea launches by exploding two V-2s on mock decks constructed at White Sands. The damage to the decks was so devastating it led to the development of solid-fuel rockets to replace the liquid fuel systems developed by the Germans.

Murphy, Dall, Vandiver, Casey, and thousands of other young men soon left Midway and the Navy. Operation Sandy became an oft-told sea story to friends and family. Their collective legacy would galvanize the development of naval missile warfare for generations to come.

CHAPTER 4

POWER AND
PURPOSE

Turkey-Russia relations simmered when Russia sent 12 troop divisions to the Turkish border and the United States responded with an increased naval presence near Istanbul. Yugoslavia was suffering exacerbated regional ethnic tensions and Italy struggled to rediscover domestic stability.

Then England stunned the world when it promised India independence within a year, abandoned its mandate in Palestine, and cut off foreign aid to Greece and Turkey. The international abdication left a tremendous and unexpected void in the European body politic, one that President Truman moved quickly to fill. The Marshall Plan became the cornerstone of American foreign policy when in 1948 Congress approved more than $5 billion in loans and outright grants, ranging from $3.2 billion to the United Kingdom to $29 million for Iceland.

But that wasn't enough. A high-profile U.S. Navy presence in the Mediterranean was critical to protecting American interests there. Midway was ordered to visibly demonstrate American power, presence, and commitment to forging a stable and recovered Europe, Asia Minor, and Middle East. Midway deployments frequently were extended, the crew's liberty ashore shortened. Midway sailed at the "Tip of the Atlantic Fleet's Sword." It was aimed at the underbelly of Europe.

Nearly illiterate, Midway's toughest work details always seemed to fall to John Pruitt, a former west-Texas runaway whose accent was as dense as a stand of ironwood. He sent most of his Navy pay to his divorced mother, two brothers, and a sister after ironing buddies' clothes, sewing buttons, and standing others' watches to make extra money.

It had been five days since Midway arrived at the French Riviera and anchored off Gulf D'Hyers, France. Nearby, Cannes, Nice, and Monte Carlo had beckoned rotating liberty shifts of Midway sailors. Pruitt welcomed the break after months of patrolling the Mediterranean.

Pruitt stomped his feet on the wharf and jammed crossed hands up into his armpits as the winter night gusted into his chest. Already the memories of a day spent on liberty in postwar France were dissipating on the wind that threatened his return to Midway as it rode building seas.

When Pruitt reached the head of the line on the pier, he jumped down into one of the liberty launches ferrying men out to Midway. The 40-foot wooden dual-purpose boat with eight rows of bench seats could hold about 50 Marines if they were seated and equipped for battle. When used for liberty transport, about 80 sailors crammed into it. As in many Mediterranean ports, Midway had anchored off shore for lack of a deep-water harbor or suitable pier. Liberty launches were the crew's private taxi service, returning mostly drunk and always exhausted men usually by 2300.

The water had glistened under clear skies on the morning of February 11, 1948. That afternoon, a mistral first whispered. It rustled leaves in the French coastal foothills, gathered itself, and rolled toward the shoreline and out into the Mediterranean. The offshore gale turned languid water into white-capped froth. By the time Pruitt and others began staggering back to the wharf that night, thousands of roiling whitecaps stood between them and the aircraft carrier. Undeterred, launches ferried the sailors back aboard and then returned for another group. Experienced boat handlers navigated the pounding breakers and made their way through worsening seas in the glow of running lights.

As Pruitt's launch pushed off, the wind tore through the men who huddled and hunkered as best they could. At first they made good headway. The waist-high gunnels kept the pulsating ocean out of the boat. Then an officer took the helm when he decided the coxswain had been drinking.

The officer was an inexperienced helmsman. Skills required for handling a 45,000-ton aircraft carrier didn't automatically translate into the fine-touch skills necessary to steer an overloaded open wooden boat in rising seas and a biting wind.

Pruitt ducked as the launch approached a breaker line. It plowed through the first wave before disaster struck. A thundering wave hit the launch hard, sweeping over the gunnel and into the boat. Men were up to their waists in cold seawater. Some tried to bail water out of the sinking boat with their hands. Others froze in terror. Less than a minute later another wave crashed onto the launch. Already low in the water, it had no chance. Dozens of men were swept out of the boat as it swamped. Only its bow bobbed among the whitecaps as men shouted and choked in the dark and looked around frantically for anything that floated in the night.

Pruitt tried to stay with the launch. Without a life jacket and soaked in a pea coat that felt like it weighed 50 pounds, he wrapped an arm around a slightly submerged seat bench. Other men scrambled and fumbled for a handhold on the swamped boat, their liberty drunk forgotten. A Marine lunged for a seat and knocked Pruitt away from the motor launch. Waves pummeled him. He knew he couldn't carry the weight of his waterlogged clothing. Pruitt shed his pea coat and took off his pants. Tying a knot at the end of one leg, he caught some air in the pant leg to create a buoy. But Pruitt weakened quickly in the frigid winter water. Another wave knocked the ballooned pants from his cramped, stiffening hands. More waves pushed him down, spinning him underwater. Between the rolling waves and blowing water, he couldn't tell which way was up to the surface. Only the roiled phosphorous, creating an eerie film of light at the surface, told Pruitt where to find air.

Other liberty launches passed in the dark night, oblivious to the men floundering in the waves. Pruitt floated away from the transport boat toward open water. He fought to keep his head above death. A half hour passed before Midway discovered one of its launches was missing.

The blowing ocean stung John Mee's eyes as he stood at the bow of one of the search launches. Only 19, he was a veteran among Midway's crew. Mee had left the family dairy farm in western New York at 16 and enlisted in time to serve on the carrier Intrepid and survive kamikaze attacks before war's end. Mee and six other brothers and sisters had enlisted in the armed services and he was proud of the family tradition.

Mee's launch climbed over wave crests and cascaded into the troughs as he searched for hours, peering into the wet night for signs of life among the froth. Every once in awhile, "Ho!" rang out over the waves' roar when a lookout spotted a floating body. Sometimes it was alive.

More ships joined the rescue attempt. Their searchlights swept the crashing sea, settling on Pruitt and other lucky crewmen. Pruitt was among the first to be yanked aboard with a hooked pole because he wasn't wearing a life jacket. Clad only in his shorts and one sock, he couldn't stop shivering. He held a Ronson lighter in one hand, an otherwise trivial trinket he somehow didn't want to lose.

The luck of others failed them. As the sun rose the following morning, John Mee and the other rescue parties returned to Midway. They had retrieved eight dead crewmen, by far the single largest loss of life in Midway's short history. Mee had helped pull 29 exhausted men into wooden boats in the middle of the Mediterranean winter storm.

The tragic capsize made headlines throughout Europe and the United States. One newspaper article got it wrong, listing rescuers such as Mee as among the dead. A devastated Mee family back on the family dairy farm read that article. Brothers and sisters who had survived the horror of war couldn't believe John had drowned in a storm. They assumed the Navy eventually would come calling.

Several months later, Mee went home on leave. A friend cried out in shock when he saw him walking down a street. "What are you doing here?" bellowed his father when the Midway bosun's mate reached the family dairy farm. "You're supposed to be dead!" His mother fainted when she walked into the kitchen and saw the 20-year-old, still a boy who had already served his country for four years in war and peace, sitting at the table.

Midway completed its first Mediterranean deployment in the spring of 1948. Six years of patrolling the Mediterranean would follow before Midway would be transferred to the Pacific Fleet. In an era of uneasy postwar peace, world politics and international dynamics changed almost daily. Some nations faded from the world stage, others filled newly created power vacuums, and some cannibalized themselves. In the middle of it sailed John Pruitt, John Mee, and thousands of shipmates ordered to project American power and purpose across the southern flank of Europe.

Sometimes it cost lives. Sometimes that mission took a back seat to compassion.

The bullet holes in the crumbling orphanage wall still looked fresh as Christmas approached. The Italian orphans inside were among the war's most pained victims. Some clung to fading memories of mothers and fathers. Others had lived their entire life among strangers, facing a future as murky as their past was unknown. Hundreds of those children called Albergo de Poveri, a battered Naples orphanage, their home. They were part of the more than ten million orphans left at war's end more than two years earlier. Not only did Europe lose most of a generation in the war, the next generation had been gutted as well.

Midway had anchored off Naples the week before Christmas. As the anchor dropped, crews mobilized. Planes in the hangar deck were pushed aside and as much equipment as possible was stowed. What was once the province of mechanics echoed with the sounds of carpenters (an odd assignment on a ship made almost entirely of steel) building a stage and electricians rigging wires and lights.

On Christmas morning there was no sun. Slate-colored clouds clung to the water as Midway launches wove through a Naples harbor archipelago of upturned ships resembling a chain of bald, rusted islands. Nearly 200 children stood on the pier watching the armada of launches approach. They shivered from the cold as they wondered what lay in store aboard the hulk on the horizon. Nuns hovered around girls dressed in identical tartan dresses, crowned by broad white collars. Each girl wore a ribbon tied in a big bow in her short hair, and a black overcoat buttoned only at the collar. The boys fidgeted under the watchful eye of nuns whose white habits' wings stretched past their shoulders. The boys wore the same topcoat as the girls. Their heads were shaved and their legs were white and scarred below knickers and above ankle-high, lace-up dress shoes. They cautiously stepped aboard Midway's launches for the ride out to the carrier.

Young eyes widened as they walked into the massive hangar deck that had been ringed with lights and decorations. Christmas songs echoed among the steel bulkheads as the youngsters spotted the Christmas tree and then the long tables with plates and bowls lined up in formation from one end to the other. Midway cooks had worked through the night, preparing

Christmas dinner not just for 4,500 men, but special Christmas treats for the orphans.

Santa settled into a chair as the nuns herded the boys and girls into lines. Each youngster had a private moment with Santa (who miraculously spoke Italian) as young men from dairy farms and prairies looked on. Santa handed each youngster a present as the next young girl or boy stepped forward, some eager, others uncertain.

Young sailors, most of whom could have been an older brother to any of the children, crowded around as their young guests sat at long tables for a special Christmas dessert. A particular favorite was Midway's chocolate chip cookies whose recipe became highly valued by departing crewmen in the years ahead. Some sailors looked down at the young faces in front of them and thought of home, a faraway look washing over their faces. Others grinned from ear to ear, sharing in the unique togetherness of that Christmas morning.

The orphans who looked on life with blank faces humbled John Mee. Coming from a home bursting with family on Christmas morning, he struggled to imagine what it must be like to be alone at the age of eight. It fell to Mee and a handful of other men to take the orphans back to the pier. The crew of Midway brightened a Christmas for a group of orphans who returned to a battered orphanage humming Christmas carols and glowing from the kindness of strangers. Two months later Midway returned to Norfolk to prepare for nuclear war.

The headwind lacing Midway's deck reddened the cheeks of more than 125 off-duty sailors off the coast of Virginia in October 1949. They stood shoulder-to-shoulder along island walkways and deck-edge catwalks and gawked at the monstrous aircraft near the stern. A P2V-3 Neptune was warming its engines, its massive wings gently flapping in the wind. Commander Frederick Ashworth eased off the brakes as the Neptune rolled forward. As it gathered speed the odd-looking canisters on each of the tail erupted in ash-colored smoke. The Neptune lurched forward, powered by the still-experimental jet-assisted takeoff engines. Ashworth lumbered off the bow, dropped a few feet, and then slowly gained altitude as Midway chased. The Neptune's nose lifted upward and Ashworth disappeared in smoke and exhaust.

More than 26 hours later, Ashworth landed in San Diego. His route had taken him south to the Panama Canal and then north over Texas before heading west and landing 4,800 miles later. The Navy proclaimed the highly publicized stunt a success, claiming it proved Navy aircraft could match the long-range nuclear weapon delivery capability of the Air Force. Both branches routinely courted supporters in the halls of Congress where make-or-break appropriation decisions were made. PR stunts were part of the game and Midway was a pawn.

Despite the flight off Midway, it was a game the Navy was losing. Its futuristic, flush-deck United States aircraft carrier had been cancelled only days after its keel was laid, prompting the resignation of the Secretary of Navy John Sullivan in protest. Meanwhile, the Navy glossed over the fact that Neptunes couldn't land on aircraft carriers. In the event of a nuclear strike mission, Midway had to make for port, load the Neptunes by crane, and then deploy. It hardly made for a quick-strike capability. Once the Neptunes took off and delivered their nuclear weapons, the pilots faced the prospect of locating a friendly airfield or ditching their aircraft and hoping for rescue.

While the Navy and Air Force fought for supremacy, politics continued to polarize the world. The North Atlantic Treaty Organization had been established to defend Europe a month before Stalin conceded defeat after a 324-day blockade of Berlin. A few months later Russia detonated its first atomic bomb and the People's Republic of China had been formally proclaimed. Uncertainty gripped a nervous crew as Midway patrolled the Mediterranean.

On a coal-black Mediterranean night, Braden Kruger leaped out of his bunk at the sound of General Quarters. He ran to his gunnery station. Silence returned, broken only by the sound of Midway slicing through the sea as he waited. "This is fun," he thought. "Nobody could get close to us out here." Minutes later, from over the horizon Kruger heard a faint bup-boomp, bup-boomp, bup-boomp. He waited, wondering. Suddenly, the night sky over Midway exploded with light from erupting night flares. Momentarily blinded, Kruger heard the British Spitfires scream toward Midway out of the darkness, simulating a strafing run. "Holy shit," he muttered. "What the hell are we doing out here on a ship?" the Marine asked himself. "Anyone tells me he's not afraid out here, he'll be lying through his teeth."

Fear and uncertainty on Midway were not uncommon as America greeted the 1950s. Russia owned the bomb, shocking American officials who thought Soviet nuclear development had been far less advanced. American war planners believed future conflicts would include the use of atomic weapons. It was time Midway go nuclear. That required major changes in Navy philosophy, resource allocation, and personnel training.

On June 14, 1950, President Truman ordered 90 nonnuclear bomb assemblies be transferred to the military from Atomic Energy Commission control. Midway was among the few carriers to receive them, because the Midway class of three carriers (Midway, FDR, and Coral Sea) could accommodate aircraft large and powerful enough to deliver nuclear weapons. With those assemblies came specially trained personnel and new security responsibilities for Kruger's Marine detachment.

Midway began training to deliver nuclear weapons. Midway also trained on defending itself against nuclear attack. Detailed and classified procedures were established for "ABC Warfare." Atomic, biological, and chemical attacks all were concerns for a carrier with a crew who might have only a few minutes' warning.

Midway's crew knew the horror they would face if attacked. Postwar atomic bomb tests had painted a graphic picture of what to expect if an enemy targeted the Navy's foremost class of carriers with nuclear weapons. Midway's officers knew the blast and heat would cause 85 percent of the injuries. They knew the temperature of the fireball would exceed one million degrees Centigrade. If a nuclear weapon detonated underwater near Midway, the underwater pressure shock wave transmitted through Midway's decks would break legs or worse—especially if loose gear had not been stowed and if sailors were caught standing. Both the ocean and mist fallout would be radioactive. The crew could expect debris to fall for 90 seconds after the blast.

Mustard gas was another worry. If missiles carrying mustard gas were fired at Midway, it would be impossible to evacuate the crew in time to avoid contamination. Protective clothing was so impractical on an aircraft carrier it was not even a consideration. So the principle of a "gas-tight envelope" emerged. In the event of attack, Midway's crew would be ordered below deck and to close every opening to the outside world. Each hatch and fitting was assigned to a crewman responsible for its closure. Every member of the crew practiced his emergency assignment, even the ship's dentist. "Collective protection" was considered vital to keeping radioactive particles, gasses, and biological agents from reaching the massive ventilation system powered by 291 motor-driven fans throughout Midway.

Detection and identification were critical. Special mustard gas–sensitive green paint turned red on contact. Mustard gas–sensitive crayons could be used on metal and turned bright blue if exposed to mustard gas. Then there was the bird-in-the-mine approach. In monthly training drills, the Navy reminded Midway's crew to "sniff and think."

Kamikaze attacks on wooden aircraft carrier decks had become ancient history. Instead, the men of Midway trained to guard, assemble, load, and launch nuclear weapons. They trained to defend themselves against fireballs and caustic gasses. Yet at the same time, a primal nautical fear dating back to the earliest days of naval warfare remained undiminished. Fire at sea.

Bob Kennedy learned just how much fire was feared at sea. As a youngster, he had been angry with the Germans and angry with the Japanese. His fury boiled when the war ended before he could settle accounts. Quick to laugh, the outgoing young man came from a poor family that played a massive practical joke on the youngster soon after he had enlisted. While he was away at the Navy's boot camp, his family's home was sold and converted into a business. Everyone thought it great fun not to tell Bob. It took him a while to find his folks when the 18-year-old came home on leave.

Kennedy tended a storeroom "so far down in the ship I heard the water rushing along the ship's hull when under way." One day an officer summoned him to get a rudder out of supply on the double so Kennedy loosely closed the hatch to the supply room and delivered the rudder. Mission completed, Kennedy went for chow and promised himself that he'd return to secure the compartment after watching a movie on the hangar deck.

The announcement "Fire, Storeroom Charlie 530 Able" turned Kennedy's blood cold. Kennedy pictured a trashcan full of uncovered oily, combustible rags in his storeroom and panicked. He ran to the fantail, fearing an explosion. Meanwhile fire crews raced to Storeroom Charlie 530 Able and doused the smoldering can, possibly caused by a cigarette dropped through the grating from the deck above.

The next day, Kennedy was headed for the rapids. Standing in dress blues in front of Captain W. M. Beakley, Kennedy told his story. The highly decorated war veteran who graduated in the first class of the National War College the year before could have ordered Kennedy's court martial. When witnesses confirmed Kennedy was ordered to leave the storeroom immediately to deliver the rudder, Captain Beakley's piercing eyes sized up the South Carolina youngster before imposing 15 days' restriction. He and his buddies in aviation supply never left combustible material unattended again.

Extended Mediterranean deployments at the epicenter of the Cold War grated nerves already frayed from spending months away from home. Toward the end of each deployment, calendars etched in passageways and alongside berths filled with X's. Midway's crew counted days down to when Midway passed Gibraltar, leaving civil wars and international sniping in their wake. Families beckoned in Norfolk.

So Darling, we only have fifty eight days between us, after that there won't be anything between us and I don't mean maybe. Darling I can hardly wait for us to be together again. It seems so long that we have been parted. I only hope that we do a lot of operating the rest of the time, as this last week went by pretty fast. The way you ended your last letter, "I'll hold you in my heart, until I can hold you in my arms." It's beautiful Darling and the feeling is mutual.

I love you Darling,
Ralph

Even when Midway returned to Norfolk for months of repairs, the carrier's crew walked a sword's edge. Frequent training exercises off the coast of Virginia carried risk and uncertainty for aviators and ship's company alike.

On July 23, 1951, the sun bounced off the Atlantic as Commander George Duncan turned his F9 Panther into his final approach and lined up to touch down "inside the box" (the area on the deck bracketed by the first and last arresting wire). Duncan's aircraft was the latest generation of the Panther. In another year it would become the backbone of carrier-based ground attacks in the Korean War. The Panther flew more than 600 miles an hour with a capacity to carry 2,000 pounds of bombs plus six rockets. Fast and deadly, it also carried four 20mm cannons with 800 rounds of ammunition mounted in its nose.

In the last few seconds of his approach, Duncan's aircraft floated to the right of centerline and sank, as if it lost power. When it drifted downward to a point below the deck, it tried to rise, sticking its nose upward as if to climb onto the deck at the last possible second. But it was too late. Duncan slammed into the stern of Midway, about six feet below the flight deck. The impact split the plane in two as cleanly as a stick snapped over a knee. The forward portion of the plane—nose, cockpit, and right wing—tumbled onto the flight deck. The rest of the plane disappeared in a ball of fire as if Midway's fantail had detonated.

The cockpit and its wing arm slammed down, pushing the nose hard onto the deck. The impact was so great the canopy flew off the plane and Duncan's helmet was ripped from the 34-year-old pilot's head. The beheaded plane skidded forward and then turned on its side, rolling, rolling, rolling down the deck in a race against the burning jet fuel chasing it. As Duncan's amputated cockpit approached the island, a tire appeared to his left, hurtling forward and out of the fireball that now spanned the width of the deck. Within seconds nearly a third of Midway had disappeared in spreading orange flames.

Duncan continued to roll as if his cockpit was part of a sadistic, brutal carnival spin ride that bounced and spun down the deck toward the bow. As the cockpit neared the island, the spectators along an outside catwalk on the island called Vulture's Row saw Duncan strapped inside, his face white in shock, defenseless against steel deck and fire. Finally, the cockpit rolled to a rest, yards from the first of two emergency barricades that had been pulled taut. Miraculously, the spreading conflagration slowed as well.

Before the carnage came to a stop, a fire suit–clad sailor sprinted toward Duncan's wreckage. Others were a few yards behind him, dragging fire hoses to beat back the flames as they billowed thick, black smoke astern. Some men with no assigned duties on the deck ran to the wreckage as well, unsure what they could or should do. The deck fire was brought under control while unseen men inside the ship's communications center directed other aircraft into an extended holding pattern. Under the smoke that lingered on Midway before drifting astern, a sheen of water and diluted jet fuel soon covered most of the deck.

The rescue crew that raced to Duncan's cockpit had expected to find a charred and probably mangled body. They were certain George C. Duncan, the pride of Tacoma, Washington, was about to be the newest name on Midway's "In Memoriam" list. George Duncan survived. He even tried to stand once he was pulled from the smoking rubble, but quickly yielded to a stretcher destined for sickbay where the ship's medical team waited.

It took hours to pick the deck clean of Panther pieces, sweep it free of even the smallest debris, and to extract the remainder of the plane that had impaled itself into the fantail. Dozens of young men gathered around the cockpit. They marveled at how the gauges, dials, and much of the cockpit's interior were unmarked. Only three feet behind it, there was no plane. Wires hung limply from the back of Duncan's seat, the entrails a flying mechanical animal violently pulled apart. George Duncan escaped death by skidding and rolling faster than hundreds of gallons of burning jet fuel could spread into the teeth of a headwind.

It was a crash and survival that the crew talked about for weeks. Only a few months later E. W. Keegan experienced a similar terror.

"Shit on a shingle" had grown old. The Navy staple of creamed beef on toast would soon give way to a traditional Thanksgiving turkey dinner, complete with dressing, mashed potatoes and gravy, candied yams, assorted vegetables, and dessert. Plenty of coffee. The printed menu even noted that cigarettes and cigars would be available after dinner.

Flight operations, though, rarely took notice of holidays.

As Midway crested one swell after another, Dominick Triola stood on the portside catwalk at the bow, watching men refuel parked aircraft. The New Jersey native wasn't big, had a long face and serious, intense eyes. Somewhere during his boyhood Triola had gotten it in his head he'd join the Navy. Nothing else would do. So Triola enlisted within days of graduating high school and months later was fueling fighter jets on Midway's bow off Virginia.

After the last aircraft had landed and was refueled, Triola planned go below to drain the fuel lines. When Triola turned to watch pilot E. W.

Keegan approach, the hair on his neck rose. Something was wrong. It looked like Keegan was coming in too parallel to the deck. Usually pilots approached heavy in the tail so the tailhook would grab an arresting wire. Keegan seemed to be flying level, just above the arresting wires. Then Keegan touched down too late. He headed for the emergency mesh barricade and wasn't slowing down.

Larry Virag stood near the bridge, daydreaming about what would be his first Thanksgiving on active duty in the Navy. Virag had grown up with a passion for the Navy, perhaps from watching his father go to work every day in a downtown Cleveland shipyard where he had helped build WWII wooden minesweepers. An electrician, Virag often was called to the upper levels of the island to work on a problem or install a piece of equipment. He got to know those who regularly worked on the bridge so it wasn't hard for him to slip up into the island to watch flight operations when he wasn't on duty.

From up in the island, Virag watched the horror unfold. Keegan had gotten a last-minute wave-off and slammed his throttle wide open. But just as the plane began to rise, the tailhook caught the most-forward cable for an instant and then broke free. Keegan's plane bounced hard on the deck, and then bounced a second time as it sliced through the emergency barricade.

James Davis didn't know a jet was headed directly at him. The former newspaper typesetter from South Carolina was the plane captain for the air group commander's Corsair. He had assumed control of his plane near the bow where it was being refueled by Triola's crew.

Davis and eight other crewmen were working on the bow among the six aircraft parked closely together and within reach of the high-pressure gas lines that snaked up over the deck's edge, delivering 120-octane fuel. He couldn't see that somehow Keegan's canopy opened as it ripped through the barricade. The wind pummeling his face, the young pilot looked back toward the bridge in shock at the very moment he realized nothing would stop his Panther from barreling into the fueled aircraft 300 feet ahead. He had lost control of his life and knew it.

Triola, Davis, and the rest of the refueling crew on the bow looked up to see an out-of-control fighter jet headed directly at them. Some sprinted to the opposite side of the bow. Triola jumped off the catwalk, slid down a ladder, and dove through a hatch. James Davis ran to the only shelter he could find, the catwalk that Triola had just abandoned. Up in the island, Virag stood mute as Keegan's Panther slammed into the parked aircraft. A fireball erupted when Keegan's plane severed one of the fueling hoses. Just as a crewman closed the hatch behind Triola, flaming jet fuel washed down onto the catwalk not far from where Davis stood.

Unidentifiable pieces of plane flew rocketed skyward and fell over the side into the Atlantic. Davis was lucky he wasn't hit by debris. A fellow plane captain had jumped off the deck into the four-foot-wide safety net below and outside the catwalk. Keegan's plane shoved two of the parked planes over the side, onto the safety net, killing the captain, and then all three planes cascaded into the ocean.

Like most bad crashes aboard Midway, a chilling thud and shudder had rolled through the ship's spine. After hearing countless routine "whumps" from routine landings, the crew instantly recognized the sound of disaster. Many were on duty and could do nothing. Others couldn't possibly get to the flight deck in time to help. Triola tried to scramble back on deck but burning fuel forced him to race through passageways, leap through knee-knockers, and cross the hangar deck before climbing back onto the flight deck. Even though emergency crews stood by when flight operations were under way, Keegan and several men trapped on the bow could not be saved that day.

Two weeks later, a somber crew stood in line for Thanksgiving dinner. The sounds and smells of death on the flight deck remained sharp. They were a sobering reminder that even routine exercises only a few hundred miles from Norfolk carried both known and uncharted risk. Each man had to navigate his own path through the uncertainty. Some wrote long and frequent letters home. Others retreated. One penned a newfound perspective discovered as they stared down Cold War threats and lived with danger at sea:

> Lo, I have slipped the surly bonds of earth
> And danced the skies on laughter-silvered wings;
> Sunward I've climbed and joined the tumbling mirth
> Of sun-split clouds – and done a hundred things
> You have not dreamed of – wheeled and soared and swung
> High in the sunlit silence, Hov'ring there
> I've chased the shouting wind along and flung

My eager craft through footless halls of air.
Up, up the long delirious, burning blue
I've tipped the wind—swept heights with easy grace
Where never lark, or even eagle flew;
And, while with silent sifting mind, I've trod
The high untrespassed sanctity of space,
Put out my hand,
And touched the face of God.

—JOHN GILLESPIE MAGEE JR.

ROWS OF STACKED AIRCRAFT batteries made the air thick and acrid. The battery locker had only two entrances, one from an interior passageway and another out onto the sponson deck. It was the perfect place to run an illegal craps game for the big winners of smaller games earlier in the day throughout Midway. On the night of March 15, 1952, Bill Grabowski sensed a killing was about to be made.

A Connecticut high school dropout, Grabowski had enlisted with some buddies in 1950, leaving behind a large Polish family headed by a hard-working, illiterate father toiling as a mill worker to feed six children. Grabowski was tall, lanky, and likeable. Very outgoing, he was quick to brag of his female conquests and enjoyed playing craps. He wasn't alone. Most of the crew earned a monthly salary of between $83.20 and $99.37, enough to fuel one of many sailors' favorite pastimes: gambling.

A sailor could gamble in any department on the ship. If it was payday, he typically got paid in the morning, grabbed some chow, and if he wasn't on duty, joined some buddies to "throw the bones" the rest of the day. It usually started about 1200, for nickels and dimes. Then halves and dollars led up to late-night showdown games between the day's winners. Among some groups, blackjack was the game of choice. Others played poker. Pots could be as much as $40, the equivalent of a two-week paycheck. But craps was king of the hill, often in the darkest and least accessible recesses of Midway.

A big winner earlier in the day, by the time Grabowski stepped through the hatch into the battery locker the betting was beginning to make some players nervous. A sailor nicknamed "Greek" ran the game after converting a workbench into a craps table, complete with backboard. A single light hung above the table, the rest of the compartment as black as a Mediterranean night sky. Nearly 20 men crowded around the table, boasting of their skill and yelling at misfortune when suddenly three cloned bandits slipped into the locker with pistols that swept the room.

Each wore his hat inside out and pulled hard over his eyes, almost down to the neckerchief that covered his face. Pea coats covered them from head to foot and all three wore gloves to hide rings or other identifying features. It was so dark even the color of the robbers' eyes was impossible to discern.

The gunmen herded the men into a single file that snaked through the locker's aisles. One after another, each player was yanked out into the light and ordered to hand over his cash. The man in front of Grabowski stuffed his wad of cash into his T-shirt before stepping out into the light. His bluff of "just getting busted" worked. Smiling, Grabowski claimed the same, only to see a pistol shoved into his nose as $200 exited his wallet. Another man, near the back of the line, tossed his cash behind a pile of spent batteries. In the darkness he wasn't spotted. But most men lost all their money that night, even two hapless innocents who walked into the locker in the midst of the heist.

Once they collected all the cash, the robbers dogged down the inside hatch and left through the one leading outside. Grabowski and the others weren't about to chase them, but had an idea. They raced back to their compartments to see if anyone there was out of breath as if they had just returned on the double. No luck. They never saw their money again.

The next day newspapers around the world carried reports of the "Dice Raid [that] Was a Real Stickup." Although early reports indicated the robbers took millions from Midway's paymaster, $4,400 was lifted, enough in 1952 to buy a new Jaguar X120 or most of a house. Rumors about the identity of the culprits abounded. The robbers dressed like ship's company enlisted men. That made some victims think "those fly-boys, with their attitude, were probably behind it."

Shore leaves were cancelled and a massive search conducted. An unexpected influx of men reported aboard at the next port (suspected by the crew to be Naval Intelligence) and a few ports later just as mysteriously disembarked. Some noticed that a number of Midway veterans suddenly transferred off as well, adding grist to the rumor mill. Weeks later FBI agents interviewed Grabowski, plying him with Camels, Chesterfields, and Luckys, hoping he'd name Greek as the mastermind of an inside job. No luck there, either.

The robbers got away clean. Captain Wendell Morrisset, the commanding officer of Midway's contingent of Marines, enforced the newly adopted Uniform Code of Military Justice. The Marines were the police force of Midway. They provided security, enforced the Code by making arrests, and even ran the jail aboard the warship. Morrisset never had anyone to bring up on charges for what became one of the most famous Midway stories of the 1950s.

Morrisset was as by-the-book as a Midway sailor could get. His eyes were filled with determination. A long, straight nose rose from a square jaw toward a receding hairline. A native of Lubbock, Texas, Captain Morrisset, USMC, was all business in a time of uncertainty. He was convinced he was doing an important job at an important time.

With more than 70 Marines under his command, Morrisset's men guarded Midway's nuclear bombs (called "special weapons" at the time), an open secret to the most of the crew. Morrisset and his detachment also trained with the Marine divisions that sometimes were aboard in the event of a sudden amphibious landing in the Mediterranean. He maintained an organizational table that converted part of the ship's crew into a pseudo-landing force to be deployed until real Marines arrived. He didn't know senior officers back at the Pentagon were discussing two possible scenarios for an emergency deployment of his Marines and perhaps part of Midway's crew.

The birch forests of the Kola Peninsula shuddered as thousands of Russian soldiers crossed marshes and bogs that were beginning to harden with frost in September 1952. On the northern coast at the edge of the Barents Sea, men worked through the lengthening late summer nights, loading ordnance and supplies aboard Russian warships berthed at Murmansk, less than 100 miles from the Norwegian border.

To the west, Norway's northernmost county, Finnmark—bordered by the Barents Sea in the north, the Norwegian Sea in the west, Russia in the southeast, and Finland in the south—sat virtually defenseless against the imminent Russian invasion. Sparsely populated along fjords and larger than Denmark, Finnmark's wide interior valleys would soon freeze for the Arctic winter, becoming a slick highway across the northern edge of NATO. A flanking invasion skirting the heart of NATO could permanently shift the delicate balance of power toward the East. The Russian Bear looked restless.

Half a world away, Chairman Mao strengthened his grip on the three-year-old People's Republic of China. He had pushed Chiang Kai-shek off the mainland onto Formosa and nearby coastal islands that included Quemoy, the Tachens, and Matsu. Most were within range of mainland communist artillery. American nerves frayed when a Chinese MiG-15 shot down a U.S. Navy patrol plane, killing two crewmen as Chiang Kai-shek actively campaigned for overt United States support of an invasion of mainland China.

One threat was real. The other, imaginary. The Russian mobilization against Norway existed only in the imaginations of war planners as the basis for Operation Mainbrace, NATO's first major naval exercise and one in which Midway would play a key role. To the east, the Sino tinderbox was real. In the years ahead, it would become even less stable. But in 1952 Midway's mission was to defend NATO. So in September Midway steamed north toward the North Atlantic alarm. The era of United States and Soviet sparring at sea began in earnest.

Dear Folks,

Had a little excitement last night. We were refueling a destroyer and as a photographer I have to be on the bridge while this is being done. Everything seemed to be going okay, and the fuel lines were put across to the destroyer. When the operation was half over, the "can" started drifting away from the Midway. First the after fuel hose snapped, then the forward fuel hose snapped. Fuel oil was spurting all over the place for a minute. Then the destroyer pulled right back toward us and sharply hit us. The bow made quite a dent in the hull and the mast broke a railing up on the island just below where I was standing. . . . Guess I'll close for now. Next time you hear from me we may be in Scotland.

Love,

Bob

Bob Haskins was as innocent as he was young. A farm kid from Savoy, Massachusetts, Haskins had watched his father eke out a living on the family farm, cutting cordwood and selling Christmas trees. Haskins was the baby of seven children. At one point, three brothers and a sister served in the Navy during World War II. It seemed inevitable that he would follow in their wake.

He didn't know that writing his parents about a minor collision during an underway replenishment (UNREP) nearly made him a national security risk. His mother passed his letter along to the hometown newspaper that ran an account of the UNREP incident with the local teenager in the middle of it. An admiral aboard Midway had barred any public disclosure of the collision and had prohibited reporters aboard from filing a story on the collision. About three weeks later, Haskins was stunned to see a copy of the *North Adams Transcript* in his chief's hand. In no uncertain terms Haskins was told to keep ship's business on the ship. Next time a security officer would be paying him a visit. *Aye-aye, sir.*

Haskins photographed the rest of Operation Mainbrace that included more than 160 ships from eight nations. More than 80,000 men participated in the exercise premised on a Russian invasion of Scandinavia through Germany and Norway. NATO ships conducted an amphibious landing of 1,500 Marines on a Danish island, deployed a task force into heart of the Baltic Sea midway between Sweden and Russia-controlled East Germany, and conducted exercises off Norway. Over the course of 13 days, Midway and fellow "blue fleet" ships defended Norway against the "orange fleet" that simulated Soviet combat tactics while the real Russian fleet patrolled the maneuvers' staging area off Norway.

Aviation gas petty officer Jim Gorman's enemy in Operation Mainbrace was the North Sea. Unending winds cut through every man on the flight deck, threatening frostbite. Day after day, Gorman "had to find ways to stay upright in a cold hurricane without getting blown overboard." North of the Arctic Circle, flight deck crews worked without gloves and were issued shoes that lacked foul weather lining. Operating under "battle conditions," the most a man could hope for was a sandwich and cup of coffee to warm his insides. During Operation Mainbrace, the weather made aircraft refueling on Midway's bow nearly impossible. Aviation gas was supplemented by 10 percent lube oil and had to be pumped by hand from 55-gallon drums into the jets. Several men came home with frostbite.

Gorman's Operation Mainbrace battle scars included frostbitten ears and a frozen tear duct.

But at least Gorman had a secret place to warm himself. Midway's command information center (CIC) had the best coffee on the ship. A secret brew, they said, and no admittance to unauthorized personnel. Gorman had a friend in CIC who gave him access to the coffee he cherished after duty on the flight deck.

One afternoon during Operation Mainbrace as the clouds gave way to a broken sky, Gorman stood in the darkened CIC, shivering hands locked around his coffee cup.

"What the hell—what was that? Did you see it?"

"Yeah, what was it? Weather balloon?"

"No way, did you see how fast that sucker flew?"

"Our jets can't do that speed can they?"

"You think it was Russian? They're not far away."

"Yeah, but what . . . ?"

Four conversations erupted at once a split second after a blip had raced across a CIC radar screen. No one had ever seen anything move so fast. There were no reports of aircraft in the immediate area—although no known jet could begin to approach the speed the sailors in CIC had just witnessed. Neither Gorman nor anyone else had an explanation for what had appeared to be the impossible.

The Midway-class carrier They all carried F-1 and B-2 packages for the newly developed Mk-7 nuclear bomb. Select Midway aircraft crews were ordered to practice loading nuclear weapons and preparing for takeoff. And they had to train in total secrecy aboard Midway.

As Christmas 1952 approached, the U.S. nuclear bomb arsenal reached 850. At least two were aboard Midway. On Christmas Eve Midway anchored near Cannes, France. A cold wind kept much of the crew aboard that night and by 2400 the last liberty launch had returned and was secured. A few minutes later the pilots and crews from two squadrons gathered around the Christmas tree in Hangar Bay Two. Marines guarded closed hatches and secured fire doors to ensure a silent night.

The Christmas tree was flanked by an AD-4B Skyraider on one side and an F2H-2N Banshee on the other. Next to the tree were Mk-7 and Mk-8 tactical nuclear bombs. Both were about 10 feet long and could be carried under the belly of a Skyraider. The Mk-7, nicknamed "Thor," was four times more powerful than the bomb dropped on Hiroshima and could explode on contact or in the air. "Elsie," the Mk-8 version, was only half as powerful but could penetrate the earth to reach underground command facilities before detonating. The aircraft crews practiced loading and wiring the bombs onto their modified planes inside the silent ship.

Heads were down and backs bowed when the screech of an opening fire door jolted them upright. A very drunk sailor under Shore Patrol escort had hit the fire door's open button so he could cross the normally deserted hangar bay. The Marines snapped to and blocked his path as the plane's crews froze as if they were cat burglars caught in the act. "We wondered if that drunk guy ever remembered what he stumbled across that night," said one of the pilots who spent the first hours of Christmas Day practicing with nuclear weapons. "If he did, we wondered if any of his buddies believed his story about pilots loading nuclear weapons next to a Christmas tree in the darkness of Christmas Day."

As some crews trained with nuclear bombs, others were put in charge of parties. Midway deployments in the Mediterranean often blended public relations with projecting American military power.

The hangar deck, mess, and wardroom were festooned with decorations, snacks, libations, and the best musicians Midway had to offer. Anticipation hung in the air as young men fidgeted in their dress blues waiting for their guests to arrive. An hour after the sun set, leaving a deepening blue nautical twilight behind, two liberty launches filled with young women rode the Mediterranean swells toward Midway.

Anchored off Barcelona, Spain, a captain's party on Midway had been planned for some of the local dignitaries and more than 110 daughters of Barcelona's leading citizens. It was part of the public relations mission of most Midway deployments. The young women didn't know they would become the source of both rumor and braggadocio.

Marine Captain Morrisset's men stayed sharp, guarding against couples sneaking away as the dancing began on the hangar deck. No one noticed when a wisp of wind first danced across the flight deck. It strengthened, pushing the Mediterranean into angry crosscurrents. The wind grew even stronger and when it came time to take the ladies ashore that night, Midway's guests found themselves stranded aboard.

Ordered by Captain F. O. O'Bierne to keep order, it fell to Morrisset to quickly devise a plan to maintain all-night control. He also had to convince the local contessa aboard that Barcelona's finest daughters were Midway safe. Ultimately Morrisset broke into Midway's store of movies and held an all-night film festival on the hangar deck. While the films were shown, Midway's radio station began broadcasting on commercial frequencies in the hope an early-morning announcement might find its way to the families that had to be wondering why the bewitching hour passed with no word their daughters. Finally, as the sun rose the next day and the winds calmed, Midway was able to return the young women to their families by 0900. It was over.

"Well, not exactly," said photographer's mate Haskins. Not long after the dance, venereal disease swept through the crew. "Now, no one could prove just where it all came from, because we had been in Gibraltar, Golfe Juan, and Marseilles before reaching Barcelona. But you had to wonder. It wasn't the kind of thing a guy bragged about, but our medical officers sure were kept busy." Between treatments, ship's physicians preached the value of taking sexual precautions.

One day a medical officer had had a bellyful of giving shots. The crew was ordered to the hangar deck in shifts to listen to lectures about venereal disease and watch horror movies of what could happen if they didn't take precautions. He became known as "Old Blood and Guts" for the way he railed at the crew. *"Now when you fellas get over there on shore, the women are gonna be interested in ya. Now the best damn thing you can do is K-Y-P-I-Y-P. Now for those of you who don't know, that's Keep Your Pecker in Your Pants. Now, if ya can't do that, use the pro kits, for chrissakes."*

"Pro kits" were prophylactics. In most ports, as Midway sailors made their way across the quarterdeck, they passed a box of pro kits from which some grabbed a few on their way ashore. Sometimes there was a reminder as part of the Plan of the Day, a daily itinerary that detailed ship and shore activities. At the very bottom was the simple reminder, "KYPIYP."

Exercises, drills, and legend-making aside, Midway cruises of 1953 and 1954 made good on the Navy promise that its recruits could see the world. Guided tours were available in most ports and on occasion multiday trips into the heart of the host country were available to those lucky enough to have liberty. When Midway made a port call at Algiers, Morocco, those on liberty could take advantage of a two-day trip (cost: $22) or an all-day tour of Algiers and the Casbah ($5). The cost "does not usually include wine, drinks, and the damage," according to the shipboard rate sheet. The two-day trip boasted "the sands of the Sahara, camels, dancing girls, mosques and minarets of the Moslem religion." The all-day tour was more sedate, offering only wild monkey feeding.

More frequently, a Midway sailor only a few months removed from Stayton, Walsenberg, or Belle Glade traveled solo or in small packs when ashore. Perhaps armed with a pro kit in his pocket, the most he and his buddies had to go on were scouting reports from Midway veterans or periodic reports in the shipboard weekly newsletter, *Midway Current.* A few days before arriving in Marseilles, the *Current*'s editors admonished, *"It is to be noted that certain districts in town are frequented by some very tough and very sharp operators. If you find yourself in one of these areas it is best to get out quick. Also it would be wise to keep a hand on your money as a sailor is considered fair game on any of these back streets."*

Life lessons were frequent and sometimes painful for young men growing into manhood aboard Midway.

A recruit's journey to Midway began with 11 weeks of basic training. It accomplished little more than acquainting young sailors with the rudiments of Midway life. For many, it began at Naval Training Center at Bainbridge, Maryland. The massive 1,000-acre, 500-building complex had been built on a bluff overlooking the Susquehanna River to train more than 250,000 sailors in WWII. Its giant Quonset regimental drill hall and massive brick headquarters greeted new recruits on a journey that began at the guarded base entrance and led to the steel flight deck of the nation's largest aircraft carrier.

In September of 1951, 17-year-old Clancy and his brother had walked across New York's Times Square to buy school clothes. They took in a movie, *Steel Helmet,* a downbeat, almost antiwar film starring Gene Evans. By the time the movie ended, Clancy had decided to enlist in the Navy as soon as he turned 18, even though it meant dropping out of high school a few months before graduation. At the training center in Bainbridge, he found himself on a path that led to the Mediterranean aboard Midway on repeated deployments through 1954.

Clancy was one of the young men aboard Midway who had much to learn as one Mediterranean patrol blended with the next. Long and gangly, he kept his thick, curly red hair long so that it cascaded down onto his forehead. (Regulations such as working attire and hair length were enforced to varying degrees, largely based on the personality of the commanding officer at any given time.) Wide, horizontal eyes often were serious. The eldest of eight children, his grin sometimes turned grimace.

The process of molding Clancy into a sailor began immediately upon arrival. He stood in line with other teenagers who arrived in long-sleeved sweaters, jackets, cuffed pants, and scuffed shoes that were promptly confiscated. He spent much of his first day in the Navy wearing only a towel as he stood in endless lines for x-rays, inoculations, eyesight tests, dental checkups, physicals, body measurements, and a haircut that left only a patch of scruffy hair on the top of his head. A skinny chest, white legs, and uncertain face were the sculptor's mud that the old salts, most about the same age as the recruits' fathers, began to recast as a seaworthy sailor.

The next day Clancy flinched as the executive officer's voice rocketed around the drill hall and across a sea of recruits. Soon the new recruits formed up into small groups that became the personal province of education petty officers. Classroom sessions were coupled with practicing how to catch a hot shell out of an antiaircraft gun. Reviewing the assembly of a rifle followed instruction in how to wear a gas mask and how to roll clothes the Navy way. Young men practiced with sound-powered telephones, dummy helms, and signal flags that looked like props on a movie set. Training in firefighting topped the list of priorities. Swimming stamina, lifesaving skills, and learning the proper way to abandon ship rounded out a young man's immersion into Navy life.

Less than three months later, nearly 150 teenagers, grins on their young faces, lined up for graduation pictures. Clancy couldn't control a boyish, toothy smile from ear to ear, eyes sparkling with pride. A few wore their white hats slightly askew suggesting an aura of invincibility and eagerness to tackle what life ahead dare offer. Yet in many ways, Clancy and the others were still boys. Men already out on the blue water awaited them, prepared to finish the job of molding them into men.

John Hipp was only a few years older than John Clancy. A Naval Academy graduate from Pennsylvania with a bright future, Hipp led the Midway's 44-man seventh division that included Clancy. Strangers all as the new men reported for duty, it was part of Hipp's job to build an effi-cient team while Midway continued its patrols. For some of the more insightful and compassionate officers, building a team often included mak-ing a personal commitment to the men under their command.

Hipp sensed that the young man from Far Rockaway, New York needed help. To no one's fanfare, Hipp decided to take Clancy under his wing. One day Clancy stood as a witness at a captain's mast after a buddy—a tough guy from New York—had gotten into a fight in Cannes. The friend had a checkered record so Clancy decided to take the fall in front of Captain W. H. Ashford. Captain Ashford saw through the teenager's charade and sent the real culprit to the brig. Clancy's attempt at becoming the fall guy couldn't go unchallenged. Hipp took Clancy on a walk down Midway's flight deck for some "catwalk counseling."

Hipp was more the older brother than senior officer as they walked into a stiff breeze that slid along Midway's deck. "That wasn't the right thing to do," said Hipp, staring ahead off the bow. "I know why you did it, but it was wrong." Clancy said little. He knew. "That guy deserved what he got. He's always deserved what he's gotten. We all do, in the end. There's always accountability and responsibility."

"Yea," said Clancy, his head down, wind rippling around him. "The friends you choose will always reflect on you. You're better than you think you are, John. You just don't know it yet. So I'm going to show you. I'll tell you when you're square and doing it the right way. When you aren't, we'll talk about it privately. You're better than you think. Give yourself a chance to prove it."

Clancy, the high school dropout, was touched. A man who had seen the world believed in him. In the following weeks they spent long nights in a gun tub just below the flight deck, talking about life goals and life fears under skies sometimes speckled with stars, other times flat black with unseen clouds. On occasion Hipp took Clancy aside and, clearly irked, chastised Clancy for his penchant of keeping his red hair too long.

One day, Clancy decided to show his gratitude. He went to the gunnery maintenance shop and asked a crewman there who moonlighted as a bar-ber to trim Clancy's cherished red hair to Navy regulation length. When Hipp next spotted the shorn Clancy, the officer slapped him on the back. "You're going to make it, Red Dog," he said, hanging a moniker on Clancy the New Yorker would proudly wear the rest of his life.

Later, when it came time to take the division's team photo on a sunny flight deck for the cruise book, Hipp yelled at Clancy to "get over here and stand right behind me. I want to always remember you." Clancy did as he was told, standing tall with his white hat down low on his brow, looking over the shoulder of John Hipp. Clancy and thousands of others found their way to manhood aboard Midway in the middle of the Mediterranean as the Cold War raged. Those who followed would have to find their manhood half a world away.

CHAPTER 6

A NEW ENEMY

FOR NEARLY SEVEN YEARS Midway had patrolled the Mediterranean, giving political and ethnic enemies a moment of pause. Yet as the Mediterranean continued to simmer, a narrow sliver of ocean half a world away suddenly threatened to boil over. Two Chinas jockeyed for a showdown in late 1954. The leader of the national Chinese on Formosa, Chiang Kai-shek, had marshaled 58,000 troops on Quemoy Island and another 15,000 on nearby Matsu, both only a few miles off the coast of mainland China. Day after day, Chairman Mao's communist artillery pounded the off-shore islands.

In Washington, a massive debated raged. On September 12, 1954, the Joint Chiefs of Staff recommended using nuclear weapons against communist China, a strategy President Eisenhower and his Security Council rejected. Yet rumors began to make rounds on the Norfolk waterfront where Midway had berthed after its latest Mediterranean deployment. Rumors that the United States was preparing for nuclear war. Rumors that Midway would depart Norfolk on a world cruise and be reassigned to the Seventh Fleet in the Pacific. The rumors were true.

In December the United States secretly shipped nuclear weapons to its base on Okinawa and nonnuclear bomb assemblies to Japan. While Chairman Mao and Chiang Kai-shek sparred, the United States loaded up for a potentially massive knockout blow. Midway might be ordered to deliver it. Just two days after Christmas, Midway cleared Norfolk and headed east as artillery shells screamed across the Formosa Strait toward off-shore targets.

On their way to the world's newest threat to peace, Midway's crew first would experience a Navy initiation rite of more than 200 years' standing.

Don McGahan couldn't sleep. The son of a barber in Somerset, Kentucky was scared. Several decks away, John Clancy similarly worried about what lay just over Midway's horizon. Soon Midway would "cross the line" at the equator on its dash across the Atlantic and then through the Indian Ocean toward its new assignment in the Pacific. "Crossing the line" was part Halloween costume party, part fraternity initiation in the Navy. Sailors who had never crossed the equator were called "pollywogs" and were required to endure a ceremony of pranks and pratfalls concocted by those who had already crossed the equator to become coveted "shellbacks." Rank held no sway. Commanders stood alongside the lowliest apprentices.

Shellbacks began hinting at what was to come. The pollywogs couldn't separate fact from fiction. Hints and innuendo fueled speculation. The night before the crossing, a few pollywogs played practical jokes on targeted shellbacks. McGahan wanted to get in a good lick. He decided to visit a machinist's mate first class who already was a shellback. In the midst of a card game, the shellback was staring intently at his cards when McGahan slapped him in the face with a handful of grease. McGahan came to regret the prank as most ill-advised decision "I ever made in my life. The guy arranged it so I repeatedly had to face swats and whacks from him all day long."

When Midway crossed the equator on January 6, 1955, more than 2,850 pollywogs tentatively climbed up onto the flight deck. They found the most powerful ship in the world dead in the water, adrift. They looked up at the mast. Next to Midway's pennants, a Jolly Roger wobbled in the morning breeze. Trembling sailors faced a sunrise-to-sunset series of shenanigans devised by shellbacks dressed as King Neptune, his Royal Court, Davy Jones, and his band of pirates. "Good lord," John Clancy thought, "What I have gotten into?"

Each pollywog was expected to survive a series of pranks in order to convince King Neptune he was worthy of becoming a shellback. It started with King Neptune's Royal Babies: five of the fattest shellbacks on board, sitting on a raised platform, each with a bare, blubbery belly slathered in heavy black grease. Every pollywog had to walk up and "kiss" (bury their face in) a baby's belly as others looked on and howled. Reeking of grease, each pollywog moved on to the Royal Doctor who slammed a fistful of flour into his blackened face.

Then it came time to visit the Royal Dentist who filled the pollywog's mouth with spicy meat sauce and vinegar. "Swallow it." Some were blindfolded and ordered to eat the contents of a bowl handed them. The shellbacks were experts at playing mind games. A voice ordered John Clancy to "eat the entire bowl of worms! Right Now!" He reached into his bowl and filled his mouth with something long, slimy, and gritty. Gagging, Clancy choked it down. "Turned out it was spaghetti covered with a ton of nonsweet cocoa powder. Your imagination ran amuck," confessed Clancy. "Even knowing later what it really was, it still tasted like worms to me."

By that point, every pollywog was a mess. So the Royal Mortician hosed each down before entombing him in a coffin mostly filled with water. Then, handcuffed, it was time to visit a Royal Barber armed with tin snips. It was a sad pollywog facing the Royal Executioner who flipped him into a makeshift swimming pool filled with ship's garbage. Finally, the gauntlet awaited. Shellbacks formed two lines, facing each other. Wet, greasy, shorn, and smelly pollywogs sprinted as fast as they could between the two lines, nearly the length of the flight deck that stretched for more than three football fields, enduring swats on rumps, legs, and the bottoms of their feet. At the end, free of the gauntlet, they dove into a cargo net. The ordeal was over.

But for some, a little extra was added. McGahan watched as some of the Marine pollywogs were given a rough time, reflecting the sometimes uneasy relations between ship's company and Midway's Marine detachment assigned to perform security and guard duties. One Marine's head was covered with a gasket sealant that gelled rock hard. It took him several days of using diesel oil as a cleaner to dissolve the black cranial cast so his head could be shaved and begin to heal. "Probably the dirtiest trick I saw pulled in the Navy. For the rest of us, by the end of the day your butt was tore up and you were pretty black and blue. When it was over, you felt a euphoria you didn't know existed. It was over. You made it through. You were a shellback. I never felt such an enormous sense of pride."

They all had survived the time-honored initiation to become "a son of Neptune." Men, regardless of rank or assignment, felt a new kinship. A new sense of unity. Days later Midway arrived at Capetown, South Africa. White and black sailors who had forged a unique bond of common experience in the middle of the Atlantic were prohibited from associating with one another ashore in a city stained by apartheid.

Midway sliced through the Indian Ocean, a setting winter sun in its wake. Ahead, thousands of miles of unbroken ocean stretched over the horizon toward Southeast Asia. All 12 boilers were on line, driving the carrier through the unending swells.

As Midway plowed ahead, an unending relay race of Navy ships took place as every few days one pulled alongside for what most Midway captains called "a major pucker event." No one looked forward to underway replenishments because Midway did not stop to take on supplies. Instead, it sailed a duet with tankers, supply ships and others, modestly slowing but never wavering from its course.

Standing at the helm, Don "Slim" Dresser made sure pucker catastrophes didn't happen. As a helmsman, he ensured Midway maintained a precise course and speed when a supply ship or tanker steamed alongside, about 150 feet away. Helmsmen on both ships matched speeds and never drifted off course more than one degree. If a ship yawed a single degree, it moved sideways 20 feet in one minute. Any more than that during a refueling UNREP, fuel lines could pull loose to create one of the three biggest worries on the bridge during an UNREP. Loss of steering and loss of propulsion were the other major concerns that could prompt an "emergency breakaway."

Tall and with a friendly, open face highlighted by bright blue eyes, Dresser had arrived on Midway after declining an offer to join the presidential yacht detail. Being on call twenty-four hours a day, always in dress whites, didn't appeal to Dresser so he transferred to Midway.

As a member of Midway's basketball team, "Slim" earned either envy or ire from shipmates. Sports were an outlet that kept much of Midway's crew in shape and fed their competitive grit. Basketball, weightlifting, baseball, softball, and boxing all were popular. Basketball tournaments and boxing matches called "smokers" were held in the hangar bays. Crowds of several hundred spectators frequently filled the hangar bays with hoots and derisive cheers. The ship's athletic teams enjoyed extra liberty, going ashore to compete against the locals which prompted shipboard jealousy on occasion.

Standing at the helm, Dresser knew hydrodynamics became uncertain when waves were compressed between the ships' hulls, building into leaping white crests that ricocheted from one ship across to the other. They often crashed up onto the deck of the oiler or destroyer alongside Midway. It was an important, dangerous, and frequent exercise because Midway consumed 5 percent of its fuel supply every day when it steamed at 18 knots. At a brisk 30 knots, Midway burned through its massive fuel stores in a week.

As long as Dresser stayed straight and true, others shot lines across to the other ship and erected the underway replenishment rigging to pass fuel, parts, dry goods, movies, people, and even ice cream from one ship to the other. Don McGahan dreaded UNREPs. No one looked forward to standing in a bucket-brigade line for hours at a time, handing one box or crate after another to the man next to him. It was both tedious and exhausting, a tough job by any man's standard. Still, an UNREP detail provided McGahan and others who worked in the bowels of Midway a diversion and some fresh air.

Misery fueled by hunger often spawned ingenuity in the UNREP lines. Stomachs growled often on Midway. The lines stretching from the mess reached legendary length. Many sailors skipped meals altogether. Sleep often took precedence over eating. So when a man had the chance to swipe something out of the UNREP line, he often would. It was easiest when Midway UNREPed during a battle condition drill as it sped across the Indian Ocean. Only a few red lights divided the ship into long stretches of darkness, perfect for diverting a crate of juice or other desirable. Cheese was best, though, because of its weeks-long shelf life.

Don McGahan had joined his buddies when they enlisted in the Navy. The southern boy with a soft accent as rounded as Kentucky's mountains became a machinist's mate. McGahan's job was to keep the guts of Midway operating. Twelve boilers fed four power plants, a massive complex of machinery that operated virtually 24 hours a day when Midway was at sea for months at a time.

McGahan sometimes lived inside the equipment. "There were miles and miles of extremely high-pressure steam pipe. A tiny leak could be so small a man couldn't see it yet it still could cut right through him. Sometimes we'd have to clear a valve and then repack the asbestos insulation around the pipe. We thought nothing of mixing flake asbestos with water to a plaster consistency as asbestos fibers floated up into our eyes and nose."

Steam was the blood of Midway. Without it, operational systems died. Steam also created brutal working conditions in a ship designed more for war and survivability than comfort. The evaporator room reeked as one of the hottest places on board. McGahan watched the temperature climb to 130 degrees where the evaporators made fresh water. "Men sat in cages wiping sweat from eyes riveted on gauges. After seeing newsreels during World War II of ships getting blown apart, we'd wonder about what death might be like deep inside Midway."

McGahan didn't know that up on the flight deck, flight operations were intensifying as Midway reached the far side of the Indian Ocean. In a matter of days Midway pilots would be patrolling within a few miles of communist Chinese airfields and dodging both communist and national Chinese fighter aircraft. Midway had to be ready for extended air operations in a very small and congested corner of the world. That placed a high priority on air traffic control and the detached voices and cool wit of men like Ken Sullivan.

It was Sullivan's job—a half deck below the bridge in the island—to organize and make sense of flight operations. Sullivan had been destined to become an air traffic controller aboard Midway. As a boy, Sullivan had been mesmerized every time he spotted a plane in the high sky above Sacramento, California. His father was an engineer who loved planes as well. After joining the Navy, it seemed natural that Sullivan would be assigned to air control.

His journey to Midway began several hundred miles south of Sacramento where the Navy operated a training school at El Centro. The farming town in the middle of the desert was only a few miles north of the Mexican border and surrounded by crusty sand, spindly ocotillo, and the aptly named Salton Sea. Dry and brutally hot, El Centro was ideal for flight training, parachute schooling, air traffic control instruction, and uncontrolled legions of cockroaches.

In many ways, Sullivan, two other controllers, and an air officer comprised the brain that made the fluid and dangerous process of landing heavily armed aircraft aboard a floating steel airfield even remotely possible. Air controllers decided which planes landed first, based on their status. If an F9-F Panther carried less than 900 pounds of fuel, the pilot likely didn't have enough fuel to stay in the pattern. He needed to land and land quickly. Air control made those judgments, called out the landing sequence to pilots (called "stacking them up"), and then communicated with the landing signal officers down on the flight deck. Controllers also stayed in near-continuous contact with the arresting wire crews so they could set the tension for each plane based on its weight the instant its tailhook slapped the deck.

Air operations played out against the backdrop of friction that sometimes developed between the ship's company and the crew assigned to the air wing. The captain of Midway reigned supreme over the entire crew, although the air wing was the province of the commander of the air group who in turn answered to the captain. Air wings were not permanently assigned to aircraft carriers. Sometimes the air wing haughtily called the carrier "Hotel Midway" which rankled ship's company. Conversely, men assigned to Midway frequently saw the air wing as egotistical and unappreciative of what it took to enable an air wing to operate on a carrier. (Later, when Midway was homeported in Yokosuka, Japan, one air wing, CVW-5, was permanently assigned to the carrier for 18 years. Such an unprecedented association overcame much of the inbred hostility between air wings and ship's companies. But in the 1950s a testy relationship between the two groups existed on Midway.) Some officers, by virtue of nerve, personality, or experience, exacerbated that relationship more than others as Midway turned toward the Formosa Strait.

Air Officer Walter Albert Haas was in his early 40s. He walked awkwardly, all elbows and knees, and his reddish hair and ruddy skin frequently disappeared behind blue smoke billowing from the cigar or pipe permanently implanted between his teeth. Haas had flown off the carrier Yorktown and fought the Battle of Midway. He was an ace who once flew Hellcats. Sullivan knew Haas had seen more air combat and carrier landings than most of the men in Pri-Fly could imagine.

For some reason, Haas didn't think much of Midway's captain and, being part of the air wing, he harassed the captain whenever he could. Smoking wasn't allowed in Pri-Fly, not that it mattered to Haas. Sullivan often watched Haas light up a cigar, smoke it down to the stub, and then stuff it into a cherry wood pipe to finish it off. Haas liked to close all the hatches to Pri-Fly and puff at flank speed. When anyone activated the sound-powered voice tube to the bridge, blue smoke poured out, raising the ire of the captain who bellowed at Haas in frustration even as flight ops continued.

The bickering took a backseat when American warships appeared on Midway's horizon.

Heavy, ashen clouds blocked the sun on the morning of February 6, 1955, and Midway was quiet. It had completed its high-speed dash across the Indian Ocean after being ordered to form up with Task Force 77 off the coast of China. Midway's sailors had been warned "this is the real deal."

Marty McCormick, a troubleshooter for the VF-12 "Flying Ubangis" squadron, was asleep when Flight Quarters sounded earlier than usual. He had grown used to making the high-stepping sprint to his duty station, avoiding men and knee knockers along the way. He scrambled up a ladder and jumped through an outside hatch onto the walkway just below the edge of the flight deck. The sight on the horizon stopped him dead in his tracks. The youngster who had decided the Navy was a better option than shift work at the Philadelphia Electric Company thought perhaps he had been transported back in time to World War II.

Warships lined the horizon in every direction. "There was the Yorktown. The Essex. The Wasp and their escort ships and men I had only read about in school. Their history from days gone by flooded over me. Even a submarine surfaced for a brief period, exchanged some signals with the bridge, and then submerged. It was truly an amazing sight. This was no training drill. The ammunition was live and it was combat conditions."

The Eisenhower administration had decided to evacuate the heavily populated Tachen Islands, relocating more 30,000 nationalist soldiers and civilians. Pilots from Midway and the other carriers of Task Force 77 were ordered to fly air cover, silencing the artillery from the mainland as thousands of families stood on the Tachens' piers, waiting for the next landing ship tank (LST). Most refugees believed communist China troops would take control of the Tachens once the evacuation was completed; they could never return home.

Fleeing civilians brought everything they could carry and drag, including livestock, onto the LSTs. Once aboard, families hauled their heavier belongings onto the tank afterdeck. Hundreds of families crammed together on the main deck of each LST as Midway aircraft circled overhead. It was a rocky, dangerous way to escape the shelling for an unknown future. On the LST Tom Green County, a child was crushed when a mountain of refugees' belongings shifted in rough seas. The youngster was buried at sea, a small boy's flight to safety cruelly cut short, a homeless family devastated.

Midway patrolled not far away, ready to launch additional aircraft if necessary. Marty McCormick could see the flashes from the communist artillery on the coast while pilots paced in their ready rooms. Men deep inside the hull repeatedly glanced at the nearest 1MC speaker box in anticipation of a call to battle stations. McCormick looked out over the water, waiting for VF-12's Banshees to return from patrol over the islands. Landing, even in good conditions, made everyone nervous. McCormick thought back to his first few days aboard Midway and the harbingers of what lay ahead.

On his first day aboard within the peaceful confines of Mayport, Florida harbor, McCormick had stopped in front of a photograph of a horrific crash on deck during the previous cruise in the Mediterranean. His breath caught in the back of his throat as he wondered if the pilot had survived and whether flight deck personnel like him had been killed. Not long after, one night he saw a returning pilot get a wave-off from the landing signal officer (LSO). For some reason, the pilot didn't break left, but flew straight down the deck and out over the bow. From McCormick's station on the flight deck, it seemed the Banshee was flying straight toward him. McCormick dove over the side of the deck and onto the narrow safety net along the starboard catwalk. Like a fish caught in a net, McCormick stared down at the white foam rushing by, 50 feet below him. "That's when it hit me, on the deck of an aircraft carrier you're at war even in peace. It's never safe."

Now, with all of two months' experience under his belt, the youngster from Philadelphia waited for his pilots to return from a game of cat and mouse with communist artillery crews and prowling enemy fighters. "Heads up! We've got a plane in the groove with a hung rocket!" A plane was about to slam down on the steel deck with a rocket that failed to fire and was dangerously "hung up" on the jet's wing. No one knew whether it would stay there when the Banshee's tailhook grabbed an arresting wire.

McCormick looked up in time to see the Banshee touch down, grab the wire, and yank the rocket free. It shot down the deck toward the bow where a number of F9 Cougars were parked for refueling.

Everyone on the flight deck dove in different directions. McCormick heard the rocket skidding down the deck, bouncing a little, until it slammed into and wedged against the tailpipe of one of the Cougars. He waited for the fireball to roll over him. "I just knew it was going to go off and we'd be grease spots." It never did. McCormick watched in amazement as ordnance men "came out of nowhere, sprinting to the Cougar. They pulled the rocket from the plane and threw it over the side of the ship. It was the last we ever saw of it."

Within a few days, Task Force 77 completed its mission, shuttling thousands of Chinese out of the Tachens, leaving the islands to the communists. Midway remained in the western Pacific as news reports grew even more alarming. Secretary of State Dulles publicly acknowledged the use of nuclear weapons was under consideration. President Eisenhower created an international uproar when he publicly stated, "A-bombs can be used . . . as you would use a bullet." The Chief of Naval Operations, Robert Carney, predicted war with China by mid-April. Midway stayed on station and its crew on edge, wondering if they soon would be ordered to launch aircraft carrying nuclear bombs against a new enemy.

Then China folded. On April 23 it announced a newfound willingness to negotiate with Formosa. About a week later communist shelling of Quemoy and Matsu stopped. War had been averted for the time being. As Midway steamed toward Yokosuka, Japan, the communists continued their military build-up along the coast while Chiang Kai-shek reinforced Quemoy and Matsu. Another Chinese crisis seemed inevitable. Perhaps Midway would return.

When the carrier steamed under the Golden Gate Bridge on July 14, 1955, it completed a 57,000-mile journey around the world. The next stop would be the Puget Sound Naval Yard for a massive two-year modernization after decommissioning.

The overhaul of Midway had been planned for years and was necessary to keep pace with explosive advances in naval aviation.

No crew would be needed during the modernization. Some Midway sailors received new orders. Others left the Navy. Ken Sullivan, the air controller in the smoke-filled Pri-Fly, left the Navy and spent the next 30 years as a practicing attorney. Don McGahan, the son of a Kentucky barber, left the Navy after making one last asbestos plaster casing and became a production director of a number of daily newspapers.

Some left Midway quietly. Others back slapped their way ashore. John Clancy, the high school dropout from Far Rockaway, received orders to transfer to another ship. He walked slowly off Midway and paused on the pier, his seabag against his leg. He turned and looked up at the carrier. There was John Hipp standing in a gun tub on the fantail. Memories of countless hours spent together, gazing out over the blue water sharing, laughing, revealing, and resolving swamped Clancy. Each raised a hand in farewell. A moment passed before they snapped their best salute to each other. One, a U.S. Naval Academy graduate, the other a young man who would spend most of his life as a power plant operator in New York. One had reached manhood on Midway and together they had faced down a common enemy. And both were part of what made the first decade of Midway magic.

CHAPTER 7

TO THE EDGE
OF WAR

MIDWAY CAPTAIN FRANCIS E. NUESSLE had been given eight months by the Navy to mold a new Midway into a fighting ship after its two-year modernization.

Midway's overhaul was unprecedented. Its $55-million modernization had required more than 1.1 million man-days of labor by thousands of welders, sheet metal workers, electricians, plumbers, naval architects, and machinists. The carrier that returned to active duty in 1957 bore little resemblance to the Midway that had been decommissioned two years earlier.

The British innovation of adding a second, angled deck to aircraft carriers had revolutionized carrier air operations. A second short, canted deck extending from the stern to the port side at about a 10-degree angle to the original centerline deck was added to Midway. It enabled aircraft to land from the stern on the angled deck while aircraft launched straight ahead off the bow.

A major benefit was safety. On a straight-deck carrier, the emergency mesh barrier almost always stopped a propeller-driven aircraft if it missed the arresting wires. Jets, though, landed at about twice the speed of a prop aircraft so they frequently plowed through the barricade and into armed and fueled aircraft parked on the bow. It was deadly. The angled deck enabled aircraft to land *to the side* of aircraft on Midway's bow. Simultaneous recoveries and takeoffs required retraining of flight deck crews. Other improvements included flight deck strengthening and the installation of a huge, 50,000-pound crane. New, more powerful steam-driven catapults were installed to launch larger jet aircraft, including a catapult on the new angled deck.

A sophisticated new primary flight control, the nerve center of flight operations, was installed. The crew assigned there faced extensive training on sophisticated new equipment. Below, crew living conditions had been the source of complaints since Midway touched water in 1945. As the crew reported aboard in late 1957, many discovered expanded air conditioning reached more of the living spaces.

Other major structural changes were made. The open bow was enclosed as a "hurricane bow" which strengthened the flight deck and reduced vulnerability to storm damage. Seven small portholes in the bow, just below the flight deck, looked like the eyes of a giant, mutant steel creature. They were part of a secondary command center constructed in case the bridge up in the island was knocked out.

The width of Midway increased by eight feet to provide massive amounts of additional fuel storage. Fuel capacity grew to one million gallons of aviation gas and jet fuel. Midway became fully jet capable. The 45,000-ton aircraft carrier launched in aviation's propeller era only 12 years earlier was now a fully loaded, 63,000-ton platform that carried the largest and most powerful jets in the Navy arsenal.

It was up to Nuessle to evaluate every improvement and component. He did it by repetition. Drills followed drills that tested 1,700 telephones, 2,000 electric motors, 242 miles of electric cable, and 230 miles of tubing inside 12 massive boilers. More than 325 separate ventilation systems were tested, as were 14,000 electric lamps, 600 loudspeakers, and the six galleys that fed an average of 34 men per minute, 24 hours a day.

Logistics were tested as well. Nowhere was that more evident than planning and preparing 10,000 meals daily by 53 cooks and 19 bakers. The supply division was critical if Midway's mess was to bake 6,500 loaves of bread a week, serve 850 gallons of ice cream weekly, and prepare 7,000 pounds of food daily.

As Midway reclaimed its operational identity off the California coast, rumblings of war rolled in from the west. In 1957, the United States installed missiles on Formosa that could deliver nuclear warheads into mainland China. Talks between the United States and communist China broke down when the U.S. replaced its ambassador with a diplomat of lower rank. Meanwhile Chiang Kai-shek sought American approval of commando raids against the communists. After three years of dormancy, nationalist and communist Chinese factions again prepared for a showdown. As Midway demonstrated its operational readiness off California, the Navy turned to Captain John Thomas Blackburn and ordered him to prepare Midway for war.

Blackburn had ridden his fame as founder of the storied Jolly Roger squadron in World War II to the rank of captain. Renowned for his 11 Japanese kills, daring and bravado, the ace had commanded the air wing aboard Midway shortly after commissioning in 1945 and was the first pilot to land aboard Midway. On June 2, 1958, he returned to Midway as its commanding officer.

One day up on the bridge, Blackburn looked down at the sleek and mean F8 Crusader. It crouched on Midway's catapult, eager to leap into the sky. In trials a pilot had flown a Crusader from a carrier off the coast of California to the carrier Saratoga off Florida less than three hours later. It begged the new captain of Midway to fly it even though Blackburn wasn't qualified.

Later when Midway was moored in Buckner Bay at Okinawa, the temptation was too much for Blackburn. Blackburn's Crusader shot off Midway's bow and rocketed for the heavens, leaving a poker-red fire trail in its wake. The Crusader was far more jet fighter than anything Blackburn had flown. Within a few minutes of takeoff, Blackburn nearly lost control of the sensitive thoroughbred. Too much speed prompted the Crusader to "porpoise" through the air. Sky and clouds blurred across the canopy as unconsciousness neared before Blackburn regained control. Midway beckoned. Blackburn knew enough to realize he had been licked and landed without incident.

The next morning, Blackburn shocked the crew when he crawled out of his captain's at-sea cabin. His eyeballs were bright red from broken blood vessels and he sported two world-class shiners from the brutal G forces the flight had produced. No one dared ask the skipper how he felt. He was back on bridge and that was that. Captain Blackburn was a man who lived life on the edge and loved it.

Blackburn also was a man who left other men awed in his wake. Diminutive at only about five feet six inches, a cigar was permanently rooted in the left corner of his mouth. He walked fast, talked fast, and expected the same from others. By many accounts Blackburn also was a four-star alcoholic who thought nothing of joining a group of lowly ensigns in any officer's club or bar at night and then riding them like hell the next day.

He also was an enlisted man's captain. His reputation as a daring Navy ace preceded him and his willingness to mix with the crew made him one of the three most popular captains in Midway's 47-year history. He had been bred to become captain of Midway. Blackburn's father had been a Navy captain 45 years earlier. A brother was a commander in the Navy and an uncle was a rear admiral. In his second tour on Midway, Blackburn knew his way around the carrier better than any captain before him. And it wasn't long before the Captain Blackburn style permeated the entire ship.

Captain's mast exemplified Blackburn's leadership style. Unlike other captains who listened to witnesses and carefully deliberated on minor offenses, Blackburn ran through 20 cases in 20 minutes. He often dispensed with the niceties of judicial protocol. "Mr. Jones!" Blackburn would yell. "I see here you were late getting back aboard. How come?" "I overslept, sir" was the common reply from a seaman whose knees had become jelly. "OVERSLEPT? Out that late the night before?" "Yessir." "Is that going to happen again, Mr. Jones?" "No, sir." "SEE THAT IT DOESN'T. NEXT!!!"

Some Blackburn dramas unfolded off the bridge. One day, gripes reached Blackburn about the sloppiness and rudeness of sailors working the chow lines. Blackburn climbed into some greasy overalls, pulled his long-billed cap low over his forehead, and sidled into one of the chow lines. Sure enough, potatoes were tossed onto his tray. Peas caromed onto the deck. His muttered request for more was ignored. Blackburn shuffled down the line toward the end. Once there, he turned on his heel to face the line, raised the full tray over his head in slow motion, and dropped it onto the floor. As the echoes of the tray's clang and skittering utensils faded, silence replaced shock as two angry mess stewards started toward him. Everyone froze when he took his cap off. Blackburn didn't say a word as he held the gaze of every man on the galley side of the chow line. He silently turned and walked out of the mess. Midway's crew received top-drawer restaurant service for weeks thereafter.

Blackburn had no patience. On Midway's first extended cruise since modernization, the catapult crews struggled to keep all three catapults operational while conducting simultaneous launch and recovery operations. The number three catapult kept malfunctioning. One day, Blackburn warned a catapult officer "to keep that catapult on line or else!" After a couple of launches, it failed again, fouling the tightly timed launch operation. Blackburn stared down at the flight deck from the bridge. He grabbed a microphone and over the flight deck's loudspeakers ordered the offending catapult officer off the ship on the next available plane. The man never set foot on Midway again. And word spread. Blackburn meant business.

He also played hard. Blackburn could have come from central casting as the hard-charging, risk-taking invincible aviator who lived for today and spit on tomorrow, often with a drink in his hand at sunset. He often jumped at the chance to join his crew as they prowled the bars in the Thieves Alley district of Yokosuka, Japan. One night after a long stay at a bar in Okinawa, Blackburn decided to pilot the captain's launch and twenty of his shipmates back out to Midway. On the way, he skippered the boat straight onto the rocks. He thought nothing of it. On nights when in port, he and his wife hosted favored Midway officers in his Quonset hut for beer and eggs as an 0200 nightcap. Midway's crew knew Blackburn invariably would be on the bridge at "oh-dark-early" the next morning, clear-eyed, and expecting everyone else to be the same.

The crew didn't always wait for liberty to have a cocktail on Blackburn's watch. A joke in "officers' country" up near the flight deck held that the massive steam catapults could barely be heard over the clinking of aviators' martini glasses. Groups of officers made the rounds from one stateroom to another after a day's flight ops. They hung names on each night's destination. "Chez May," and "Timby's Tavern" were among the favorites. Some enlisted a collaborator from the dentist's office to assure access to large containers used as martini shakers and other implements suitable as swizzle sticks. A conspirator from supply could provide fruit juices as mixers.

Much of the alcohol came aboard in the bellies of Demons. Demon pilots smuggled cases of beer aboard in the gun tub of their aircraft, trusting plane crews to slip the beer into canvass bags, sneak it below, and then run back and forth to the wardroom for bags of ice. The priorities of men in their twenties, full of life, daring, and themselves.

Fate would soon test that attitude. The day after Midway arrived in Pearl Harbor in August 1958, mainland China launched a massive artillery attack on the nationalist Quemoy and Matsu Islands only six miles offshore where Chiang Kai-shek had stationed 100,000 troops. Communist ships blockaded the islands to prevent their resupply. The communist government publicly stated it intended to "liberate" Formosa. Midway was ordered to impose a moment of reflection on both sides. Only four days after arriving in Hawaii, Midway steamed southwest toward Formosa for a 37-day deployment at sea, much of it spent by Midway pilots flying with Chinese MiGs.

As Midway approached Formosa, Midway's loudspeakers blared, "Men, this is the captain. In a few hours we will be on station and within range of artillery on the mainland. Be ready, stay sharp, and know this: if we are fired upon it will be the start of World War III. I know Midway is ready. I know each of you is ready. Good luck. That is all."

The crew didn't know Blackburn's brief speech emanated from the Pentagon where the Joint Chiefs of Staff had discussed a war plan for defending Quemoy and Matsu. The Joint Chiefs called for nuclear strikes deep into mainland China, targeting military complexes in Shanghai, Hangchow, Nanking, and Canton. All had large civilian populations. They planned to use nuclear weapons as powerful as those dropped on Hiroshima and Nagasaki. In 1958, those bombs were considered low yield. Even at that, State Department officials estimated "there would be millions of non-combatant casualties." One State Department policy planner predicted that if Midway's aircraft bombed China, Russia "would probably feel compelled to react with nuclear attacks at least on Formosa and on the Seventh Fleet. Under our present strategic concept, this would be the signal for nuclear war between the U.S. and USSR."

One night aboard Midway, that call nearly came. After a day of routine operations, squadron VAH-8 pilots were summoned to their ready room. Nicknamed the "Fireballers," VAH-8 aviators flew Skywarriors and trained to drop nuclear weapons. Commander Hal Woodson stood rock still and for a long time looked out across the faces of his pilots. They grew antsy as the silence lengthened. Woodson took a deep breath and somberly told his men that orders may be issued in a few hours to attack an airfield in China. War could ensue. "Here's what I want you to do," Woodson told flight crews whose faces had paled. "I want everyone to write their last letter home, right now, before you leave this room. No excuses. Right now. Give me your letters. Those of you who come back will get their letters back. I'll mail the letters of those who don't return."

As thousands of Marines prepared to invade Okinawa, Midway was christened on March 20, 1945. It would be the largest ship in the world for 10 years and the first too large for the Panama Canal. (NATIONAL ARCHIVES)

Above, the dawn of naval missile warfare broke on Midway's stern when a captured German V-2 rocket was successfully launched near Bermuda. It promptly veered off course and was detonated as it approached a nearby destroyer. (NATIONAL ARCHIVES)

Above, humanitarian missions were frequently assigned to Midway. Here more than 100 Italian war orphans arrive for a Christmas dinner aboard the carrier on Christmas morning, December 25, 1947. (NATIONAL ARCHIVES)

Left, a variation of the P-2V Neptune was one of the first aircraft capable of delivering nuclear weapons off the deck of Midway. Midway's nuclear capability was one reason it was kept patrolling in the Mediterranean throughout the Korean War. (NATIONAL ARCHIVES)

Lt. Cdr. George Duncan's test flight of an F9 Panther in 1951 ended in disaster when Duncan's jet slammed into the stern, shattered, and cartwheeled down the flight deck. Note airborne canopy left center. (NATIONAL ARCHIVES)

Above, incredibly, Duncan walked away with burns on his face and hands. Within four hours normal flight operations resumed. (NATIONAL ARCHIVES)

Above, in the Navy, almost every occasion is worthy of a cake. The 50,000th landing aboard Midway in 1953 called for a cake 9 feet long ceremoniously cut by Cdr. E. J. Kroeger.

A young Midway sailor from Savoy, Mass. posed with Edward G. Robinson when Midway made a port call during the Cannes Film Festival in 1953.
(ROBERT HASKINS)

Adventures on liberty: photographer's mate Robert Haskins captured a 19-year-old Bridgette Bardot on the beach at Cannes, France.

(ROBERT HASKINS)

Once nicknamed "Paddles," landing signal officers near Midway's stern later became lighted caricatures with lights strapped to their bodies as they coached aviators aboard at night.

(NATIONAL ARCHIVES)

More than 175 American young men died aboard Midway. William D. Henry II of squadron VFA-31 was committed to the deep in May, 1954. (National Archives)

As each letter was finished and handed to Woodson, pilots headed to their bunks to try to sleep in their flight gear, sidearms strapped tightly to their sides. If the call came at dawn, time would not be wasted getting dressed. The call never came. The sun rose and routine air operations resumed. Perhaps someone in Washington changed his mind. After a sleepless night, the flight crews of VAH-8 were never told why. They all got their letters back as Midway remained on station and routine patrols continued.

Midway's VF-64 squadron was saddled with the F3H Demon, a fighter most pilots called "the pig" because of its unreliability. The Demon sucked jet fuel so badly it lacked what Joe Corsi and the pilots called "legs." The pilots were even more worried about the Demon's integrity. Sometimes a locking pin on the cockpit control panel broke loose during a cat shot. The control panel would then slam into the face and chest of the pilot, jamming the throttle as he rocketed toward the bow. Other times the unreliable Demon's J71 engine nozzle stuck in the open position, robbing the pilot of critically needed thrust. Allegedly an all-weather fighter, Demons were notorious for losing power when it rained. Some pilots said it was even dangerous to fly a Demon into clouds due to their moisture. As a result, VF-64 was plagued with casualties under Captain Blackburn as Joe Corsi and other aviation machinists struggled to keep the pigs in the air.

It was Corsi's job to keep pigs flying over Formosa. One day Corsi was near the island watching his roommate, Gary Bergevin, take a cat shot at dusk to get night qualified. The catapult fired and the Demon hurtled toward the bow, spent catapult steam trailing behind. Bergevin reached the bow and dropped. Corsi lost sight of him but expected him to pop up into view. He never did. The next time Corsi saw his roommate's plane, it was floating in the water as Midway passed by. He never saw Bergevin again. Perhaps part of the Demon's panel of gauges had broken loose. No one could be sure.

Another Demon pilot became preoccupied with pleasing Blackburn who had grown unhappy with the lengthening intervals between landings. The commander of Corsi's squadron, W. H. Heider, spread the word to taxi "smartly" after landing so the next plane could land. Later, after Heider had landed, he "goosed" the throttle too quickly to get out of the way of his squadron's pilots on approach. Heider's plane lurched across the deck much too fast. Just as he passed the island heading forward, the plane careened to the right and headed for Corsi who was standing in his favorite position to watch flight deck operations. As Corsi dove out of the way, Heider's Demon went over the side. He hit a gun mount on the way down and flipped upside down. He drowned only a few feet from Midway's hull. Perhaps the throttle stuck. No one could be sure.

It fell on the shoulders of Commander Glen Even to take over the VF-64 squadron and get it back on an even keel. It wasn't easy. Tall, lanky, and a fitness fanatic, Even was deeply respected by his squadron. But the pilots had seen enough. There were rumblings of refusals to fly. The new commander climbed up to the bridge to advise Blackburn of the situation. "I don't care how you do it, get them over it. I need them back over the islands. Dismissed," was Blackburn's terse reply. The rumor among ship's crew was that Even gathered up all the (illicit) Scotch he could find, assembled his pilots inside their ready room, locked it, and had a proper wake for their fallen aviators. Later, when the door opened, the pilots of VF-64 were ready to fly.

They rejoined other Midway squadrons as airborne referees, flying long, looping laps around Formosa and splitting the Formosa Strait at the edge of communist air space. Midway also had other aircraft in the air. One in particular tried to make the aircraft carrier invisible.

Alan Beddoe thought of his wife and four children at home as the Skyraider arched out of the clouds and screamed toward the waves off Formosa. The plane's shudder chilled Beddoe as the sea filled the pilot's windscreen. The gauges and dials in front of Beddoe blurred as the pilot cinched back on the Skyraider's controls at the last possible second to keep from slamming into the sea.

As Midway sailed the Formosa Strait, one of its missions was to act as a listening post. An auxiliary radio room was appropriated by a group of radio operators who came aboard—rumored to be CIA—with their own equipment. They kept to themselves, heightening the mystery and fueling speculation. At the same time, the United States didn't want communist China eavesdropping on Midway's message traffic. One idea was to fly more than 100 miles away from the ship, unleash a 1,000-foot antenna behind the plane, and transmit messages to Manila or Okinawa. That way, the location of Midway remained secret. Chief radioman Beddoe had volunteered to transmit the messages from the belly of a Skyraider in what was named Operation Pigeon Post.

As the Skyraider rose up off the waves, Beddoe exhaled slowly and his heart slowed. But he still had a problem. The trailing antenna remained wrapped around the Skyraider's tail, making it impossible to land aboard Midway. The plane was too far away from any friendly airfields on land. Beddoe's pilot had only one option. Time and again he pushed the Skyraider high into the clouds and then dove straight down toward the Pacific, pulling out at the last possible second, hoping the jarring would unwrap the antenna. Once, twice, a third time, and no luck. Midway sent up a chase plane that was powerless to help. Finally, after another screaming dive to the wave tops, the antenna slid off the tail as the pilot brought it to level. Beddoe landed a shaken man. It was the end of Pigeon Post.

Meanwhile President Eisenhower played a game of international brinkmanship with Chairman Mao as Midway aircraft patrolled overhead and other Navy ships escorted nationalist supply ships to Quemoy and Matsu. Finally, on October 6, 1958, communist China stepped back, unilaterally suspending the shelling for one week on the condition that supply ships would no longer be escorted by Navy warships. Over Chiang Kai-shek's objections the United States agreed, laying the foundation for what became a de facto cease-fire agreement.

When the carrier Ranger relieved Midway, Captain Blackburn left his mark on his replacement as well. A Midway helicopter paid a visit to the Ranger, dropping a can of yellow chromate paint that splattered square in the middle of the Ranger's deck. Attached was a note: "Our captain can beat up your captain." The air wing's final mission accomplished, Midway departed Chinese waters for the second time in four years.

Although Blackburn would soon transfer command of Midway to another captain, his specter would cast a long shadow over what would become known as the "Disaster Cruise" under the command of his successor, James Mini.

Like Blackburn, Captain Mini owned a stellar war record. Mini had led one of three units of Air Group 15 off the carrier *Essex* in the battle for the Philippine Sea. Mini and his group of Helldiver pilots faced brutal opposition, losing one-third of the squadron. Despite intense enemy fire, Mini's squadron completed 75 sorties and scored 30 direct hits on Japanese carriers and battleships, a remarkable accuracy record.

There the similarities ceased. Mini was wound as tight as Blackburn had been swashbuckling. Mini constantly worried about what might happen on his watch. He found it difficult to sit still in his perched captain's chair and the bridge was far too narrow and congested to pace. On many occasions he broke into a profound sweat. Body odor filled the bridge. While Blackburn often mingled among the crew, Mini spent far more time in his cabin, away from his men.

Cotton-white clouds drifted across Subic Bay on November 9, 1959. Midway rested. Most of the crew was ashore on liberty and only a faint hum vibrated through the ship. "Fire! Fire! In the after heath pump room, fifth deck!" shattered the lazy Philippine morning.

Men assigned to damage control rolled out of bunks and broke through chow lines to race to their stations. Others on duty in their respective departments barely listened, paused, and went back to work. Small fires were common aboard Midway.

The hum returned and minutes passed. "All Hands. All Hands. Abandon ship. Abandon ship. Report to the pier immediately!" More than 1,000 men flinched, then mobilized. They thundered down passageways, jumped through hatches, scrambled up ladders, and raced across the brows onto the pier. Not far away, thin hints of smoke wafted out of the ventilation shafts near the island. Then it turned black and thick as it mixed with the tropical air.

Below, damage control parties sprinted through smoke-filled spaces, searching for the source. Some stopped to strap on face masks while others squinted as they ran through the noxious, gray haze to join a fire hose line. Their white T-shirts were soon stained coal-miner black with oil, soot, and sweat. The heat watered men's eyes inside scratched face masks as they neared the fire. There it was. Inside a space that pumped jet fuel. Few places on Midway were more inaccessible. Few were more dangerous.

High in the island, Captain Mini grew increasingly worried as reports came in indicating that the fire was building momentum and heating the deck immediately above. Nuclear weapons, ordnance and guided missiles were stored on that deck. Mini realized this was a fire that could send Midway to the bottom of the bay, or worse.

Not far away, Dick Singer started gathering up Midway's classified codes, manuals, and message traffic in communications in case essential personnel were evacuated. Behind him men speculated as wisps of a far-off campfire floated in the darkened red-hued air. "You think we're going to abandon ship?" "Dunno." "Maybe tugs will pull us out of Subic." "Focus people, pull your materials together and wait for orders . . ."

Singer asked permission to help the men who already were falling in the fight against the fire. It choked several into unconsciousness as Singer and others ran down deserted passageways searching for metal litters to carry downed firefighters to safety. His boots echoed through what had become a smoldering, smothering ghost ship.

Meanwhile, D. T. Blakeslee's head pounded. His W Division was responsible for the safekeeping of Midway's nuclear weapons. "W" was the most mysterious division on the ship. Its men were trained as a Naval Special Weapons Unit at a base near Albuquerque and then received additional training from the Nuclear Weapons Training Group in San Diego. They came aboard Midway as a team with top-secret clearance that kept to itself and worked behind hatches guarded night and day by armed Marines. The Marines never knew when Midway carried nuclear weapons on board so airtight security procedures were maintained regardless of what might be behind the gray hatches they guarded. The weapons' compartment grew hotter as the hours passed and the fire below blazed. Blakeslee ordered the compartment flooded with seawater to cool the weapons that no one said were there.

Not far away, another secret world existed on Midway. More than two dozen men who were assigned to the guided missile division worked at the forefront of naval ordnance technology. They were responsible for assembling, loading and arming Midway's Sidewinder and Sparrow guided missiles. GM Division was located directly above the fire. Its compartment, too, was flooded, swamping the missiles and assembly equipment.

There was chaos on the hangar deck. Plane crews and elevator operators scrambled to bring as many planes as possible up to the flight deck so the ship's crane operators could lift Midway's most accessible aircraft onto the pier as hundreds watched. Hours passed and the smoke continued to pour out of Midway. Tugs and fireboats idled several hundred yards away, prepared to pull the carrier out to sea. Men stood on the pier, axes in hand, ready to cut Midway free if the order came. Captain Mini paced on the hangar deck, worry rolling in waves across his face. He knew it was impossible to offload all of Midway's ordnance. If the tons of bombs, rockets, and missiles detonated, the damage and loss of life would be catastrophic. As most of the crew watched from the pier, Midway began to ride low in the water under billowing smoke.

Eight hours after the fire was discovered, damage control crews brought it under control. Decks began to cool as night fell on the Philippines. Almost immediately a damage control specialist was arrested. Later Mini said Phillip Cunningham, who Mini claimed had a "hero complex," had been arrested on charges of arson. Cunningham had come under suspicion of setting a number of fires aboard Midway because he frequently was among the first on the scene once the fires were discovered.

Captain Mini was beside himself. Midway had nearly been towed out to sea for fear of detonation because of an out-of-control firebug in his ship's company. The implications to crew morale and Mini's career, to say nothing of the safety of the ship, were enormous. Mini ordered his legal officer to sign the complaint as the "accuser" against Cunningham. Justice would be swift.

Legal officer Barney Cochran spoke with Mini more than most. A law student at George Washington University when he enlisted, Cochran and a staff of five ran the criminal justice system aboard Midway. Nicknamed "the Judge," he assigned officers to court martial proceedings, duty that few officers enjoyed performing. In essence, Cochran acted as the state's attorney.

At first Cochran refused, telling Mini that as ship's investigating officer, Cochran could not be the accuser as well. It was a clear violation of the military's criminal justice process. Mini insisted. The former law student relented and signed the form. After several years of incarceration, Phillip Cunningham was freed "on a procedural technicality."

The fire in the Philippines was enough to label it "The Disaster Cruise of 1959–60" with Mini at the helm. But the fire was only one of several misfortunes. In Okinawa, a sudden squall sank a launch carrying 12 Midway sailors on a scuba diving adventure. Two of them died.

Joe Ingram was a member of Midway VA-24 squadron whose executive officer was a young aviator named James B. Stockdale. Only five years later, Stockdale would exhibit extraordinary bravery as a North Vietnamese prisoner of war and earn the Congressional Medal of Honor. Ingram's duties included respotting aircraft. One afternoon he towed one of VA-24's F8 Crusaders, the sleek, long-legged fighter whose fuselage rode high off the ground, to a new location on the flight deck. The tow bar broke free and the nose of the Crusader dropped, crushing Ingram against the steering wheel of his tractor.

Ultimately seven members of Midway's crew died on what appeared to many as a jinxed cruise. Midway twice crossed typhoons' paths. Investigators arrested a sailor on charges of involuntary manslaughter. Midway was searched for drugs. Mini called the search a routine matter because of the prevalence of drugs on the streets of Japan. Many crewmen scoffed at Mini's version, knowing illegal drugs were much more available in other countries where Midway visited.

Calamities aside, Mini was haunted by Blackburn. In an odd quirk of assignments, Blackburn had remained on Midway as chief of staff to Rear Admiral David J. Welsh. As commander of Carrier Task Force 77, Welsh had made Midway his flagship. Welsh had distinguished himself in World War II, earning a Bronze Star, a Silver Star, and Purple Heart. Captain Blackburn, was an even bigger hero with his Navy Cross, Distinguished Flying Cross, and Air Medal with two gold stars. Blackburn's personality and swagger remained unabated. Together, Welsh and Blackburn cast a long and dark shadow over the worrisome Captain Mini.

Midway's crew constantly came in contact with their beloved former skipper. The difference between the backslapping Blackburn and the taciturn Mini was driven home one night when Midway was in port. An officers' party filled most of a bay on the hangar deck as two sailors headed for shore on liberty. As they tried to cut across the hangar deck, an ensign barked at them to take the long way around. Gene Coulter and Don Lockwood were more than a little irked. As they navigated the detour, one of them reached up and opened a valve that activated hangar deck sprinklers. The party came to a water-soaked halt as Mini sputtered in anger. "That's my boys!" Blackburn chortled, a few tables away.

In the early 1960s Midway took on a different personality, in part due to standard Navy policy to rotate duty every 12 to 18 months and in part due to the evolution of the missions assigned to the carrier. Midway typically split its time between Japan and the Philippines on annual western Pacific deployments. The cruises carried several missions. One was to demonstrate both power and presence off the coasts of China, North

Korea, and Russia in Cold War currents. Another was training. Most sailors rotated off Midway after a year and a half, making training a constant and high-priority mission.

One of those responsible for some of Midway's most critical training was the son of a Los Angeles albacore fisherman. On the small side with bright, intelligent eyes, perhaps more than anyone else he was responsible for getting pilots back aboard Midway safely. He was a landing signal officer. His name was Vern Jumper.

"I just wanted to thank you. You saved my life last night." It was a sentiment most aviators voiced at least once to an LSO.

Each squadron's landing signal officer aboard Midway possessed the power of a god—power that sometimes saved a man's life. Usually one of the best pilots in the squadron, the LSO talked each pilot down onto the deck. He had a ringside seat, standing on a platform next to the landing area as the LSO stayed in voice contact with every pilot on every landing. The LSO taught, coached, and sometimes yelled.

The conversation was always one way. A pilot never talked back to an LSO, other than to acknowledge he had visual contact and to inform the carrier of his fuel status. Instead he listened, responded to the LSO calls, and prayed his tailhook grabbed the No. 3 wire for an "OK" trap. The absence of extensive LSO-pilot conversation made for some mysterious mishaps during recovery operations as Midway patrolled the western Pacific.

One night Jumper stood on the LSO platform near the stern bringing pilots aboard as the wind pounded his back. A Crusader dropped too low early in his approach as the deck pitched heavily. He seemed to stay there a full five seconds. Jumper waved him off using the "pickle switch" which activated bright red warning lights. At that point, the pilot was 1,000 feet from the ship, but stayed low, and kept coming. Then he drifted toward the LSO platform. Jumper and two other LSOs dove into their safety net. The pilot hit the ramp 15 feet left of the centerline. The fuselage sheared off the LSO's windscreen and destroyed nearby landing equipment. The pilot died. Jumper couldn't explain it. That night stayed with him a long time.

Another time Lou Page (who later would shoot down one of the first MiGs in the Vietnam War), neared Midway on approach when he dropped too low. "Power," said Jumper. Page didn't pull up. Jumper repeated his command, "Power!!" Page remained too low. "Goddamn it, WAVE OFF, WAVE OFF!!!" At the last instant, Page climbed up and over Midway's stern, took the wave-off, and came around again to land safely. The next day, Page summoned Jumper. The LSO expected a royal chewing out for the language and tone he had used with a senior officer. Instead, it was a private, man-to-man thank you as Jumper turned to leave, smiling.

In the early 1960s, half of all Navy crashes occurred when pilots were landing. One of the biggest causes for landing accidents was a low approach. One night off Hawaii, Dick Tucker, the executive officer of Jumper's VF-21 squadron, practiced night landings. Newly assigned, Tucker and his radar intercept officer (RIO), Ron Sterret, were getting used to Midway's small landing window. Tucker drifted too low as he closed on Midway. He, too, stayed there for some reason. His F-4 Phantom disintegrated against Midway's stern, killing both men. Seven children in the Sterret family lost their father in the crash.

The LSO evaluated every landing and entered the grade in his canvas-covered logbook. OK-3 was the best a pilot could get because pilots were trained to aim for the third of four arresting wires. An LSO's shorthand notes in his logbook told entire stories. For example, OWO-RD meant as a pilot neared Midway, he saw the deck rolling from side to side and the flight deck crew bracing themselves as the pitching worsened. He checked his fuel status and decided not to land, go around, and take his chances that the flight deck would have settled minutes later.

In the squadron's ready room, the LSO posted grades for all landings under each pilot's name on the "greenie board." It was a simple system. Green meant okay (highest grade possible), yellow signified fair, and red was a color no pilot wanted to see near his name on the greenie board. The grades of the LSO were final. No one successfully challenged a landing's rating. It was the LSO's job to help the air wing's crews get back aboard safely while earning their trust, even if it required commands that sometimes ignored officer protocol.

Sometimes the judgment of an LSO and the teamwork of flight deck crews failed to measure up against fate. One night a Crusader pilot practiced touch-and-goes off the canted deck while other aircraft were near the catapult, preparing to launch. The pilot hit the deck so hard his plane came apart and a missile was knocked free. He ejected as the plane went over the side.

Vines Haughan was Officer of the Deck at the time and from the bridge watched the horror unfold. Midway's plane guard destroyer came along-side to search for the pilot as the Crusader sank. Almost as the jet went over the side, Haughan noticed one of the planes positioned for launch shower-ing sparks from its engine. The plane's takeoff was scrubbed and he saw an injured man carried below. Haughan assumed the pilot had been hurt by some kind of engine malfunction or from flying debris from the nearby crash just prior to takeoff.

The next day when he went to visit the pilot in the infirmary, he was nowhere to be found. Instead the pilot of the sunken Crusader looked up at Haughan. When the Crusader pilot ejected at the edge of the flight deck, his trajectory had carried him directly over the deck and onto the aircraft that was ready for takeoff. He slammed into the plane, breaking bones. When the pilot's parachute had been sucked into the jet's intake it produced the spray of sparks that Haughan saw on the darkened deck.

A chief petty officer had sprinted to the aviator's aid and cut the para-chute's shroud lines before the pilot was sucked into the jet engine. The Crusader pilot attributed his good luck to the Almighty. Haughan was in no position to disagree.

The "Whale," parked near the island was one of the most menacing aircraft aboard Midway. The massive A3D Skywarrior was intended to deliver nuclear weapons as Midway sailed toward the edge of war in the early 1960s. It was one of the most flexible and frequently modified air-craft flown by the Navy. And it was a plane its crew said A-3D meant "all three dead" because it didn't have a crew ejection system. To save weight, aircraft designers expected the crew to slide down a chute before opening their parachutes. Crewmen who were departing the Whale had to remem-ber to clear its tail before opening their chutes.

Odds weren't much better if the crew had to ditch in the ocean. The wings were set high on the fuselage to create a larger bomb bay. If a Skywarrior made an emergency landing in the water, the wings' buoyancy pushed much of the fuselage underwater. A crew that had seconds before slammed into the ocean faced swimming up to the surface to survive.

Because Skywarriors took a long time to reach flying speed, pilots landed at 95 percent of full power in case they didn't grab an arresting wire and needed to "bolt" back into the air. Skywarrior crews likened landing the 35,000-pound aircraft at nearly full power to being strapped into a comfortable easy chair and then being dropped off the roof of a house.

Midway's Skywarrior crews learned to make the most of new aircraft technology. When they discovered a shortcoming, they used ingenuity to overcome it. Some solutions worked better than others. Skywarrior crews flew at high altitudes for up to four hours at a stretch. They breathed concentrated oxygen that tended to dehydrate them. Flight surgeons were worried about pilots' mental alertness in the absence of nourishment after a grueling four-hour flight. One surgeon had an idea. He rigged an enema bag with a tube that fit under the pilot's oxygen mask. The notion was the pilot could ingest some stewed prunes or baby food before he got busy landing on Midway. One time the enema bag was inadvertently punctured, spraying prune juice across the pilot's visor. The idea never took hold.

Novel ideas required increasingly greater coordination and carried higher risks as the Navy constantly designed multiple missions for Midway's air wing. One day off the coast of California, a Midway Skywarrior was ordered to drop paratroopers instead of nuclear bombs, a concept had been tested with dummies at the El Centro Naval Aerospace Recovery Facility, about 200 miles east of where Midway steamed near San Diego. Skywarrior modifications that included bench seats to carry the paratroopers proved unsatisfactory in early trials. Finally it was decided a Skywarrior might be able to deliver two Marines to the target if one member of the flight crew stayed on the ship so that there would be enough room for two paratroopers.

The reconnaissance Marines boarded Midway in full combat gear. Faces smeared with grease, they were chiseled and on edge. In a few hours they would see if they could drop through the Skywarrior's bomb bay to make night parachute drops under simulated combat conditions. At the final brief aboard the carrier, they silently nodded "no" when asked if any wanted to pull out of the volunteer mission.

After launching off Midway, the Skywarrior approached Camp Pendleton, the Marine Corp's massive 15,000-acre kingdom of coastal scrub and manzanita-covered foothills separating San Diego from Los Angeles. As the Skywarrior approached the football field–sized drop zone, it slowed to near-stall speed and descended to 1,200 feet. A Marine sat on the lip of the bomb bay, his legs dangling in the jet stream below. The second Marine dropped down to his haunches directly behind his buddy and wrapped his arms around him. Together, they dropped through the bomb bay feet first and away from the Skywarrior. Once aground, their mission was to evade "enemy" troops, make their way to Camp Pendleton's beach, and swim out to a waiting submarine. The first two attempts went off without a hitch. The third and final drop would be different. It would be at night.

As the Skywarrior from Midway's VAH-8 squadron made its third approach over the rugged terrain, the Marines' jump light blinked from red to amber. In seconds it would turn green, the signal to drop into the black. But when the Skywarrior's computer indicated he was over the drop zone, the pilot couldn't find the confirming landmark lake. Just as the red "abort" light brightened, the first Marine jumped. The remaining paratrooper screamed he couldn't hold his buddy back from jumping. "Gotta get with my buddy. Gotta get down there with my buddy! Gotta get to my buddy!!" he kept yelling over the growl of the engines as he moved past the red light and dove headfirst into the black sky below.

Later, as Midway prepared for another western Pacific deployment, the Skywarrior crew heard both Marines had landed safely in the drop zone.

Midway returned to Alameda from another western Pacific cruise in May of 1964, the last peacetime cruise it would make over the next decade. The Vietnam War loomed. After almost 20 years of endless drills and practice, more than 50,000 landings, near-war, unpublicized skirmishes, and 23 commanding officers, the Midway mission soon would turn from defense to offense. The plan of the day would be driven by battle plans against an unseen enemy.

DAVID CHRISTIAN AND JOHN McKAMEY flew side by side over the North Vietnamese jungle in what was Midway's first combat deployment in its 20-year history. The sun bounced off their canopies as they searched for an invisible enemy below.

Half a world away, Kansas farmers drove out to their wheat fields to the sounds of "I've Got You, Babe" and "Eve of Destruction" on their truck radios. June 2, 1965, promised to be hot and humid. It was the land of farmhouses, and home to David Marion Christian. They didn't know that ground fire had erupted from a clearing and riddled Christian's Skyhawk. As his plane twisted toward the jungle, Christian's commander thought maybe Christian had ejected, but no emergency beeper signals were heard.

Not far away, Fillmore, Indiana greeted the same day. It was home to McKamey, the son of rural mail carrier Oscar McKamey and Mary Bryan McKamey. Like their neighbors to the southwest, the McKameys didn't yet know the enemy also had drawn a bead on their son. As his Skyhawk shuddered a bone-jarring death rattle, John McKamey yanked hard and prayed the ejection seat would fire. Seconds later his Skyhawk exploded inside the Vietnamese jungle.

Midway's bow was a blur to M. D. McMican. Ocean spray lifted over the deck and sparkled in the sun as Midway dug into one swell after another. As the massive rotary engine on the nose of his Skyraider warmed, vibrations coursed through the canopy, making gauges jiggle and jump. McMican was anxious to get off Midway's deck and turn toward the coast. The lives of Midway pilots Christian and McKamey were at stake. He looked down at the catapult officer for the signal to launch.

McMican was at the controls of a single propeller-driven dinosaur in a Midway air wing dominated by fighter jets. Nicknamed "Spad," his Skyraider had a long and storied career in the Navy, dating back to the summer of 1944 when it literally had been designed in one night. It became the workhorse of the Korean War and a vital part of the air war over Vietnam. It patrolled, bombed, and strafed. It also saved lives.

Three crewmen were also aboard. One was a copilot and two others were wedged into a small space under the rear canopy, operating counter-measure and search-and-rescue equipment. Conversations were clipped short. Midway had two pilots down. Their rescue would nearly be impossible until McMican's Skyraider was circling overhead.

Once he was off the deck, McMican figured it would be about 30 minutes before he'd be over the crash sites of Christian and McKamey. The Spad's long-loiter capability made it ideal as an on-scene command post, directing helicopters and other support craft to downed pilots. Getting to the site of a pilot downed in the Tonkin Gulf to direct rescue operations was critical because crashing into the sea carried huge risk. Nearly one in three pilots who crashed in the gulf drowned by impact or exhaustion. The odds of surviving a crash in the jungle were little better.

The trade-off to stamina, said Spad pilots, was its slow speed. There was only one speed a pilot had to remember flying a Spad: 120 knots. "You launched at 120 knots, cruised at 120 knots, and landed at 120 knots." Spads were easy targets.

It wasn't long before the Spad was circling over what the crew believed to be Christian's crash site. A wispy column of ash-gray smoke escaped the jungle canopy. As McMican scanned the green expanse below, movement off to one side caught his eye. Bright red tracers crossed in front of the Spad's canopy. A second later, the crew jumped at the gut-wrenching staccato of enemy bullets slamming into the Spad's fuselage. McMican pulled hard on the controls to turn for the coast but it seemed like minutes before the lumbering Skyraider responded. McMican struggled to control the aircraft as enemy fire again sliced through the plane. Within sight of the

Tonkin Gulf, the death spiral began. The jungle rushed up at the four young men. One of them managed to eject seconds before the Spad crashed and burned on the coast. He free fell into the sea. His parachute never opened.

Midway Captain James M. O'Brien lost six aviators that day in June. A week later, intelligence officers reported a body had washed ashore in the vicinity of the three crashes. They didn't know whether the body was Christian or the Spad crewman who had dropped into the sea. All four Spad crewmen were designated as "Killed in Action/Body Not Recovered." Because neither Christian's parachute was seen nor his emergency beeper heard, he too, was listed as "Killed in Action." Officially, only John Bryan McKamey of Fillmore, Indiana, might be alive. His parachute had been spotted. He was "Missing in Action."

Tropical sweat rolled down Paul Hauschild's forehead and into his eyes that morning in 1965. A photographer's mate third class, he maintained the reconnaissance cameras on RF-8A Crusaders. It was his job to cram large-capacity, 16mm cameras into Crusaders that had been converted from day fighter to reconnaissance. Occasionally it was so tight Hauschild sat down and pushed the camera station doors closed with his feet. The son of a credit manager for Reynolds Aluminum in St. Louis, Hauschild also processed the Crusaders' film before turning it over to Naval Intelligence. He spent a lot of time in the ship's camera repair shop, near the Spad crews' ready room.

He could feel the shock spreading like a toxic cloud as men silently arrived and then left the ready room. Conversations were hushed and phrased.

"Did you hear?"

"Yeah."

"Christ, all four? "You talk to the skipper yet?"

"No, heard there's a brief at 1300."

"'Bout what?"

"Dunno. Maybe intel."

"Christ."

Hauschild saw grief blanket aviators' frozen faces, paled by the shock of losing so many so quickly.

"Attention, this is the captain." There was a long pause, prompting men to look up. Most of the crew still oblivious to the losses. Captain O'Brien gave them the word. Some men gasped. Others sat down, their eyes suddenly watering. Some wiped a grimey sleeve across a forehead, sighed, and turned back to their work. Grief could not be allowed to interfere with mission.

Tic Toc Martin didn't have time to allow reflection to interfere with duty. The backseater in an F-4 Phantom had a schedule to keep. Dave Martin exuded a quiet confidence that some called "nerdy." The one-time reporter for the *Rocky Mountain News* had coveted the Phantom's front seat but a slight case of myopia had prevented him from becoming a pilot. A precise man who spoke in measured, soft tones, he was immensely liked throughout his squadron. The massive Rolex wristwatch he had purchased in Hong Kong appeased a yen to always know the time and made a perfect target for razzing.

The pace of combat exhausted Martin and the other aviators on Midway's first combat deployment. A pilot sometimes flew as many as three missions in a single day and averaged up to 25 missions over North Vietnam a month. For most, it became numbing routine capped by a few moments of terror and then nerve-fraying recovery.

A typical mission began with an overall briefing by the air wing commander about 90 minutes ahead of launch. The big picture, latest intelligence, and weather were discussed. Then pilots reported to their squadron ready rooms to review the tactical plans of attack and designated search-and-rescue areas. Briefers rarely acknowledged when a particular mission carried unusual danger. But Martin learned to spot the clues. Unusual emphasis on safe areas and rescue procedures. Reminders about procedures for refueling if the aircraft had been hit by enemy fire. Repeated emphasis on maintaining flight integrity. Then there was the 120 Rule. "Remember, if you take fire and have to get out of Dodge, report to Red Crown. Stick it on the 120 heading. Almost always that will be your shortest route to the ocean." Water improved a pilot's long odds of rescue. No pilot liked his chances of rescue if he crashed inside the "Iron Triangle" bordered by Haiphong, Hanoi, and Thanh Hoa.

Then topside to the aircraft. Most aviators walked around their plane looking for hydraulic leaks and unsecured panel doors. The plane captain gave them the latest on that aircraft's most recent "gripes" reported by other crews and what repairs had been made. Pilots then strapped in, placing their lives in the hands of the air boss, plane handlers, shooters, and others before facing an enemy that filled the air with fire.

North Vietnamese gunners learned *not* to aim at Midway aircraft. Instead, they filled a five-mile square column of flak from 3,000 to 20,000 feet above the ground, daring Midway pilots to fly through it. Nearly three-fourths of the Navy planes lost in Vietnam to known causes were due to small arms and antiaircraft artillery (AAA) fire. Pilot Jerry Sawatzky attained legend status when, after landing aboard Midway, he climbed out of his cockpit, crawled underneath a wing, and stood up through a hole carved by vicious ground fire.

The real worry, though, was enemy MiGs.

"Hey! Lookit down there! Those are MiGs on the tarmac!!! Jesus Christ! Let's go get them!" "Are you nuts? No way. ROE says they have to attack us first." "Yea, but . . ." " Button it . . ."

Politically inspired Rules of Engagement imposed on American pilots in 1965 stuck in Dave Martin's throat. A macabre Midway air wing joke claimed pilots needed a law degree to understand who or what could be attacked and under what limited circumstances. Midway fighters flew over enemy MiG airfields but were forbidden from attacking unless the MiGs rose up to meet them. If a MiG approached Martin's Phantom, he had to get close enough to make a visual identification, report it, and then wait for permission before engaging. That put the cannon-less Phantom at a serious disadvantage against swarming MiGs. Authorization to engage usually came so late that the F-4 pilots found themselves largely limited to firing the short-range Sidewinder missiles in dogfights. They fought with one hand behind their back. The MiG-17 was a relatively primitive fighter built according to traditional dogfighting schools of thought. It lacked the more sophisticated, long-range missile capability of the F-4 Phantom but had maneuverability and cannon armament going for it. Its automatic cannons made it a formidable close-in combat foe against American fighters dependent on air-to-air missiles.

On occasion pilots rewrote rules of engagement on the fly. One day a Midway Phantom pilot loitered over a target in hopes of spotting a MiG. The pilot got hit with small arms fire under his ejection seat, knocking out his radio. With no word from him, another pilot heading for Midway reversed course, took fuel from a nearby Marine airborne tanker, and returned to search for his friend. He scanned the jungle canopy for smoke. He dropped to the deck, flew low and raced through enemy-filled valleys desperately looking for any sign of a crash. No luck. "No joy for 102" was his message back to Midway before making a solemn, quiet flight to the carrier. Only after landing and walking into his squadron's ready room did the pilot learn his buddy had limped to an air base near Danang, and was comfortably seated in the officers' club, beer in hand.

Midway pilots often rolled their eyes when they learned of bombing restrictions that defied military explanation. Bridges were a strategic target in North Vietnam but nothing could be bombed within a mile of a Red Cross symbol. It wasn't long before North Vietnamese bridges sported red crosses at one end. Midway pilots were forbidden from attacking surface-to-air missile (SAM) sites under construction, sites the pilots knew would be firing at them in a few weeks.

Sometimes Midway pilots used Sidewinders for target practice. When they flew missions over Binh at night, defenders turned on searchlights and swept the skies. To face small arms fire, artillery, and even surface-to-air missiles was one thing. Being frozen in a spotlight that reached to the stars angered many aviators. More than one searchlight was knocked out by a Midway Sidewinder, not exactly what war planners had envisioned.

Each aircraft could only land aboard Midway with a prescribed remaining fuel load. Rather than jettison surplus fuel over the ocean on their way back to Midway, pilots sometimes made a quick 15-minute side trip to an area about 50 miles north of Hanoi and a known MiG airfield, hoping to lure the enemy into a dogfight. They usually trolled only for a few minutes before fuel status forced them back to the Tonkin Gulf and the carrier.

On June 17, 1965, the radio room supervisor from Ft. Collins, Colorado leaned forward at the nervousness he had heard in the Midway pilot's voice. The shouted "Tallyho!" nearly knocked Jim Bell out of his seat. Bell could almost hear the sounds of tracers splitting the sky over North Vietnam, even though he was nearly 100 miles away. Bell sat in a sea of toggle switches and dials. With the flip of a switch he monitored communications with the omnipresent plane guard destroyer off Midway's stern. With another switch he could talk with Red Crown, a ship high in the Tonkin Gulf that coordinated air attacks over North Vietnam. Yet another switch connected him with Midway pilots "up north." He heard unbridled excitement when Midway pilots spotted a MiG and the frustration in their voices when permission to engage the enemy came too late. Untold numbers of outhouses and oxen were blown out of existence when furious aviators let go their ordnance on their way back to Midway.

While attacking enemy barracks, the Midway Phantom pilot was reporting four MiGs approaching from the north, fast. Commander Lou Page and his radar intercept officer, Lieutenant John Smith, were in one Phantom, on patrol above the strike aircraft. On their wing were Lieutenant Dave Batson and his RIO, Lieutenant Commander Bob Doremus. In seconds they would be outnumbered, two to one.

At first the four MiGs were tiny specks in the sky. Then they turned toward the Midway jets to attack. The first real dogfight of the Vietnam War was on.

Countless times before, Page and Batson had sat in their ready room and talked about a game plan if they ever engaged the enemy. Both, of course, wanted a kill. Their plan had been that if MiGs were spotted, Page would accelerate to visually identify and Batson as wingman would have first shot. If more than one enemy appeared, then Page had the MiG on the left, and Batson would take the fighter on the right. Two of the four MiGs followed the Americans' playbook precisely. After accelerating to make the identification Page turned left, locked on, and drove a Sidewinder into one of the MiGs. Batson went right, one of his missiles racing ahead straight and true into a second MiG.

The other two MiGs disengaged and escaped, although there were reports that possibly one had been damaged by debris from one of the destroyed MiGs. It was possible the third MiG succumbed, especially when pilots learned later only one of the four MiGs had returned to base. They were the first two MiGs shot down by American pilots in the Vietnam War. The skirmish lasted only 29 seconds.

It was a day to celebrate aboard the Midway. Sailors whose assignments supported the air wing all shared in the jubilation. The heroes of the hour, Page, Smith, Batson, and Doremus, received Silver Stars from Vice Admiral Paul P. Blackburn, commander of the Seventh Fleet. All four flew to Saigon for press conferences commonly called the "Five O'clock

Follies" and were featured in *Stars & Stripes*. Doremus would receive an added—and wholly unwanted—measure of fame only two months later.

Meanwhile Midway's marathon of sorties continued, some flown by vintage propeller aircraft whose pilots knew their odds of survival could be bleak if the enemy found them.

Lieutenant Commander Edwin Greathouse constantly scanned the skies around him as he held the controls of one of the four Skyraiders headed toward a target south of Hanoi. If he was lucky, Red Crown would alert him if MiGs rose from Hoa Lac or Kep airfields. But MiGs could appear in the blink of an eye.

It had been only three days since Midway's MiG shootdowns. As Greathouse approached the target, the words he dreaded exploded inside his helmet. A hollow, detached voice told him two MiG-17s were closing fast. Where? Where? There! Small and built for speed, the hawklike, 600-mph enemy jets circled in front of the Skyraiders, as if taking the measure of a hapless prey. Then they banked hard and turned directly toward Greathouse and the others, closing at a frightening pace. The plodding Skyraiders were badly overmatched and their pilots knew it because the expected Air Force cover had not arrived. They were on their own. As the MiGs approached, they fired their missiles at the lumbering Skyraiders. Greathouse kept his group together as the missiles screamed toward them, whitish smoke trailing behind. At the last second he ordered the pilots to dive to the treetops, nearly brushing the jungle canopy along a ridge. The missiles missed.

Now the Skyraiders had a handful of seconds to convert their weakness of slowness into an advantage. The foursome split into pairs, each turning in tight defensive circles as the MiGs' tracers "the size of tennis balls" blazed by the Skyraiders' canopies. Then the MiG pilots made a mistake. They failed to account for the Skyraiders' superior turning ability. Lieutenant C. B. Johnson turned hard into a MiG and unloaded his 20mm cannons when the MiG accepted the challenge by turning toward him. Taking gunfire almost head on, the MiG continued toward Johnson. Smoke began to trail away. Passing within 30 feet of Johnson's plane, the Skyraider shuddered as the MiG thundered past before nosing into the ground and exploding.

It was a remarkable dogfight of World War I aerial combat tactics, one that Greathouse later called "a very personal war of survival." It was almost inconceivable a propeller-driven Skyraider could survive against a MiG. Greathouse and Johnson and their backseaters, Jim Lynne and Charles Hartman, received the Vietnamese Air Gallantry Medal and joined their Phantom colleagues as the newest media celebrities aboard Midway.

Only two months later, the jubilation of killing the enemy would take a back seat to sorrow as the number of Midway pilots dwindled.

Even in the face of endless missions deep into enemy territory, Bill Franke's eyes burned with confidence. He was a cut above most aviators on Midway in 1965. Fellow pilots admired him and considered Franke in line to make captain. He had returned from countless missions to land on aircraft carriers, including Midway 15 years earlier in the Mediterranean.

Franke had called Oklahoma City home as a young boy. He often said that he "wanted to be a pilot something fierce" and in 1943 tried to join the Royal Canadian Air Force because he could fly Spitfires after 12 weeks of training. But Georgia Franke Smith had refused sign the papers allowing her only child to go off to combat flight school as a 16-year-old. When he turned 17, parental permission wasn't necessary so Franke promptly enlisted in the Navy, and became an ensign in August 1948.

He planned strikes in the war room aboard Midway. Franke stewed over Washington's limitations on what could be attacked and what was off limits. He had lost track of how many times he put together strike plans, routed them through Pearl Harbor headquarters and on to the Pentagon, only to see them denied. Some of those plans called for strikes against the missile sites Midway's pilots could see being built on their way to targets. They watched the SAM sites take shape but could not attack because Russians were there. Washington had given the enemy immunity.

On August 24, 1965, Franke flew high above a North Vietnamese bridge, watching for MiGs as the weather turned sour. The mission profile had been changed at the last minute. In the seat behind him as naval flight officer sat the same Robert Doremus who had downed a MiG-17 two months earlier. Doremus wasn't supposed to fly with Franke that day. Franke's regular back-seater, Jim Mills, was being rested and Doremus wanted to accumulate some flying time after having been delayed on a trip back from Japan.

As Franke and Doremus provided cover for attack jets, one of the SAM sites that had worried Franke earlier fired on his Phantom. The telephone pole–sized missile raced into the sky, seemingly destined for Franke and Doremus. It buried itself in Franke's F-4 before exploding. One of the Phantom's wings had disappeared, throwing the aircraft out of control and into the jungle. Franke's wingman saw the plane explode. He didn't spot any parachutes.

The wingman radioed Midway's combat information center that F. A. W. "Bill" Franke, and Robert Bartsch Doremus were likely dead. Midway could add two more names to its growing list of dead pilots.

Red lights glowed in the clammy dark air. A man moved silently to a Plexiglas wall, grease pen in hand. He updated its neatly printed chart with a shorthand that was the day's combat line score. Midway's command information center showed two more pilots had been lost to enemy fire. Others peered into the radar scopes, adjusting dials to track multiple flights of Midway aircraft. Their movements were ghostly, shrouded in a red gloom. A few looked up at the updated Plexiglas mission scoreboard. To some it was a series of abbreviations. To others, it represented life and death aboard Midway.

Two of them were typical of young men thrown together aboard Midway. Both Ron McPhail and Oscar Granger were radarmen in 1965. McPhail was an army brat who had already had seen part of the world. He enlisted in the Navy only days after he had seen John Wayne piloting a brown-water Navy boat in a movie whose title he soon forgot. Taller than many of his buddies with a square face and sturdy jaw, McPhail was one of those men who wore his hat low over his eyes. Granger was a farm boy who had outgrown a family farm that produced corn and alfalfa between long South Dakota winters. When he heard a Navy recruiter promise San Diego, he had signed up immediately.

McPhail was a strike controller. He maintained communications contact with the pilots starting at 50 miles out from Midway until they were in-country over land. Then, when they returned, McPhail had them until they hit the 50-mile mark from Midway's deck, when he turned them over to carrier-controlled approach. Granger carried similar responsibilities. The two virtually lived in CIC, keeping score on the endless series of missions that sometimes extended from 0500 to 2400.

McPhail and Granger set in motion a chain of decisions and actions each time Midway pilots turned into the homeward leg of their mission. They assessed the status of each aircraft and crew as they headed toward the carrier. Tone of voice said as much as words. Some reported damage in a voice made thin by unrelenting enemy fire. Some leaked fuel from flak damage and needed an airborne tanker fast.

McPhail and Granger also were among the first to know if a pilot had been lost. For some in CIC it became mechanical as they tracked the planes outbound, waited 90 minutes to four hours depending upon the mission, and then picked them back up on their return. They tallied the score, focusing on numbers rather than the men those notations represented. Time for reflection would come later. Their job was to react to circumstances as they unfolded on the radarscopes and in headsets in a blackened room.

"Sundowner 1, rolling in."

Bombing runs and air battles, however brief, mesmerized Granger. Hollow, detached voices drifted down from the overhead speakers and cut through his headset. He always felt the excitement, his heart pounding. He rode a roller coaster of nervousness, anticipation, exhilaration, and anguish. He knew when a Midway aircrew went down, whether other pilots saw them eject, and whether parachutes opened. Yet emotion couldn't interfere with snap search-and-rescue decisions that could save a pilot's life. Granger knew it didn't look good for Franke and Doremus.

Both had ejected from the Phantom before it crashed and were captured within minutes of landing in a rice paddy. They were destined for the "Hanoi Hilton" prisoner of war camp. Hundreds of American airmen spent a brutal part of their lives there. For most, days of pain strung together as time blurred. Pain at the hands of the enemy, pain of powerlessness, and the pain from imagining what wives, children, and parents must be enduring back home.

One day, a newly arrived POW gasped when he saw Franke. "Back home, they think you're dead," he whispered under Franke's cell door. The words shot through Franke. The imagined conversations at home haunted him. *"Kids, your dad's not coming home."* He ached knowing his family believed he was dead, that his wife, Jackie Louise, believed she had to find a way to move on. She was even paid the insurance money. Meanwhile his wife could only pray and hope for a miracle while trying to focus on raising William, Debra, and Valerie. Franke and the other prisoners waited, persevered, and held on to their faith.

Perseverance and faith were just as important to the men who rolled themselves out of sticky bunks on Midway that smelled of mildew every morning in the Tonkin Gulf.

At sea, carrier combat operations were relentless. They typically lasted a month at a time, with one-week breaks for liberty and resupply in Hong Kong or Subic Bay in the Philippines. The regimen made for long, hot stretches in the tropics. Many crewmen, even those assigned to brutal tasks, worked 12-hour shifts.

Rick Janes, a skinny youngster from Minnesota, was assigned the bizarre task of climbing down inside the steam catapult canal just below the flight deck when maintenance was necessary. The steel cooked in the sun. In sweltering tropical humidity, Janes covered himself from head to toe with overalls, shirts, and gloves to prevent any skin from touching the blistering metal. Heat stroke then became the worry. Whenever Janes squeezed into the long, narrow catapult chamber, a chief petty officer stood by and insisted that Janes keep talking as he worked so the chief knew Janes had not passed out from the heat.

"Janes, you okay?"

"Yeah."

"Janes! Are you all right? You still breathin' in there? Speak up, son!"

"Yes, sir."

For most sailors the only salvation was talcum powder. Pounds of talcum. Without it, itching became unbearable and rashes spread like wildfire. The smell of sweat and talc drifted through the passageways. General Quarters drills made a bad situation unbearable. Ventilation systems shut down during GQ, forcing sailors to wear wet rags around their heads in search of relief as powdered faces, arms, and necks caked with sweat.

Below deck, the humid heat sucked the energy out of a man as jets thundered overhead. Dominic Finazzo thought he knew about summer humidity. Born in Casablanca, he grew up in Brooklyn. He was the kind of kid who went to church every Sunday but might swipe a candy bar along the way. On Midway, he assembled bombs. Midway aircraft dropped more than 16 million pounds of ordnance during its 1965 combat deployment. A routine day for Finazzo consisted of using a hammer and chisel to break free the frozen nuts of 250- and 500-pound bombs in humidity that made hands and hammers slick with sweat.

The engineering spaces in Midway seemed closer to hell than the wet air that swept across the flight deck. Engineering was the land of the bloated. Pipes covered with countless layers of insulation were barely recognizable under uncounted coats of paint. Hundreds of crusty cables were clumped together, running from one overhead brace to the next toward an unknown destination. Heat hung in the air, drifting up through open metal grates that separated one level from the next. The smell of sweat blended with grease, steel, and rubber. Yet many engineering spaces were spotless. No oiled footprints. Dozens of white-faced, industrial-style dials sparkled. The thundering rumble of equipment echoed off whitewashed walls, settled in a man's heels, and rolled up his spine. It was a land where man was humbled by raw, hot power.

Midway was a confederation of departments and sections and the men permanently assigned to Midway's bowel worked in another dimension. Deep inside the hull and well below the waterline, daylight was a rarity, a wisp of fresh air a faded memory. Many felt underappreciated by those who lived "up on the roof," and ignored by those who "drilled holes in the sky." The primary loyalty of most young men repairing jet engines, mixing kegs of bread dough, or monitoring hundreds of gauges in engineering rested with their department and the men who shared their cramped, musty quarters. Terms used sanctimoniously by outsiders ("snipes" for those in engineering) became badges of honor among those so branded. Some placed pen to their plight:

ODE TO A SNIPE

Now each of us from time to time has looked upon the sea
and watched the warships pulling out to keep our country free.

And most of us have read a book or heard a lusty tale
about the men who sail these ships through lightning, wind or hail.

But there's a place within each ship that stories never reach
and there's a special breed of man that legends rarely teach.

It's down below the water line and it takes a living toll—
a hot metallic living room that sailors call "the hole."

It houses engines run by steam that make the screws go 'round,
a place of fire and noise that beats your spirits down.

Where boilers make a hellish roar and blood of angry steam,
they're armored gods without remorse that haunt your every dream.

They have no time for man or god nor tolerance for fear,
their honor pays no living thing the tribute of a tear.

For there's not much that men can do that these men haven't done
beneath the deck—deep in the hole—to make the engines run.

A constant threat from boiler fires is like a living doubt
that any minute would with scorn escape and rub you out.

The men who keep the life-fires lit and make the engines run
are strangers to the world of light and rarely see the sun.

And every breath of every day they stand their watch in hell,
for if the fires should ever fail, the ship's a useless well.

They're locked below like men foredoomed who hear no battle cry,
it's just assumed that if we're hit the men below will die.

There's not much difference in the hole whatever the war will bring,
for threats of violent, ugly death down there are a common thing.

Every day is a war for snipes when gauges read red,
twelve hundred pounds of heating steam can kill you mighty dead.

So every man down in the hole has learned to hate so well
that when you speak to them of fear, their laughter's heard in hell.

Sweat-soaked men fight down below in superheated air
to keep their ship alive and well, though no one knows they're there.

And they'll fight strong for ages on, 'til warships sail no more
through boilers' heat and deadly mist and hellish turbine roar.

I can talk about this place and try to make you see
the hopeless life of men down there, because one of them is me.

                                    —*Author Unknown*

The blanket of fog brought tears to some men's eyes. They were
home. They had survived. After six months at war, an exhausted Midway

steamed under the Golden Gate Bridge on November 23, 1965. More than 11,500 sorties had been launched from a deck worn down to bare steel. Seventeen aircraft were lost, 14 of its pilots were believed dead, and three others missing.

As preparations were made in late 1965 to again decommission Midway, this time for a four-year overhaul, the skies over Vietnam quieted when the United States suspended air operations during Christmas. The North Vietnamese took advantage of the lull, rebuilding many of the bridges Midway pilots had destroyed.

Midway's modernization would affect the entire Navy. Plans called for an $88 million overhaul, the most comprehensive overhaul ever undertaken. They were not universally endorsed by the entire Navy leadership. Some admirals felt Midway's life expectancy would reach only to the end of the Vietnam War. That made a near-$100 million overhaul a dubious investment at best.

The design and construction of Midway nearly 20 years earlier posed major challenges to cost-effective modernization. The deck's armor plating varied in size and steel quality. Below, engineers and workmen faced the prospect of working in and cutting through more than 1,300 compartments below the waterline. Massive amounts of steel cutting were necessary, sometimes every four or five feet through the 1,000-foot length of the ship in order to install new electronics.It was a slow, laborious process. The simultaneous construction on the carrier Hornet and the guided missile cruiser Chicago interfered with modernization. The arrival of the fire-ravaged Oriskany from Vietnam for extensive repairs caused a major delay. As both the delays and price tag mounted while the war continued in Vietnam, the nation took notice. A national debate erupted over whether to spend tax dollars on new ships or to modernize older ships.

The Navy recognized it had a major problem on its hands. In 1968, it assigned a veteran shipyard naval officer, Captain James Kaune, to take over as Midway's project manager. When Kaune assumed command, he noted "no one was in a real hurry to get back to work" after long, repetitive meetings that seemed to go nowhere. A major priority became one of simply increasing the tempo of reconstruction. Kaune took several actions to step up the pace on Midway.

Short lead-times between ideas and implementation were praised, creating a culture where accomplishment became the basis for commendation. Kaune created an "action group concept" in which workers acquired a greater ability to direct their own activities and take responsibility for their actions. He then promoted the concept internally and externally with posters, matchbooks, buttons, bumper stickers, billboards, awards, and editorials in the local newspapers. Kaune had become the CEO of a business called Midway.

Midway had become the world's largest rat nest. *Star Trek*–inspired visions of a futuristic warship vanished when the new crew began to report in August 1969, more than three years and $175 million into its renovation. They found a barely recognizable steel hulk awash in electrical cables, acetylene hoses, and wires.

Some young men like Charles Paige of Michigan reported long before Midway was ready to sail. At first they were given duties that had nothing to do with their official assignment. Paige, a radioman, spent his early days as the driver for Captain E. J. Carroll, an even-tempered man who often asked Paige to slide over so Carroll could drive back to the ship. It gave Paige a chance to take a good look at Hunter's Point where Midway was berthed, a chunk of land that extended out into San Francisco Bay. The bullet holes in the Marine guards' Crisp Avenue entrance shelter were testament to the rule that sailors at Hunter's Point were not allowed to leave the base on foot. Hunter's Point was aptly named.

San Francisco beckoned only 20 minutes away by bus, an intoxicating blend of self-absorbed sophistication and Haight-Ashbury at the close of the 1960s. Midway sailors learned it wasn't always wise to wear a uniform on liberty. But Paige and others were prohibited from having civilian clothes aboard ship. There were two solutions. Smuggle civvies on and off ship in tote bags or rent a locker over a clothing store in downtown San Francisco for quick changes. Some sailors wanted to look like civilians so badly they wore men's wigs to hide their short hair in the summer of Woodstock and the year before Kent State.

The ultimate price tag to complete the four-year modernization of Midway by 1970 was $202 million, a huge sum that didn't include the ship's engineering plant that powered Midway. But the project's defenders argued the Navy came away with a nearly all-new ship sitting on a 25-year-old hull.

Meanwhile as fresh young men prepared to take Midway back into combat, the families of those who preceded them prayed, wondered, and wept. It would be as long as a quarter century before some families learned what became of sons on Midway who had fought by the deadly rules of combat.

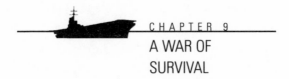

CHAPTER 9

A WAR OF SURVIVAL

Jim Sawyer could hardly believe his luck as he lay on a Navy hospital bed in Danang. The mattress above him shook each time a predawn Viet Cong rocket exploded nearby. Dust drifted in darkened night air. Between blasts, he ached from a newly set left arm that had been shattered only hours before. His leg throbbed where 158 stitches weaved sinew and muscle as one. Toughened by a west Texas oilfield childhood, he knew the pain would ease in time. He wondered how many Midway shipmates weren't as lucky. He wondered who had died off the coast of Vietnam as a light rain dressed Midway's flight deck.

His arms hung heavy. His boots kept catching on the rippled flight deck. Crusted ocean spray made his face brittle. Crewman Tony Dennig was exhausted. October 24, 1972, had been another long day of flight operations aboard the carrier. For nearly 12 hours sorties of Midway aircraft cycled off and back onto the carrier after completing bombing, SAM suppression, and photo reconnaissance missions over South Vietnam. The brutal routine repeated every 90 minutes as one raft of aircraft shot off the bow shortly before an earlier group was stacked up for recovery. Flight deck crews barely caught their breath from one launch as they turned to see Corsairs and Phantoms, Crusaders and Intruders, inbound off the stern at incremental elevations of 1,000 feet. They reorganized to direct the aircraft to the bow to be refueled, rearmed, and then cycled back into position for another cat shot toward the enemy.

By 2000 hours on October 24, more than a dozen aircraft had safely made it back aboard. Jim "Buzzard" Sawyer, Vic Wood, Tony Dennig, and others were on the edge of collapse. Only one aircraft remained in the air, an A-6 Intruder on its final approach. Only a few men on the flight deck paid any attention to what appeared to be a routine approach. Most focused on stabilizing aircraft with tie-down chains, refueling, a hot meal, and sleep.

Tony Dennig, though, looked back as the Intruder neared. He had been struggling with a panel under an F-4 Phantom when he heard "in the ball," in his headset, the indication the pilot was about to land. Just as Dennig looked astern, the Intruder seemed to dip slightly to his left. As the plane came over the deck, the stern rode up over the top of a swell. The plane's right wheel slammed down onto the deck ahead of the rest of the aircraft. Instantly it snapped off, spraying sparks as the broken strut grabbed an arresting wire for an instant before breaking free. The Intruder pivoted into a sideways slide straight down the deck toward more than 30 men and their planes. Dennig stood square in the path of the sliding monster.

"It's coming! It's coming!" screamed Dennig as he scrambled out from under the Phantom. He ran headlong into a plane captain, throwing a perfect chest block that sent him flying. Dennig's best friend, Fred Goterotti, scrambled down off the same F-4's canopy where he had been securing flight systems. He frantically looked for a safe place to hide from the horrible screech headed toward him.

Only a few feet away, Sawyer, attached to the ordnance shop, was standing between two F-4s. He had no time to think. He sprinted toward the island, the only safe haven on a flight deck. Sawyer faced a long run across a flight deck that spanned more than four acres. He might have made it, had the Intruder not changed directions in midskid.

Vic Wood should have been in the path of the Intruder. Also a member of the ordnance crew, he stood talking with Clayton Blankenship as the Intruder approached. Told the Intruder carried no ordnance, Wood remembered one of the cardinal rules of the flight deck. "If you don't have any business on the flight deck, get off!" So Wood stepped down onto the catwalk, leaving Blankenship to finish up the last recovery. Wood didn't know the approaching Intruder was saddled with two "hung bombs," a pair of

Mk-82s that had failed to release from its wing. Later, men shuddered at the thought of 500-pound bombs bouncing their way into a pack of parked aircraft on the bow of an aircraft carrier.

The bone-jarring grind of the Intruder sliding down the deck cut through headsets alerting the flight deck crew to an unfolding disaster. They barely had time to turn toward the sound when the Intruder slammed into a Phantom. The Intruder split in two, its tail section severed and starting its own slide forward. Meanwhile, the Intruder's fuselage caromed off the Phantom and continued forward toward men as flames poured out. Men were trapped as the Intruder drove into the middle of a pack of aircraft parked forward. Ordnance crews, refuelers, troubleshooters, and plane captains were surrounded by flames and crushing wreckage. Metal-searing hell had landed on Midway.

The heavy clouds over Midway glowed from the flaming jet fuel as fire crews chased the skidding Intruder past the island and toward the parked planes. One aircraft's fuel cell had punctured, shooting JP-5 fuel and flames into the air. As emergency crews opened their fire hoses, the air boss up in the island directed them into the smoke and flames so that the wind across the deck didn't blow their fire-retardant spray uselessly over the side. Within two minutes, the fire was brought under control.

Another drama had already begun over the water only a few hundred yards away. As the Intruder skidded down the deck, observers on the bridge were shocked when bomber-navigator Michael Bixel ejected from the careening aircraft. He soared out of the eerie glow of Midway's yellow flight deck lights and disappeared into the rainy gloom.

As the sounds of the crash died, the screams and moans of injured men pierced the night air. Some lay motionless on the deck made slick by a blend of jet fuel and fire-retardant water. Others writhed in agony. Some still tried to crawl to safety, pulling themselves with bloodied fingertips across the ribbed asphaltlike nonskid surface that tore through leather as easily as a man's muscle. Lucky, healthy shipmates sprinted to their stricken buddies, doing what they could to ease their horror until medical personnel arrived.

Dr. Donald Vance shouldn't have been on the flight deck that night. Normally during a mass casualty drill, his station was the aft mess deck.

But within seconds of the crash, he found himself sprinting through the rain, kneeling near one victim, shouting orders, and then racing to the next. In his wake, corpsmen and flight deck crew administered emergency triage and sometimes carried victims in wire baskets over to the aircraft elevator that would take them below for treatment.

One of those victims was Jim Sawyer, whose sprint toward the island had kept him in the path of the swerving Intruder. At the last second, he dove onto the flight deck. Something "like hot golf balls being dropped on me" pounded his back briefly. It passed and thinking he was okay, Sawyer rose to his feet. With an arm hanging at a gut-wrenching angle, his stumble on a shredded leg brought help who carried him to a wire litter on the elevator.

Sawyer looked up into the rain peppering his face. He heard men nearby screaming as he waited to be taken below. A corpsman stopped, gave him a shot of morphine, and wrote a "1" on his forehead. The morphine stood no chance against the pain. A second shot and a "2" calmed the waves of pain from his shattered arm and badly lacerated leg. Once the elevator was filled with injured, including one man screaming from the pain of blinded eyes, Sawyer was taken below. JP-5 jet fuel was often the killer in flight deck crashes. That night it blinded one man and another drowned when he inhaled fuel that coated the lining of his lungs and asphyxiated him.

Only a week earlier, officials from Clark Air Base had briefed Vance and his medical department on mass casualty procedures. Those procedures saved a number of lives that October night. In the end, four men sacrificed their lives on the deck of Midway. Serious injuries totaled 27, requiring three emergency operations in Midway's operating room. Eleven others were flown off to Danang within hours of the crash, just in time for the rocket attack. An unsung hero was an Air Force colonel who grounded his planes despite enemy fire at the Danang airport so the inbound flights from Midway could land with the badly wounded.

One of those flown ashore, Tony Dennig, never woke up in the Danang Naval Hospital. After blocking his plane captain over the side, Dennig's world went black. Shipmates found him 32 feet away from his plane, unconscious. Nearly three days later he awoke in the Clark Air Base Regional Medical Center. He had five broken ribs, two cracked vertebrae, suffered temporary paralysis, a leg wound, and punctured left lung. His plane captain later was found in the deck-edge safety net, unconscious, and suffering only a broken leg. Years later, he thanked Dennig for saving his life.

Other survivors were haunted by the experience. Vic Wood couldn't believe his luck. He had followed his early-Navy training by leaving the deck in the belief there was no more ordnance to tend. His buddy, Clayton Blankenship, stayed on deck and was instantly killed.

Open leg fractures were the most common injury that night as heavy tie-down chains snapped off wings and padeyes and whipped ankle-high across the flight deck. Shrapnel from shattered chain links sliced through muscle and bone. The Intruder's pilot, Michael Bixel, was never found and declared "lost at sea."

Two days later military notification teams began to make their rounds. Two teams, usually an officer and a chaplain, went to Omaha and Minneapolis to inform families that Robert Haakenson Jr. and Robert Yankoski also had died on Midway's flight deck that night.

A third team drove to Spring City, a quiet hamlet set among the rolling hills, horse farms, and woodlands of southeastern Pennsylvania, to call on the Dennig family. The team could have been calling about a Dennig son who was fighting in the rice paddies of Vietnam. Perhaps they carried news about another son who flew helicopters in combat. Instead, they told the Dennig family that Tony had survived a horrific crash on Midway, had been flown off the carrier with serious injuries, and that the Navy had no other immediate information.

The day before, air strikes against North Vietnam had been suspended as prospects for a negotiated peace brightened. It soon proved to be a mirage. Midway's last combat deployment to Vietnam typified much of the uncertainty, frustration, fear, anger, and exhaustion that gripped many Americans, both in service and at home. A floating chunk of America a fifth of a mile long, Midway embodied all that confronted the country in 1972 after nearly a decade of war and social turbulence. Vietnam had become a lost cause. All that mattered now to most of the crew was coping with the needless waste and surviving a war that had no end in sight.

Midway had been training off the coast of California in the spring of 1972 when the final turning point of the Vietnam War took place. On March 30, massive numbers of North Vietnamese troops swarmed south across the demilitarized zone. The United States countered with renewed bombing over the north as 12 of North Vietnam's 13 army divisions, approximately 120,000 men, charged south that Easter weekend.

Midway was ordered to rejoin the war. With only two days' notice and nearly two months ahead of its scheduled deployment, Midway's crew had scrambled to ready the carrier for its return to battle. On April 10, California disappeared off Midway's stern as the carrier set a course for Hawaii. Less than three weeks from the day deployment orders had been received, Midway was on station 7,800 miles from home, launching aircraft toward the coast of Vietnam.

Life aboard Midway was far different than when the carrier had left the war zone in 1966 for its four-year overhaul. In the face of low enlistment rates, the Navy had relaxed both recruitment standards and service regulations. Beards were now allowed. Enlisted men had a private lounge aboard Midway, no officers allowed. Recruiters faced heavy pressure to meet quotas. A popular rumor held some recruiters made their quotas by striking deals with small-town judges to accept petty criminals into the service as an alternative to a few months in the county jail. Old salts groused over the new Navy and its lowered standards. Several recalled a time when valuables could be left out in the open. Not so in the Navy of the early 1970s. At the same time, reenlistment incentives were sweetened. One year 101 sailors reenlisted on Midway. They received more than $250,000 in bonuses in return for service obligations that totaled more than 525 years.

Drugs infected the Navy and Midway. In 1966, the Navy had discharged 150 sailors for drug offenses. Only four years later, 5,000 sailors were discharged. Rumors swept Midway about how the deployment of a West Coast destroyer had been delayed when more than 100 of its 2,400-man crew were found to be part of a drug ring.

The drug culture was no less insidious aboard Midway. Prodigious amounts of drugs were consumed ashore on liberty, particularly in the Philippines. For many, "speed," "smoke," and "grass" topped the list of most popular drugs. Sometimes LSD was smuggled onto the carrier as microdots hidden under stamps. Some believed that several of Midway's Marines were the primary dealers. Few were willing to rat on Midway drug offenders, run the risk of being implicated, and be sent to a brig guarded by their buddies.

As Midway steamed off the coast of Vietnam in the last year of the war, an aide to Secretary of Defense Melvin Laird opened a letter postmarked USS Midway. Inside was a cartoon of Snoopy sitting on his doghouse, writing a letter a few days after actress Jane Fonda had visited Hanoi. It came at a time when Midway's pilots fumed over the Pentagon's prohibition against bombing North Vietnam's rice-economy irrigation system. *"Dear Jane,"* wrote Snoopy. *"After going and returning from North Vietnam unscathed, you must be convinced we don't bomb dikes."*

Frustration on Midway grew as prospects for a settlement brightened and then dimmed. The steady pulse of routine continued. Regardless of whether bombing North Vietnam had been suspended for a few weeks, meals had to be prepared, patients seen, boilers tended, and message traffic decoded and delivered.

Men devised different ways to ease the strain. One source of entertainment was the ship's flush-deck pilot landing assist television (PLAT) system. Facing aft, it gave viewers a head-on view of every aircraft as it landed. On occasion a bomb or rocket broke free when a plane touched down. It was an unnerving sight to see a bomb skidding directly at the PLAT lens, skim over it, and skitter off the flight deck and down into Midway's bow wave.

Those working in the PLAT shop sometimes considered the equipment their personal entertainment center. They amused themselves by watching porn tapes on their closed-circuit system. One day PLAT operators received a call from Air Intelligence, politely inquiring when the next porn tape would be broadcast. The operators muttered a nonreply, fearing it was a setup to get them to confirm possession and broadcast. They didn't know that at some point in the past, someone had tapped into the system and surreptitiously installed a PLAT monitor in Air Intelligence so they could watch the landings. PLAT operators hadn't known their private screenings were being broadcast elsewhere inside Midway.

Snoopy provided the comic relief thanks to Wally Girard, the most junior of three assistant air controllers on Midway. Upon reporting aboard, it fell to him to prepare the flight plan each day and get it to the print shop for duplication. But prior to delivery, the flight plan had to be approved. The first day, Girard dutifully wrote the plan and stood before operations officer Al Johnson awaiting his approval.

"What's this?" asked Johnson after a quick scan of the document. "Where's Snoopy?" New to air plan writing, Girard had no idea what Johnson was talking about. The silence lengthened before Johnson explained the facts of air wing life to Girard. "Get this straight. Each air plan must have a Snoopy cartoon. I don't care who draws it and it doesn't matter too much what it says. But it must be there, every day, and without it no air plan will be approved. Dismissed."

Girard beat a hasty retreat and went to work. It wasn't too long before he mastered Snoopy and his doghouse, added a bubbled comment by Snoopy, and again stood before Commander Johnson. "Approved." With that, a Midway tradition continued. Every day, the air wing looked forward to seeing what Snoopy had to say. No department was immune from Snoopy's sarcasm. LSOs, the "weather guessers," pilots, captain, navigator, and others all came in for their share of the daily barbs—even the ship's physicians, Midway's sentinels in the war of survival.

"What? You're my what?" fumed Midway Captain William L. Harris Jr.

"I'm the new senior medical officer," stammered Donald Vance, fresh from his internship after finishing medical school at the University of Arkansas. "The hell you are! Hear this, *Doctor* Vance. I have a senior medical officer aboard. Jim Wells. *He* is in charge of my medical department. *He* will attend my senior officers' meetings and *he* will remain in charge. I don't give a damn about what the Navy thinks. On my ship, Dr. Jim Wells is in charge. Are we clear on that?"

"Yes, sir," was all that Vance could muster before turning on his heel and departing Captain Harris' bridge.

Vance was part of a short-lived Navy experiment that accelerated training of new physicians so they could immediately be assigned to ships as senior medical officers. The Navy hoped the accelerated training would entice more physicians to consider the Navy as a career. Vance, one of the first four physicians in the program, had received orders for Midway as its senior medical officer even though the carrier had a physician senior in rank to Vance. But out in blue water, Midway's captain ruled supreme. He already had his senior medical officer and it was up to Vance and Wells to work it out.

Midway's medical department was a complete health care complex that included x-ray machines, a pharmacy, and an operating room. About 90 patients were seen each day. Most ailments could be handled aboard ship. Others required visits to specialists who were few and far between in Southeast Asia. The Navy was especially short of ophthalmologists, urologists, and otolarangologists. At times, the backlog of Midway sailors requiring specialized attention became so acute that ship's doctors tried flying them to Japan for diagnosis and treatment. The logistics became so cumbersome the practice was quickly discontinued.

Ship's medical officers could also count on epidemics, some expected and others a surprise. In August and September of 1972, the Hong Kong flu swept through the crew, sending more than 800 sailors to sickbay before the bug finally ran its course. Venereal disease outbreaks, on the other hand, were something the ship's medical corps could set its calendar to. No other Midway port rivaled Olongapo City, just outside the gate of the base at Subic Bay in the Philippines, as a sexual fantasyland.

The medical staff could count on a massive outbreak of VD after leaving Olongapo. It was so prevalent one of the three daily clinics on Midway was designated VD-only for several days after departing the Philippines. During the 1972–73 cruise, ship's medical staff treated 36 percent of the crew for VD. They celebrated their 1,000th case of VD in classic Navy tradition by ordering a uniquely shaped cake.

It was far more difficult to monitor the health of Midway's pilots.

One by one, a dozen pilots trudged into the ready room and fell into their seats. Their missions for the day completed, they had opted for two hours of a mindless movie in place of sleep. The lights dimmed in a room that had grown stale in the tropical humidity. Once the movie started, "Quack" slipped into the room and stood silently in the back, listening. There it was. In the darkness a man had cleared his throat. Again. Quack moved toward the muffled cough, leaned over, and quietly asked the pilot to step outside.

Physicians aboard Midway constantly monitored the physical health of Midway's aviators. They knew that simply holding three walk-in clinics a day was no way to keep tabs on the air wing. No self-respecting pilot sat himself down unless he was very, very ill. Yet even modest ailments such as a head cold could put a crew in danger. Equilibrium and clear wits were critical when flying a jet.

A "cat shot" launch strained both man and aircraft. Adrenaline tingled the senses as a pilot approached the catapult, his plane captain "knee walking" the aircraft under the nose. Once he was attached to the cat, a pilot scanned his instruments one last time, his aircraft at full power and held in place by a single bolt. At launch, nearly eight Gs froze him against his ejection seat. His cheeks flattened and vision blurred. One hand locked on the throttle, the other within inches of his ejection handle, the pilot had no control for about four seconds as his jet rocketed off the bow and seemed to hang in the air. Only then could he regain control before the aircraft began to sink, getting the nose to about a ten-degree up angle. Landing gear up, raise the flaps, and begin to fly.

At night, there was no horizon as a point of orientation. Pilots had to clear their heads quickly and focus on their main attitude gyro to position their aircraft to fly. It was no place for a sick pilot vulnerable to vertigo.

No pilot ever argued with Vance's judgment when he put the aviator on the "down list." Rarely, though, did a pilot suggest that he might be too ill to fly.

The two flight surgeons of the air wing, too, had their own methods in treating the ills of air crews. Fatigue, stress, and combat pressure were always a concern. Night flying was particularly stressful, especially upon completion of a combat mission that saw SAMs and automatic weapons fire sizzling past the canopy. It wasn't uncommon for a flight surgeon to "prescribe" a little Benadryl or Valium to help pilots sleep. Others dispensed an array of numbing, airline-sized bottles of bourbon, scotch, and vodka.

Vance rubbed his pounding temples. The number of Midway crew needing a psychiatrist had become overwhelming. A recommendation that a psychiatrist spend time aboard Midway had been denied. As a result, ship's doctors found themselves playing the roles of father confessor, psychiatrist, big brother, and counselor as men fought to overcome growing demons.

Donald Vance often set his stethoscope aside to have a heart-to-heart talk with a young Midway sailor who might be homesick, lonely, or simply scared of not surviving. When a sailor paid a visit to Vance, the young doctor sat so that a large poster of a drill instructor yelling into the face of a petrified recruit was visible over Vance's shoulder. The caption read, "We didn't promise you a rose garden." It was a message Vance found himself reinforcing with his visitors. Vance often reminded the 19-year-old sitting across from him that the young man had signed a contract, was duty-bound to honor it, and someday would look back on its fulfillment with a measure of pride.

Later, some of those private talks haunted Vance at 0200 when he tried to sleep.

Ray "Buzzy" Donnelly had been a polite and stellar athlete at Villanova University who once shared an American swimming medley relay record. He was the kind of pilot who crouched under an aircraft on the hangar deck to hand wrenches to a mechanic working on a fuel drop tank. He made rounds through the aircraft intermediate maintenance department, explaining that day's flight operations or periodically showing mechanics the photos taken on reconnaissance missions. He wanted everyone to know how they helped meet Midway's mission.

One day Ray Donnelly and Mike McCormick climbed aboard their Intruder for another mission over Vietnam. They knew they would likely have to fly through small–automatic weapons fire by men unseen in the jungle below. Sometimes a single bullet found a hydraulic system knuckle that knocked a sophisticated F-4 Phantom out of the sky. Other times pilots flinched at the *brrrpppp* of bullets that harmlessly pierced the length of their fuselage as they continued toward their target.

As Donnelly and McCormick prepared to attack their assigned target, a handful of bullets thudded into the Intruder's nose. Before either could react, a few found the canopy. Donnelly seemed to jump in his seat when they found his neck and head.

Mike McCormick was horrified. His canopy shattered and his buddy covered in blood, McCormick flew as fast as he could back to Midway, screaming into his headset Donnelly was badly hurt. The wind and decompression from the gaping canopy swirled Donnelly's blood throughout the cockpit. McCormick disarmed the ejection system so that he couldn't accidentally eject from the stricken aircraft. Helpless to stem the flow of blood, the most he could do was get Donnelly back to Midway before Donnelly bled to death.

On board, Donald Vance knew he might only have seconds to save Donnelly's life if McCormick made it back aboard. "Get me a forklift and put a pallet on it! Now! You, get us up against that Intruder before he comes to a stop. You, get up here with me and hang on. No matter what you see inside that cockpit, I want you to secure the ejection seat when we get to the canopy. Ignore what you see or smell. Secure the cockpit!"

The doctor's emergency team stood ready as McCormick vectored toward Midway. As onlookers held their breaths and the LSO coached him down, McCormick somehow brought his plane aboard in a haze of gore and grizzle. In seconds Vance and his team were at Donnelly's side. Cockpit systems were secured while Vance tended to Donnelly. It was too late. Too much blood had been lost. Donnelly was dead from a few bullets on their way up from the jungle toward the clouds.

Gently, Donnelly was lifted out of the plane. McCormick climbed out white with shock. Later the aircraft was taken below to the hangar deck to a knot of hushed men. It fell to Petty Officer John Mscisz and his five-man crew to clean up the horror. Blood and tissue had been sprayed and sucked into every crevice. Seats, flight instruments, and access panels were taken out of the aircraft in order to clean it. Mscisz and his team took turns on the gruesome detail. Frequently they stopped and sat on the wing or took a walk across the hangar deck to collect their thoughts and settle stomachs. Weeks later, Mscisz marveled when another bullet-riddled plane returned from a combat mission. He counted 97 holes from one end of the aircraft to the other. No serious damage was done, and the flight crew returned unharmed.

Meanwhile, the sight of his navigator's blood spewed across his cockpit haunted McCormick. He had seen enough and decided to quit flying. Maybe that would end his nightmares. Donald Vance sat McCormick down for a long talk. They talked about life and death, perspective, and purpose. In time, McCormick decided to keep flying. He rejoined the endless cycles of launches and recoveries, daring fate by flying through enemy fire as the peace talks dragged on.

Six months later, another two-man Intruder crew headed for a heavily forested North Vietnam valley dotted with surface-to-air missile sites. The mission schedule was tight. The Intruder had only seconds to spare in suppressing SAM fire before the massive B-52 bombers arrived. As the Intruder approached the target, the dense cloud cover began to glow. More than a dozen SAMs rose to meet the American attackers. Undeterred, the bombers pounded the target, turned, and headed for their base. The Intruder also turned toward the Tonkin Gulf. It never arrived.

The Intruder's wingman, circling off the coast waiting for the missing aircraft to join up, had heard nothing. No one had seen it hit by enemy fire. He retraced his inbound route and searched the jungle canopy for any sign of a ground fire that indicated a crash. Despite the lack of a single hopeful clue, search teams flew hard for four days. Nothing was found. The Intruder had disappeared without a trace.

The Intruder's two-man crew was listed as missing in action. One was Robert Alan Clark, a likeable and funny navigator who hailed from North Hollywood, California. Friends said he left behind a son he never saw. The pilot was Michael Timothy McCormick, the aviator who had decided to keep flying. Long after the war had become a marathon of survival, McCormick had kept flying—right up to the moment he was shot down, only 17 days before the SAM sites fell silent when peace was declared in Vietnam.

CHAPTER 10

FATE, FREEDOM, AND FLIGHT

"THE WORLD'S GREATEST FIGHTER PILOT" lived for the pressure of combat. Ron "Mugs" McKeown was on his fourth Vietnam tour aboard Midway as a lieutenant commander in 1972 with the VF-161 Chargers, better known as the "Rock Rivers." His ego was legendary, built on more than 400 combat missions. At home, even his eight-year-old daughter answered the phone, "McKeown residence, home of the world's greatest fighter pilot." His cockiness and belief in fate inspired some and thoroughly irked others in the uncertain skies over North Vietnam.

McKeown had long been accustomed to commanding the center of attention. He was a running back on one of the best Navy football teams ever, leading the Midshipmen to the 1961 Orange Bowl and a top-three national ranking. In his early days, he flew F8 Crusaders, nicknamed "ensign eaters" because of their high accident rate. He had flown as a test pilot and was a member of VX-4, the squadron that tested new planes and avionic systems. There, he was in charge of writing the fighter tactics manual for the F-4 Phantom. Over Groom Lake, Nevada, he had been one of a handful of pilots who accumulated more than 90 hours of flight time in captured Russian MiG-17s and -21s. It was a classified program that provided approximately 50 Navy flight crews with personal flight experience against the enemy aircraft they would face in Vietnam. By the time McKeown was aboard Midway in 1972 he was lobbying to be named the first commanding officer of the Navy's Fighter Weapons School (Top Gun) at Miramar.

McKeown trained at NAS Miramar earlier in his career, sparring with pilots who later became shipmates assigned to other squadrons on Midway during its final combat deployment to Vietnam. He had learned how to fly a Phantom outside its envelope, and knew the necessity of taking the "who" out of a dogfight and to think in terms of the "whys" and "hows" of winning an engagement. McKeown was driven to win. He delighted in sending an opposing pilot his "Piece of Cake Award" the day after besting him in a mock battle. It fed McKeown's confidence as much as it irritated other pilots. He liked to brag that he "could drop it down a chimney if they wanted me to."

On Midway, VF-161 was a flying frat house comprised of about two dozen 25-year-olds, all under the charge of Deacon Connell, a leader revered by his pilots. "We can beat anyone at anything, anytime," Connell frequently boasted. Whether recording the highest number of "Okay, 3" trap ratings or a "friendly" game of football or basketball, the competitive streak of squadron VF-161 bristled at any challenge. The Rock Rivers took pride in wearing red baseball caps and red turtlenecks. For most, the "uniform" wasn't complete without a Marsh Wheeling cheroot wedged between their teeth. After a wire service photo of VF-161 with clenched cigars appeared, the cigar manufacturer sent the Rock Rivers a case every month, no charge.

Competitive fire fueled their souls as they lined up for as many as 45 consecutive days of combat missions, missions they flew at all hours of the day and night. Usually the Rock Rivers flew their F-4s on air defense missions, either in defense of Midway or to protect attack squadrons against MiGs deep into "Indian country" north of Hanoi. The F-4 Phantom dwarfed the enemy's MiG-17. The weight of an F-4's internal fuel load equaled the total gross weight of a fully armed MiG-17. Typically, heavy-weight versus flyweight air battles lasted less than two minutes before one or the other gained a potentially deadly advantage.

Connell, a former football player at Texas A&M, took a gridiron approach to assigning missions as the squadron's skipper. He liked to say he wanted his first-string pilots on the missions that defended the large alpha strikes. "Those bomber pukes deserve our very best." He sometimes named McKeown to the first string on a mission, even over Connell's executive officer. Other times the Phantoms flew "flak absorption" missions, racing ahead of the bombers to draw fire from SAM sites and then knocking out the sites seconds before the attack squadrons arrived. Learning how to avoid a SAM was an art. While some pilots waited until the last second before executing a barrel roll over the missile, McKeown preferred to fly toward the oncoming SAM and then dive hard toward the deck at the last second. His technique frayed the nerves of lesser pilots.

Sometimes terror came at the very end of a night mission when the Midway was less than a mile in front of a pilot. McKeown occasionally approached Midway at about 150 miles per hour, 200 feet off the water on a dark, moonless, overcast night. In those conditions, he couldn't see the ship and the landing signal officer only about 15 yards from the centerline of the angle deck couldn't see McKeown. Many times McKeown and his RIO, Jack Ensch, heard the LSO say, "I can't see you, but you sound good so keep it coming." "Keep it coming" were the words no aviator wanted to hear. They usually meant visibility was a wish. They flew through the clouds and trusted their instruments. Seconds before landing, the deck appeared through the gray mist, the stern looking like it was drawing figure eights as it rode the swells.

For the first 250 missions McKeown tried not to think about the risk. "You relied on your training and hoped you made it back in one piece. There was a lot of hope in the early missions. But along at about the 250th mission, I ran out of guts. Recognizing the thin line of death. It was tough completing those missions until I settled on a 'thy will be done' kind of fatalism and only asked that if it happened, it happen quick. Then, after about 300 missions, you think you're bulletproof. You can't get hurt. You're invincible." McKeown's call sign was "Bullet."

The most experienced pilots knew better than to blindly believe in invincibility. Before every mission, McKeown gently removed his Naval Academy ring and placed it on a letter meant for his wife and two daughters if he didn't return from the mission. He took the ring off because he didn't want the enemy to cut off his finger to get it.

Even with flight operations lasting 12 to 18 hours a day, there were far more hours between missions than time in the air. Diversion and camaraderie restored a sense of balance and perspective in prolonged combat. VF-161's approach to entertainment became nearly as legendary as McKeown's ego. During those precious five-day stays in port, parties and pranks prevailed. The Rock Rivers formed their own band, chorale, and song list of dirty songs when they took over the Hilton and Sheraton hotel bars in Hong Kong. One time, they convinced hotel staff to haul a piano up to the 14th floor for a party.

On board Midway, the practical jokes and pratfalls continued. When the squadron discovered one of its own had an irregular heartbeat, it became several pilots' mission to see if they could make it skip a beat on command. They wrapped a rubber snake around a pipe the pilot grabbed to haul himself out of bed. The conspirators yelled "General quarters!" and watched. Sure enough he grabbed the snake and jumped a foot, but remained steady as a rock. Another time, the pranksters bought a stuffed cobra and placed it in the officer's stateroom. No luck. His heart remained as strong as a lion's. It was one mission the pilots of VF-161 failed to complete.

Meanwhile the bond between a pilot and his radar intercept officer was the glue that kept most aviators centered in prolonged combat conditions. McKeown and Ensch's bond was stronger than most. Facing danger, sacrifice, and the enemy together spawned a lifelong friendship. It was fortified by a counter-punching humor. One time while on a mission McKeown dared to try a touch and go on an enemy airfield. He asked Ensch if he'd brought along his camera. Ensch said he had never believing that even McKeown might pull such a stunt. McKeown called his bluff and seconds before the Phantom's wheels touched enemy ground, Ensch confessed there was no camera aboard. McKeown swore, stoked the afterburners, and raced toward safer skies.

Pilots placed tremendous trust in their equipment and those who maintained it. Just the same, they often checked to make sure different systems were functioning properly. Periodically McKeown would check the onboard fire warning system. When pilots tested that circuit, they were supposed to warn their crew. One day McKeown thought it would be funny to skip the notification part and see Ensch's reaction to the unexpected alarms. Ensch failed to see the humor.

But Ensch had ways to rein in the world's greatest fighter pilot. Once on a flight when the two faced a very difficult landing in near-typhoon conditions, all the lights in the cockpit blinked out. "I need lights! I need lights!" McKeown screamed as he aimed for an area on the flight deck the size of a basketball court. In high seas, the deck was actually higher than the aircraft when the stern rode up over a swell. In seconds he would be hitting the deck at nearly 150 miles an hour, hoping an eight-foot tailhook would yank his 20-ton aircraft to a halt. A pause, then, "You want them back?" asked Ensch. McKeown started breathing again just as the Phantom touched down with a fully illuminated cockpit and a grinning Jack Ensch. McKeown trimmed his prankster horns for a few days after that.

Practical jokes killed time between the missions that most Midway pilots hoped would lead to a confrontation with a Russian-made MiG. Most yearned for combat and few were content with escort duty. On May 23 while on the lookout for enemy MiGs high above an attack by Midway jets, the world's greatest fighter pilot got his wish.

McKeown and Ensch along with their wingman, Mike Rabb and radar intercept officer Ken Crandall, were directed by an offshore American guided missile cruiser to inbound enemy MiGs, only 38 miles away. A request to engage was quickly approved as McKeown dropped in altitude, eyes sweeping the horizon ahead of him. "Holy shit!" yelled McKeown. He had flown directly over the enemy's Kep airfield. He was flying straight down the runway toward the setting sun when "Tallyho!" pierced Ensch's headset. McKeown had spotted two MiG-19s only 10 miles ahead and low, the sinking sun bouncing off their wings. In the next instant, the enemy jets thundered between McKeown and his wingman. The battle was on.

McKeown and Rabb went into a hard cross turn, looked up, and saw a sky full of MiG-17s. Apparently they had been trailing the MiG-19s in hopes of springing a trap on the American fighters. It worked. McKeown found a MiG-17 nearly on his tail, unloading its 37mm cannon at McKeown's Phantom. Dire straits dictated daring. McKeown savagely reversed his controls, throwing his F-4 tumbling end over end. Jungle, horizon, ridges, and sky flashed across the canopy. Brutal G forces rocked the crew's bodies into their seats and then against their chest straps. As time and breathing stopped, McKeown regained control with his nose low and looked up. The MiG-17 was directly ahead.

After a quick tone a Sidewinder was on its way toward the MiG. It missed. McKeown turned hard, got another lock-on, and fired again. It, too, missed. Now McKeown and Ensch were worried. Back on Midway they had tested their Sidewinders and one of the four had malfunctioned. They were down to one operational missile with a MiG-17 at their four o'clock position, fire belching 90 feet ahead of its nose cannon as its tracers carved the sky in front of McKeown's Phantom.

As McKeown hit the F-4's speed brakes, the MiG-17 barely avoided a midair collision as it rocketed ahead, so close that its aircraft number "triple sticks" 111 stood out from its green, mottled camouflage paint. Now the prey was the predator. McKeown fired his third Sidewinder. The MiG pilot apparently had lost track of the Phantom, turning into the missile's path. His tail disintegrated as he ejected to safety.

McKeown and Ensch now believed they were out of functioning missiles. But their wingman still battled a MiG that had remained on his tail. As Rabb broke hard trying to disengage, the enemy pilot did the same, crossing McKeown's path. He tried to lock on and was surprised to hear a tone. McKeown fired and the Sidewinder raced off its rail, burying itself in the MiG. Almost on impact, the MiG's canopy separated with the pilot following it into the air. The MiG exploded.

It was over. The remaining MiGs disengaged toward Chinese airspace. McKeown and Rabb dropped down to the treetops and wove their way through valleys and between ridges toward the ocean and safety. In less than five minutes, only 2,000 feet off the ground, "the world's greatest pilot" had killed two MiGs. Two months later he left Midway to become the first commanding officer of Top Gun.

Less than a year earlier, four eager pilots had stood at the bottom of the aviation food chain. On Christmas Day 1971 Gary Shank, Mike Penn, John Lindahl, and Mike Cobb had huddled around the television in Lindahl's home, watching the Dolphins beat the Chiefs in pro football's longest-ever game, a double-overtime 27–24 thriller. None knew Midway was in their future. They were part of a replacement air group, training for deployment in 1972. The four grew close in training, and together with their wives, rotated parties at each couple's home. Vietnam was just over the horizon and in a few months they would fly onto Midway in time for its final combat deployment. All four flew the A-7 Corsair, a rugged all-weather attack plane that carried up to 15,000 pounds of missiles, bombs, rockets, and cluster bombs. Four hard-charging young men, their lives in front of them, were trained, eager, confident, and anxious. The four were as much a cross section of Midway's combat pilots on its final Vietnam War deployment as the fates that befell them.

On board Midway one morning, Gary Shank learned he'd been paired with his squadron's executive officer for a two-plane afternoon attack "on targets of opportunity" which usually were bridges and truck convoys. As a junior officer to the executive officer (XO), protocol dictated that Shank's aircraft arrive second on the target. The XO's job was to fly in first and get out as Shank made his run toward alerted gunners who anticipated the second aircraft of the strike. As Shank made his run, the world exploded just outside his canopy. Less than a minute later his Corsair slammed into North Vietnam. No one saw the Kansas native eject.

Yet after the crash an international magazine claimed Shank had been executed after surviving the shootdown and being captured. The article included a photo of what it said was Shank's identification and helmet with a bullet hole in it. It was another 12 years before Shank's family could be certain—when North Vietnamese officials returned his remains. By then a tree planted in Shank's memory in Kansas City stood tall and wide.

Only two weeks later, the flight plan called for a major strike near Hanoi. Nearly 20 aircraft attacked, supported by Mike Penn whose assignment was to engage and occupy the SAM sites so the bombers could attack through clear skies. Attacking a surface-to-air missile site was a heart-stopping test of nerves. Penn tried to entice a SAM missile to start tracking him with its radar systems so he could fire an antiradiation Shrike missile at the SAM site. He had the get to shot off before the gunners could lock onto Penn and launch their missiles. It was crucial that Penn get the first shot off because SAMs flew at twice the speed of Penn's ordnance. It was a deadly game of quick-draw.

As he neared the target, Penn jinked across the sky as SAMs chased. Perhaps Penn never saw the SAM that hit him. Midway pilots frequently said it was the SAM they didn't see that they feared most. Although primitive, a SAM could follow an airplane if its three radar operators maintained a good lock. Pilots joked that bullets flew straight so they had to be fired by a good shot, but SAMs just had to get close.

"Oh no, you're on fire!" Penn's wingman cried, just before Penn ejected. After landing in a swamp, Penn radioed he was alive. North Vietnamese troops then activated captured survival radio beacons in hopes of luring rescuers into a trap or, at the very least, making it difficult to find Penn. Penn's single transmission was the last time anyone heard from him.

John Lindahl was the "old man" in the quartet of pilots. By the time he turned 26, he had flown nearly 300 combat missions over North Vietnam, South Vietnam, and Laos. The former high school football quarterback and member of the National Honor Society hailed from Lindsborg, Kansas. He was nearing the end of his third tour in Vietnam. He inspired enormous respect from his fellow pilots and was known as a man of integrity.

It was a bright, sunny day on January 6, 1973, as Lindahl sat in his Corsair, waiting to be shot off on his 326th combat mission. It was supposed to be an easy one. Fly over enemy territory to a designated road and bomb trucks and bridges. All systems were go as the cat officer touched the deck of Midway, pointed forward, and Lindahl rocketed toward the bow. Nose slightly up, he began to turn right. About a half-mile in front of the bow, he veered sharply right, turned over, dropped, and slammed into the Pacific as shocked men on the flight deck watched.

In his few airborne seconds Lindahl barely had enough time to eject. His trajectory angled so sharply toward the ocean that his parachute deployed and swung him only once before he hit the water, still belted to his seat. By then Midway's alarms had sounded. Midway's helicopter hovered over the crash site almost immediately. The helicopter pilot saw part of Lindahl's life preserver in the water.

But Lindahl had already sunk below the surface. The diver saw the top of Lindahl's parachute descending into the black depth. He nosed downward and swam furiously toward the fading chute. He grabbed a handful of silk and was yanked downward into darker water. The diver couldn't pull Lindahl, his chute, and seat up to the surface. Instead Lindahl dragged him down. Finally, the diver had to let go and turn toward the surface as Lindahl sank out of sight. Back aboard Midway, those who had watched the crash were shocked to learn Lindahl had not survived a near-instantaneous rescue effort. It fell to an investigation team to explain why.

The team realized a string of unrelated policies, actions, and failures killed Lindahl. In talking with maintenance crews, investigators discovered buoyant plastic plugs designed for pilots' seat pans had not been installed. That placed additional pressure on Lindahl's personal flotation device. The life jacket did not automatically inflate in seawater. Pilots had to pull on two separate cords in the proper sequence so that both sides of the life jacket inflated. That wasn't always easy after a pilot had been knocked nearly senseless. Finally, most pilots did not have adequate practice with their flotation device. Most completed their flight training using surplus World War II life jackets. They bore little resemblance to the flotation devices used in the early 1970s. Add 50 pounds of emergency gear (flares, weapon, radio, ammo, etc.) worn by most pilots and Lindahl had little chance when he rode his seat into the water, even with a diver jumping in right after him. Later the Navy began using life preservers that automatically inflated and trained pilots in more realistic conditions.

Services for Lindahl were held on Midway. The ceremony honored one of the most admired pilots on the ship, a man the commanding officer of VA-56 called "a gentleman's gentleman."

By early 1973, only Mike Cobb remained on Midway. He had lost one friend flying a combat mission. Another had disappeared. The third was killed on what should have been a routine launch. In the incredibly small world that is the U.S. Navy, Cobb also lost a former roommate. In basic jet training, a young man named Mike McCormick had roomed with Cobb, the same Mike McCormick who heroically had flown his Intruder back to Midway as his bombardier–navigator bled to death next to him; the same McCormick who thought about quitting but returned to active status only to be killed as he flew along the hilltops of North Vietnam.

Against the backdrop of peace negotiations, no pilot wanted to die for a lost cause. Survival became all important, loss all the more needless. Yet the missions continued. On November 10, Cobb was on his second mission of the day. It was only midmorning. His first flight had been at 0200.

His mission was to find holes in the North Vietnamese cloud cover and attack trucks making the run to the south. Cobb lined up on a target and as he pulled out of his run, an AAA shell slammed into his plane, throwing Cobb into the side of his canopy. He fought to regain control of the aircraft and turn it toward the ocean and a better chance for rescue. Time was short. His plane, most of it on fire behind the cockpit, carried two cluster bombs, an Mk-82 on one wing, and 700 gallons of jet fuel.

"EJECT, EJECT!!!" screamed Bill Pickavance who accompanied Cobb on the mission. Cobb did not hear the plea. With his plane in a violent vertical spin and headed for the water, Cobb ejected from an awkward position. Once clear, he watched his wounded jet fly into the water. There was no explosion, just the sound of a giant blowtorch being extinguished by the Pacific.

As he floated down toward the water, Cobb counted nine North Vietnamese fishing boats whose crews had been known to kill downed American pilots. Eight of the nine changed course and headed for Cobb as he climbed into his emergency raft. The odds weren't good. Overhead, three American pilots raced to his aid. Pickavance flew high to help direct the search-and-rescue helicopter to Cobb. Two others, Charlie "Hack" Hokenson and Gene Goodrow, flew low to buy Cobb precious time. But how? American pilots were not allowed to fire on fishing boats without authorization. If Hokenson and Goodrow waited for permission, Cobb could be captured or worse.

So like many pilots who found it necessary to rewrite the rules of engagement in the air, Charlie Hokenson took matters into his own gun sights. The cannon of both Pickavance's and Goodrow's aircraft weren't working. Only Hokenson could defend Cobb, with or without permission. Hokenson turned toward the lead boat of the approaching armada. A second later his Shrike missile blew it out of existence. The others continued toward Cobb. One got close enough that a man on the bow opened fire on Cobb. With bullets cutting into the heavy chop around him, Cobb watched Hokenson make another pass. Hokenson's cannon chewed the water around the approaching enemy. When the ocean spray settled, the attacker's boat quietly bobbed in the water. The attacker with the gun had disappeared in an explosion of splinters. After few more passes with his cannon roaring, Hokenson reported all the attackers had been stopped. Only then did permission to attack the enemy fishing fleet arrive.

Cobb was pulled from the water by the rescue helicopter and by midafternoon was back in his squadron's ready room. With three compression fractures in his back, eight weeks passed before the flight surgeon cleared him to fly again.

Cobb continued to fly missions until Midway finally left Southeast Asia in February 1973—a few weeks after the Paris Peace Accords had been signed, ending the war. Sorrow and solitude had become pervasive on Midway. Of the 17 pilots in one squadron, five had died and two more were taken prisoner. Only 10 of the squadron's original 17 pilots at the start of the cruise were aboard to see the Golden Gate Bridge as Midway tied up at Alameda on March 3, 1973.

The sun warmed the waters of San Francisco Bay as Midway arrived in Alameda. Thousands welcomed exhausted sailors who cherished their survival. The war was over. On its last combat mission of the war, two dozen shipmates had failed to come home. Eleven had been killed outright. Another seven were listed as missing in action, and six more were confirmed prisoners of war. Midway had paid a stiff price in its final 10 months of combat.

It would be another three weeks before Midway's POWs were freed and returned home. In addition to the six Midway pilots captured in 1972, five others had endured nearly eight years of hellish captivity in North Vietnam. They rediscovered their freedom with integrity and discipline.

The word had been passed that all POWs were to conduct themselves in the best military fashion possible upon release. The sick and injured left the prison camps first, followed by the others in the order of their shoot-down date. No emotion was to be displayed. No gestures. Head up and chest out on the way to the buses that took them to the airport for the flight to Clark Air Base in the Philippines. Only when the transports left North Vietnamese air space and their pilots announced "feet wet," did emotion erupt. Joy, anger, relief, fear, and incredulity saturated the air as the transports flew over the water where Midway had sailed.

Every man on Midway had sacrificed in his own way. Below deck, on the roof, in the sky, or in a prison cell. With peace, each man and his family navigated a personal course toward home and inner peace. Mugs McKeown had come home early and was training Navy pilots in how to conquer the chaos of combat when peace finally came in Vietnam. He ached for his best friend, Jack Ensch, who had been taken prisoner. The day after the Paris Peace Accords were signed on January 28, 1973, Lindahl was eulogized in Lindsborg. It was a difficult day for his parents, Hugo and Dorothy. It was a day filled with frightening, hollow emptiness for his widow, Virginia, and a 15-month-old little girl, Christine Marie, the family John Carl Lindahl left behind.

Fresh young men replaced most of the war veterans on Midway, setting a new course that would navigate détente, the death of the Cold War, and an international conflict tidal shift toward the Middle East. It would be

a course that began one night when thousands of frightened Vietnamese
stormed Midway in what became the final epitaph of the Vietnam War.

Vern Jumper gazed out toward sea and sky. Both were blackish gray,
merging at a horizon that smelled of defeat. He thought about counting the
black specks suspended just below the heavy cloud cover. It was impossible and didn't matter anyway. Soon Midway would be surrounded by
dozens of unauthorized helicopters, their pilots determined to land either
on Midway's flight deck or as close to the carrier as possible in the sea. It
would be up to Midway's crew to rescue the hundreds of refugees they carried before they drowned. The Vietnam War was over. All that mattered
now was survival, either on a wet flight deck or in the Tonkin Gulf.

Jumper was the air boss on Midway in 1975. It had been nearly eight
years since he had been aboard as an LSO and now as air boss he was the
supreme being of the flight deck and the air department's 300 young men
who comprised it. For nearly two years he had ruled the flight deck day and
night, and was proud there had been no serious crashes on his watch.

The air boss was responsible for everything that took place on the
flight deck of a carrier, from fueling aircraft to positioning them for launch
and recovery operations. Safety was paramount, followed by efficiency. If
the air boss was the ringmaster, the flight deck was center ring. Equipment
breakdown, human error, and bad luck were magnified because the ultimate purpose of Midway was to launch and recover aircraft. Nothing else
mattered. The air boss made sure that destiny was fulfilled, usually 12
hours a day, nearly seven days a week, even in peacetime. It was also one
of the most grueling jobs and, according to some, the most thankless
responsibility aboard an aircraft carrier.

Jumper rarely sat when in Pri-Fly as he directed the choreography on
the flight deck below. A small man with a head that seemed oversized for
his slight build, he often planted his hands on his hips while carrying on
several conversations simultaneously. An FM radio headset that creased his
crew cut enabled him to talk directly with the flight deck crew, ordering
respots, and directing the flow of aircraft. In one hand was a UHF radio for
contact with aircraft in the air. Within arm's length was another headset, a
direct connection to Midway's captain. His eyes constantly danced from
stern to bow and around again.

Timing drove every decision, every movement when an average of 15 aircraft landed and took off every 90 minutes. It was a cycle that could continue for 12 consecutive hours only if the timing held up. The speed of launching and recovering aircraft was 10 times the normal pace at conventional airports. The air boss and his staff in Pri-Fly were constantly on edge in the event a catapult went down, a plane bolted (missed the arresting wires) and was making a final approach on "a wing and no fuel," or the weather turned foul.

Midway had been ordered to a point 20 miles off the Vietnam coast on April 18. It was part of a 40-ship armada called Task Force 76. That same day the last Americans in Saigon prepared for evacuation, perhaps to Midway. Ashes coated the water in the U.S. Embassy's swimming pool as incinerators burned day and night, destroying secret documents. In Washington, the Senate rejected President Gerald Ford's request for $722 million in emergency aid for South Vietnam. Six days later, Ford told the country the Vietnam War "is finished as far as America is concerned." All that mattered was getting out. Only two years earlier, Midway pilots bombed Vietnam day and night. Now Midway was back on station, this time to save lives.

As Jumper looked down on April 29, 1975, he knew flight deck procedures that had been written in blood over the years soon would face an extraordinary test. On April 29, Vietnam was lost. The North Vietnamese dash toward Saigon that began three weeks earlier was ending at the gates of the American Embassy.

The day broke hot and muggy. A light rain coated the ships off the coast. How much longer could chaos ashore continue as the enemy's artillery shells tattooed Saigon? Only a few hours. Just before 1100, Armed Services Radio played "I'm Dreaming of a White Christmas." It was the signal to evacuate Saigon. Midway received its orders four hours later to evacuate Americans and refugees. Nine helicopters immediately departed for Saigon, the start of an aerial marathon that lasted through the night. Pilots made the 40-minute round-trips almost nonstop for 15 hours, disgorging dozens of scared refugees each time they returned to Midway. The refugees were frisked for weapons on the flight deck and then escorted below as one helicopter after another landed, sometimes only seconds apart. Many were loaded well beyond safety limits. Flight deck crews counted 50 refugees climbing out of one helicopter designed to carry 12 infantrymen. A few minutes later another helicopter landed, this one filled with 80 prone refugees stacked like kindling. Young American men, most of them 19 or 20 years of age, escorted shrunken old men leaning on scarred bamboo canes, women white with shock, and howling toddlers below to safety. They had just left everything and nearly everyone behind. Forever.

> *Inside the planes (helicopters), all people murmured, praying with tears silently run over their faces. So did I!* wrote one Vietnamese refugee in her diary. *Bending down the last time to see my poor country, and my beloved people and things, and all my souvenirs and memories which I have ever been with for twenty-one years. Thinking of my family and my relatives and my friends who were left behind. I felt sick at heart! An immense and unimagined pain appeared to cut my heart slowly to pieces!! What an undescribable feeling!! Adieu, my Vietnam! Adieu, my house, my office, my familiar roads. Adieu, my relatives and friends. God bless me to see my family in USA!*

Jumper and his air department worked frantically to maintain order. Not only were helicopters landing with refugees, others were departing for other ships filled with early arrivals. Before long, South Vietnamese helicopters joined the stream of American helicopters out to Midway. They had no authorization to land. Some asked for permission before touching down. Others lacked radio communication and simply trusted luck and the Americans. A few had skids instead of wheels so a bosun's mate invented a dolly on the spot that could be wedged under a Vietnamese helicopter to shove it out of the way once it landed. Some South Vietnamese helicopters hovered over the water as their passengers jumped into the ocean, betting on survival with the lives of their children.

The flood of refugees seemed endless. Exhausted, Midway's crew worked through the night as 2,074 refugees were brought aboard in the first 24 hours of the evacuation. About 10 percent required medical attention, outstripping the capacity of sick bay. Many crewmen gave up their berthing spaces so families could at least have the comfort of staying together on the first night of their trek toward forever. Other refugees slept on bubble wrap under the wings of fighters in the hangar bays. Fear and exhaustion filled the hangar deck as the *whop* of incoming helicopters pulsed through the night and past dawn.

Just before 0800 on April 30, the last of the American Embassy's Marine guards boarded a rescue helicopter, marking the official end of the evacuation. The final North Vietnamese push into the heart of Saigon began an hour later. Rescue flights from area airfields continued as Midway helicopters brought another 999 refugees aboard.

Almost invisible in the swarm of helicopters that stretched across the horizon on the second day was a tiny fixed-wing observation plane. The Cessna 0-1 "Bird Dog" had sneaked off Con Son Island, when South Vietnamese Air Force major Bung Ly learned his country's president had resigned. Crammed into the single-engine plane's backseat were his wife and five children. Their flight out to sea was as desperate as it was courageous.

Midway's flight deck was filled with helicopters, their rotary wings the fingers of giant interlocking hands. More than a 110 crewmen milled about, dazed after working through the night. Jumper was shocked to see the Cessna approach Midway. There was no room for another helicopter, much less a fixed-wing plane that required a runway. The pilot circled Midway twice and on the second pass, dropped a note. *"Can you move those helicopters to the other side? I can land on your runway. I can fly one more hour. We have enough time to move. Please rescue me."* It was written across a VFR Route map of South Vietnam. Jumper grabbed the line to the skipper, Captain Lawrence Chambers. "Can you clear space?" asked Chambers. After a moment, Jumper said he could. It took crewmen 45 minutes to clear space on the angle deck. Some helicopters had to be pushed over the side. Meanwhile, a yeoman from engineering who spoke Vietnamese was summoned to the bridge to pass along landing instructions.

With only 15 minutes' fuel remaining in the Bird Dog, Midway was ready. The carrier turned into the best possible wind. The pilot faced the prospect of landing on a wet angle deck with no tailhook and no barricade. If he failed, he and his family faced a 50-foot fall over the narrow safety nets at the front edge of the angle deck into the ocean below. Exhausted crewmen tensed. From above, Jumper reminded the flight deck crew that this was a plane with a propeller. Stay clear. Low and slow, the Cessna approached from astern. Buffeted by the wind, it wavered as it came over the deck, dropped, wavered some more, bounced, and then settled onto the rain-slick deck. The pilot killed the engine as the headwind pushed the Cessna to a halt. It came to a stop with plenty of room to spare.

The flight deck crew that had held its collective breath broke into applause as their shoulders slumped with relief. Nearly 75 flight deck crewmen rushed the plane to hold it steady and welcome the family aboard. Others raised hands over their heads in jubilation. Eyes moistened as exhausted young men carried frightened, tiny children to warmth and safety.

As the last refugee was taken below, air boss Jumper started breathing again. Midway's final mission in the waters off Vietnam had been an act of the defeated. It left Jumper with an ache in his stomach. Years earlier he eagerly had flown "up north" off the deck of Midway, hoping to engage a MiG over the skies of North Vietnam. He had seen countless threats go unchallenged because of the suffocating rules of engagement. He and his fellow aviators believed they had the "chance to knock them flat. Instead we just pricked at the enemy. It became such a waste, such a sacrifice." In the end, the most he could do was to help as many refugees as possible abandon their homes, flee their country, and trust in fate and the Americans who had failed them.

Midway's population doubled with 3,073 refugees filling berths and bays. It marked the end of a massive evacuation from the country. In the preceding month, more than 120,000 Vietnamese and 20,000 Americans had fled Vietnam. Jumper had flown dozens of combat missions, directed countless recoveries as a landing signal officer, and served nearly two years as Midway's air boss. When he left Pri-Fly after what became known as the "Night of the Helicopters," Jumper heard something from beyond the horizon of his imagination. Echoes of compassion in the jet wash of combat. The father of three listened to the sounds of infants aboard his warship.

"THE SOVIETS HAVE LOCK-ON!" shattered the exhaustion of Tom Utterback at the end of his 12-hour surface warfare watch in the command information center. The intermittent sound of the Soviet guided missile cruiser's radar monitored by Midway had changed to a constant, fixed squeal. Color drained from the faces of Utterback's surface watch team as they looked up from their short-range and long-range plots.

The Russian cruiser had remained a steady 1,500 yards off Midway's starboard quarter for hours. It was one of dozens of Russian, Korean, and Chinese ships sailing off the Koreas in August 1976. Not far away, Midway led the Pacific Fleet's Task Force 77.4. Tension had frayed nerves for days following the brutal murder of two American soldiers in the Korean demilitarized zone on August 18. While they supervised the annual pruning of an 80-foot poplar that partially blocked a checkpoint's line of sight, North Korean soldiers had ambushed Captain Arthur Bonifas and Lieutenant Mark Barrett, beating them to death with axes and rifle butts.

The United States had responded three days later with Operation Paul Bunyan supported by a Navy task force. AH-1 Cobra gunships cruised behind nearby ridges and F-111s and B-52 Stratofortresses patrolled high overhead while an engineering battalion cut down the tree. Just off the coast, Midway's F-4 Phantoms were on alert. And Midway remained on edge.

Utterback punched buttons on the console in front of him, informing the bridge, air operations, the flag, and others of the lock-on. Another crewman turned to Midway's classified files to learn the ship's capabilities, armament, and even the name of its captain. Captain Lawrence Chambers moved quickly. The two pilots in the "ready alert" F-4 Phantoms on the catapult were ordered into the air. Chambers then turned his attention to the Russians. He ordered a flashing light message be sent to his Russian escort, advising the ship that Midway was launching aircraft and to break off radar contact or Midway would attack. Minutes passed as the Phantoms circled overhead, waiting for orders to attack. The radar squeal stopped and the Russian cruiser began to drift away from Midway's course.

Hearts slowed but it would be days before restful sleep returned as Midway returned to its station at the "tip of the sword," duty that had begun three years earlier as the Navy's only carrier homeported in a foreign country.

James Auer's secret mission several years earlier had made that possible. The political advisor to the commander of U.S. Naval Forces in Japan, Auer carried back-channel messages to Funada Naka, Japanese Speaker of the House of Representatives, who in turn passed them on to the Japanese prime minister. Auer's mission was to circumnavigate Japanese laws that forbid the manufacture, possession, storage, or introduction of nuclear weapons.

Japan and the United States had signed a treaty more than a decade earlier in which the U.S. promised to defend Japanese interests in return for American military bases in Japan. Auer and Naka facilitated another, unpublicized agreement, struck between Japan and Edwin Reischauer, the U.S. ambassador to Japan. That accord stipulated that nuclear weapon–carrying Navy ships in Japanese ports would not be seen as "introducing" nuclear weapons into Japan. The United States maintained a policy of "neither confirming nor denying" the presence of nuclear weapons aboard Midway or other ships and the Japanese government agreed not to press for a specific answer.

Navy ships had been putting in briefly at Yokosuka for more than 20 years. But the dynamics of American support of the military, the nation's defense funding, Japanese attitudes, and the international chessboard had changed as the Vietnam War had drawn to a close. War planners believed the Middle East and Far East represented the new threats to peace in the post-Vietnam era. The Indian Ocean was half a world away from Navy bases in the United States. Steaming at 20 knots, it took a carrier almost a month to get from San Diego to the Persian Gulf. By contrast, when the Cold War centered on Europe a carrier transited from Norfolk to the eastern Mediterranean in about 10 days.

Bases in Japan, the Philippines, and a primitive staging area on Diego Garcia in the middle of the Indian Ocean took on increased strategic significance. Homeporting Midway in Japan had become critical and the Japanese government agreed to look the other way when Midway docked at Yokosuka.

The flight from Chicago to Los Angeles to Tokyo the day before had drained Anita of every ounce of energy. But sleep proved elusive. Midway was only a few hours away as she stood near Drydock No. 6 in Yokosuka. She hoped she could spot her husband, Steve, at deck's edge when Midway tied up. He looked taller in his dress whites. They ached for each other's arms, desperate to end a six-month separation.

Anita stood among several hundred wives, sons, daughters, and grandparents. Many carried signs and banners. Midway loomed only a few hundred yards away as Japanese tugs sidled up under the overhanging flight deck to nudge the carrier toward its new home port on October 5, 1973. Sodden clouds overhead flattened the light, casting everything in a gray hue. More than a dozen news helicopters swarmed around Midway. Homeporting an aircraft carrier widely believed to carry nuclear weapons was major news in Japan.

We don't want the Midway here, in our country . . . Why? . . . We now know that Midway *carries nuclear weapons. For more than twenty years we have been lied to about this. We have been told that the U.S. had promised not to bring nuclear weapons into our country, and that the promise was being kept. Now we have learned that the promise is not being kept, or maybe that no such promise was ever made. It was all a lie. If some foreign government brought dangerous weapons into your country, weapons that you particularly hated without ever telling the American people about it, would you be angry? If so, you should be able to understand our anger.*

—YOKOSUKA CITIZENS' GROUP

Not everyone welcomed Midway to Japan. Not far from where Anita stood, more than 20,000 Japanese carried signs and banners. Their anti-U.S. fliers fluttered in the air. The opposition to Midway's permanent homeporting was partially based on what was called "kichi kogai," loosely translated as "base pollution," which referred to aircraft noise, unruly conduct in bars and nightclubs, and the sometimes violent crimes committed by sailors in Japan. More vehement protests were voiced over Midway's nuclear weapon arsenal. "Midway Walk Out" graffiti appeared near Midway's berth.

More than 1,000 Japanese riot police kept order under skies that turned to rain as Midway tied up and Japanese television stations broke away from regular programming to cover Midway's arrival live. Their cameras panned Anita and the others on the pier, some of whom wore buttons that read "Midway Gets It Together."

Many sailors aboard Midway weren't so sure. For some, their first exposure to Japan came at 0100 in the old Hanida airport after a "Flying Tiger 747" flight from California, via Alaska. They disembarked into stale, thick air in search of transportation to Yokosuka. Culture shock hit with full force within minutes of their arrival. Air boss Vern Jumper's wife, Becky, and their three children arrived several months after Jumper's transfer to Midway. The Jumper family watched in shock as an old Japanese man stood on a bench in the middle of the terminal and serenely changed his clothes. Welcome to Japan, home of Midway for the next 18 years, during which a strong bond between Midway and the Japanese people ultimately developed.

Midway families faced a difficult transition. They had to learn a new traffic system, cope with suffocating congestion, and overcome a language barrier. With their husbands away, wives were responsible for finding housing, learning how to shop for groceries, and getting a driver's license. Most wives could not work because they did not speak Japanese. Some failed to make the transition. Divorce was common aboard Midway.

On average, only one in four Midway crewmen was married. Unlike the bachelors on other Navy ships homeported in Alameda, San Diego, or Norfolk, few of Midway's 3,000 bachelors had someone to meet them on the pier at Yokosuka. The concept of personal email accounts aboard ship was still more than 10 years away. Duty on Midway meant extended separation from loved ones. The most they could look forward to was the mail.

Mail was the lifeline that connected a sailor with his family in Abilene or a girlfriend in another port. No matter how short or innocuous, sailors cherished every letter. After countless readings, a sailor frequently taped his latest letter in a corner of his cramped berthing space. It became the first and last thing he saw each night:

Smiley J,

I got your letter this morning (Dec. 17). Thanks a lot. I love your letter so much. That letter is the sweetest one I've ever got. How could so much love be inside of you?

This is how I feel now J. I've been thinking about you all this week. I missed you. But you'll be coming back soon anyway. I made a tape for you. I'm still bad at my English. I don't think I can express my feelings enough.

So just listen to the tape. I love you so much. Kiss, kiss, kiss, my Smiley J.

Others taped photographs of home, square snippets from another life, that brought joy some days, a soulful ache on others. They were a portal to the only privacy enlisted men enjoyed on Midway. Most bunks were stacked three high on green linoleum. Only the shortest sailors could stretch out when lying down. A man's locker was only 10 inches wide by 36 inches high by 30 inches deep. It resembled a desk drawer stood on end. An area that housed 30 to 50 men looked at first glance to be three-quarters scale.

Escape lived deep within each picture a man taped up next to his bunk. A photo of a black woman standing in front of a cinder-block house, hands on cocked hips, smiling at the camera. A grinning one-year-old, festooned in a lacy white Easter outfit and with bright, innocent brown eyes sat in the lap of a giant Easter bunny. "Love you, daddy!" Whitney Bain Hogue "wrote" on the back of her picture. A snapshot of a bearded, serious young man dressed in archer's hunting camouflage down on one knee in the middle of a wide lawn, a freshly shot mule deer propped against his thigh. Faded color memories that connected young men with family, perspective and purpose.

Soon after transferring to Japan, Midway became known as the "USS Neverdock." In its first six years in Japan, each of 31 deployments was separated by an average of only a month in port. Sailors sought an escape as the years of deployments and training exercises strung together.

Intelligence officer J. R. Reddig began writing The Collected Adventures of Nick Danger, Third Eye, a serial spoof in the 1940s style of Raymond Chandler. Reddig's tales of danger appeared in the carrier's daily *Multiplex* editions.

> *This was going to be a hard one. I could tell because I was running out of air speed, altitude and ideas at the same time. Never a good thing. The best I could do was line up my airplane on the funny little square flight deck of the USS Stein and hope for the best. Matilda had given up scolding me and was sitting still as a stone in the front cockpit. If she hadn't been a religious woman before, I had every reason to believe that she was one now. I could have paused for a moment to reflect on my own sordid past, but there was no time for cheap thrills now. I had to use every ounce of my vast experience to get that little plane down in more or less one piece.*
>
> *I figure I couldn't have been doing more than about thirty miles an hour as I came up behind the proud naval warship. I could look down and count the sharks trailing along, tearing at garbage sacks. I saw one that was easily longer than the airplane. It was giant and gray and the teeth look like a dirty white picket fence.*

Reddig's tales helped provide perspective when Midway assumed additional duty after newer carriers broke down and limped into port for repairs, something that happened surprisingly often. It was the era when the reputation of "Midway Magic" began to take hold, both aboard ship and throughout the Navy. It became a badge of pride among the crew, one that extended from one Midway captain's 18-month reign to the next. An appropriate Japanese flavor was added to the mantra. "Midway Majutsu" stickers began appearing on equipment and supplies shuttled halfway around the world to Midway as it steamed off Kirachi or Mombasa.

Midway's homeporting in Japan reflected two major changes in Navy doctrine. One was to marry an air wing to a specific aircraft carrier. Usually air wings rotated onto and off carriers. In 1971, however, CVW-5 was permanently assigned to Midway. As a result, the 1,500-man air wing crew constantly lived and trained with the ship's crew. Aircraft support crews got to know Midway's configuration, quirks, and capabilities intimately. Instead of two teams (air wing and ship's company) learning to work together aboard ship, Midway essentially had one team of nearly 4,500 men, constantly working, training, and deploying together.

Midway became known as one of the best-operating carriers in the Navy in the 1970s and 1980s. Each year the Navy awarded a highly coveted Battle Efficiency "E" pennant to the most efficient and battle-ready carrier in the fleet, usually based on six to 18 months of inspections and exercises. Each department was evaluated and the carrier with the highest cumulative score was declared the winner. Four years after arriving in Yokosuka and over the course of six cruises in *18* months, Midway received the "E" in mid-1977. Eventually, Midway earned the right to fly the Battle Efficiency E's red triangular pennant with a black "meatball" in the center high above its flight deck five times.

Midway, though, carried a deservedly mixed reputation within the aviator community. Midway's air wing flew some of the oldest and most antiquated aircraft in the Navy inventory because Midway lacked the size and capability to maintain newer generations of airplanes. The ship's aircraft intermediate maintenance department couldn't house some of the testing equipment for newer aircraft. The hangar deck's clearance was too low for some aircraft equipment as well. On the other hand, if an aviator wanted to fly, assignment to the Midway with its unending series of cruises afforded ample opportunity.

The other fundamental change in Navy doctrine placed Midway in a constant state of overhaul, despite its brutal schedule of deployments. Each time Midway put in at the Yokosuka ship repair facility, Japanese shipyard workers overhauled a designated portion of the carrier. Every few months, part of Midway was enhanced, repaired, or replaced. Other carriers went into the yard periodically for two-year overhauls. Midway was usually in port for no more than a month. Hundreds of Japanese ship workers descended on Midway upon each arrival in Yokosuka. The honesty and dedication of Japanese welders, electricians, pipe fitters, and plumbers working on Midway became legendary.

Ed Spearly had one of the hundreds of seemingly insignificant jobs that formed the mosaic of an aircraft carrier's operation. He maintained the engines on the admiral's barge and the captain's gig. Spearly had followed his father into the Navy. When he finished training he had filled out his "dream sheet" asking for duty in the engineering plant of a large ship on the East Coast. Instead, the Navy sent him to a yard tug in San Diego Bay, a "McHale's Navy" assignment, reminiscent of the television sitcom where chiefs ran the show with no commissioned officer in sight. It was a back-water assignment with little future. But it was duty that soon led to a trans-fer to Midway in Yokosuka.

In port, Spearly came to respect the Japanese workers deeply, despite a language barrier that required pantomimic creativity. One day Spearly deduced that a worker's quick sweeps with his arm was a request for a hacksaw. He was flabbergasted two hours later when the man walked up to him on a distant part of the ship, intent on personally handing over the bor-rowed hacksaw as he bowed. No self-respecting Japanese ship worker left a tool on the job site. He returned every tool to storage, every time. It was quite a change of pace from the Philippines where Spearly knew "if we left dirty socks out in port they mysteriously grew legs and walked away."

"Midway sailor: Please keep hands off equipment." The note had been attached to a piece of equipment deep inside Midway. Several days after Midway had left Yokosuka, Spearly found it stuck to a particularly sensi-tive piece of equipment. It was another reflection of the extraordinary rela-tionship between Midway and Yokosuka that enabled near-constant deployment in the western Pacific, Indian Ocean, and Sea of Japan in the decade following the end of the Vietnam War. Those deployments required near-continuous air operations that strained the crew of Midway. Sometimes Midway's alert status took on humanitarian overtones.

Gary Dunbar was an old man on Midway. At 28, he was halfway through what would become a 20-year Navy career. Wide-bodied with a wife and two children living in Japan, Dunbar grew up in Palo Alto. His parents divorced when he was young and during one short, turbulent period he spent a week in an orphanage.

The one constant aboard Midway was waiting in line. Dunbar stood in a line to eat, a line to see the ship's doctor, a line to take a shower. The longest lines developed when Midway made a port of call where pier-side facilities were inadequate. They snaked through the hangar bays as sailors waited their turn to board liberty boats bound for shore. Rank brought priv-ileges so the youngest, greenest, first-tour nuggets always lost several hours of liberty by starting at the back of the line.

Dunbar was in a line that stretched into tomorrow. Inspiration followed. He could wait his turn in line or join the ship's chaplain at the head of the line if he agreed to accompany the chaplain's repair party destined for an orphanage. Dunbar figured even a work detail at an orphanage was better than standing in another line. When Dunbar reached the orphanage, he was aghast.

Barbed wire surrounded the Korean orphans. Rust-tinged diapers hung heavy between the barbs. The 16-seat outhouse overflowed. No water flowed from the well. The Korean winter wind pierced through cracks in barracks-turned-dormitories. The abandoned military base was home to more than 100 orphans. Their shivering legs were covered with cuts and scars from using a rusty slide, the orphans' only source of playground entertainment. They were in the charge of a woman whose father once ran an orphanage in the early 1950s in what became Korea's demilitarized zone. He had marched his 80 children south to safety. More than 25 years later his daughter cared for a new generation of orphans. They were badly overmatched by nature and poverty.

"Midway Magic" went to work for the youngsters when Midway's crew adopted the orphans. Over the course of several ports of call at Pusan, more than $35,000 was given to the orphanage. Masons, carpenters, electricians, and metal smiths all volunteered precious liberty time when Midway called on Pusan. New playground equipment was made. Some of the volunteers enlisted a Midway helicopter to haul the orphanage's bus engine out to the ship for an overhaul. Others scrounged nearby American military installations. One Midway "task force" mysteriously filled three flatbed trucks with several army field kitchens, beds, and lockers for the orphanage. No one dared ask how they managed it.

Before long, the Korean news media got wind of Midway visits to the orphanage. Dunbar found himself in front of TV cameras when reporters mistakenly got the idea that he had been an orphan in America. It made for a poignant, albeit erroneous, basis for news coverage of an aircraft carrier coming to the aid of Korean orphans. Usually Midway left its mark on the Korean landscape by projecting American power and purpose from offshore when civil unrest erupted or shots flew across the DMZ. Korean children felt the presence of American power and purpose in a way that inspired hope before Midway turned its attention back to the Russians with aircraft in the air and ship's crew at the ready.

It was raining. Hard. Phil Conroy stood on the hangar deck, looking out at the black sky as rain filled the air. The Nebraska native flew an A-6 Intruder with the VA-115 Arabs. He was the greenest sprig in a family tree of aviators whose roots extended back to his father and World War II bombers. As Conroy gazed toward a fuzzy horizon, the sky turned cherry orange. A thundering grind had passed overhead, reverberating through the carrier's steel and burrowing into Conroy's bones. Conroy knew Midway's arresting wires hadn't played out as they normally did when a plane trapped. The landing must have gone horribly wrong. The sound of the General Quarters alarm splintered his thoughts.

Minutes earlier, two fellow VA-115 Arabs, Dale Turner and Roger Burbrink, had been on final approach to Midway, intent on landing their Intruder that served as an airborne tanker. They could carry as much as 10,000 pounds of fuel, enough to power four F-4 Phantoms for extended flights. It was 0200 as Turner and Burbrink struggled to see the optical "meatball" that led them to Midway's deck. It was a blur. An air blower that cleared rain from the pilot's side of the windscreen had frozen.

Turner and Burbrink had pressed on through the mist and rain, even as Turner lost sight of the ship and the meatball. They dropped, lower and lower, trying to spot the flight deck. Just as Midway's lights began to take shape in the wet night air, the LSO screamed, "Power!" into Turner's ear. Too late. Nose up, the A-6 slammed into the ramp at the stern, beheading the aircraft just behind the cockpit. The severed capsule with two aviators inside screeched down the angle deck. A billowing, expanding bloom of 6,000 pounds of burning fuel chased them.

"I'm dead," Turner thought as he and Burbrink shot along the deck. Without wheels and a tailhook, the arresting wires were useless. A black ocean loomed ahead as the Intruder's cockpit raced ahead of the flames. If the fire didn't engulf them, the ocean would.

Turner and Burbrink glanced at each other. Without a word, they ejected from the deck of Midway. A millisecond before their cockpit dropped off the angle deck, two terrified aviators had shot up over the fireball, and into the black blanket of clouds and rain.

Everyone was riveted on the fireball spreading from the stern forward on the flight deck. Except one man. A phone talker in Pri-Fly followed the

A-6 capsule racing ahead of the fireball. In the blinding glare of the fire, he thought he saw something rocket up from the deck and into the clouds. He couldn't be sure.

The phone talker reported what he saw to the air boss. Midway's search-and-rescue helicopter was alerted to scan the water for the bodies of Turner and Burbrink. As the fire was brought under control, the helicopter crew searched, with little hope that anyone could have survived a flight deck ejection.

Turner and Burbrink had floated free of the fire. When they slammed into the black Pacific, their life jackets failed to inflate completely. Barely able to keep their heads above water, each time Turner and Burbrink sunk beneath the waves, they furiously kicked up toward the surface and a gulp of air. Exhaustion soon overtook fear. At one point Burbrink began to experience what he thought was death. A sudden peace washed across him in the middle of the ocean. "If this is death," he thought, "it's not so bad."

As the rain lifted the helicopter crew spotted the reflective tape on one of the pilots' helmets. Maneuvering for a rescue, the helicopter's Doppler radar auto-hover system failed, nearly drowning one of the aviators as he was about to be hoisted out of the sea. After regaining manual control, the helicopter crew hauled both airmen to safety. The crew was later awarded medals for bravery and heroism.

Minutes after the fire was out and as the rain drifted away, it became deathly quiet under a sky black as ink. Midway steamed toward another rain shower. Only a muttered "holy shit" or "mother of God" could be heard as crewmen lined up at the angled round-down at the stern to walk the 1,000-foot length of the flight deck, clearing it of debris. Midway resumed scheduled operations within hours with a crew keenly aware of the thin line between numbing routine and the suddenness of death. As the sun rose the following day, they turned their attention back to the Russian "tattletales" that always seemed to be in their wake.

"What the hell? You see this? Goddamn helo's off course! Where the hell's he going?" "Dunno!" Midway's helicopter pilot had received orders to change both his course and radio frequency. The orders rode on a soft Texas twang. The kind of voice that was easy to listen to. Homestyle and genuine.

Randy Kittilson couldn't figure out why Midway's helo had veered off the flight plan. Less than two years removed from Colorado, he sat a small dark room adjacent to Midway's combat information center tracking Russian ships and aircraft, the constant companions of Midway's battle group in a chess game that played itself out from the start of most cruises to their conclusion throughout the 1970s. Midway and the Russians moved and counter-moved, parried each other's change in course, and sometimes ran and hid. It was a subplot played out inside the ostensible mission of each deployment.

Midway's crew jammed their helicopter's alternate frequencies until the pilot finally returned to the designated Midway frequency, only to conclude he had followed flight instructions from a Russian with a panhandle twang. The Midway pilot had been following orders broadcast by a Russian ship.

Sometimes Midway contact with the Russians was nearly face to face. Many Midway crewmen came home with stories about the day a massive Russian Tu-95 turbo-prop "Bear" or a Tu-16 Russian "Badger" buzzed Midway, so close that crewmen high in the island swore they saw the faces of the Russian air crews. When either a Bear or Badger appeared on Midway's radar, Midway aircraft launched or vectored toward the Russians. Typically an Intruder or Phantom settled in on each wingtip of the inbound Russian aircraft, a little behind and below, making sure the Russian pilots knew they had company. Oftentimes a third Midway aircraft flew almost directly above the escorted Russian, taking photographs of the former long-range bombers with sleek American fighter escorts on either side, much to the delight of Midway crew as they passed the photos around later.

The Russian air crews wanted collectible photos as well. One day Phil Conroy launched his Intruder tanker to refuel two Phantoms before they headed toward a Russian Bear. Once the Phantoms were tanked, Conroy sought and received permission to accompany the Phantoms to the Bear. As the two F-4s settled in on their adversary's wingtips, Conroy slipped his Intruder up close to the Bear's rudder. From 60 feet away, flying at more than 300 miles an hour, Conroy could see members of the Bear's seven-man crew peering out the convex Plexiglas bubble near its tail. They were taking pictures of Conroy and the rare sight of an airborne U.S. Navy A-6 Intruder tanker only 20 yards away.

Sometimes Midway's contact with the Russians took place at the edge of space. The Russians' watchful vigilance of Midway provided opportunities to conduct classified exercises. Midway's intelligence department knew Russia possessed radar ocean reconnaissance satellites. The low-orbit satellites tracked American ships to within two kilometers, downloading the information to listening stations or Russian ships. The 30-foot-long, missile-shaped radar ocean reconnaissance satellites (RORSATs) also could serve as forward observation posts during a naval battle. One of Midway's classified experiments captured the signals sent by RORSATs and returned bogus signals to the satellite with misinformation about Midway's location and heading.

When electronic games of chess were being played, 20-hour shifts for Kittilson and others were common as he tracked as many as 20 ships, some very close and others over the horizon. Kittilson sometimes fought boredom when Midway and its Russian escorts plowed through the ocean on a steady, unchanging course. With only eight hours between most shifts, Kittilson could spend an hour and a half standing in the chow line or he could grab as much sleep as possible and get by on Snickers and coffee. He and others often chose the latter so ship's medical personnel frequently made rounds through CIC to dispense vitamins.

The point of most exercises was to see who could spot the other guy first. In the nuclear era, the first punch in a war of missiles at sea probably would be the knockout punch. Midway won when it kept track of the Russians and Russians won when they sneaked up on Midway's battle group. Usually that happened only when the carrier was running EMCON. EMCON was an operational status when radar, tracking systems, and any other equipment that emitted electromagnetic signals from Midway were shut down. To lose a persistent Russian trawler that tracked Midway's emissions, Midway limited active sweeps to about three every 10 minutes—hopefully enough to keep from running into anything but not enough to enable the Russians to track the carrier. Usually it was an effective tactic. But one night it spelled disaster for a freighter from Panama filled with telephone poles.

The massive, black silhouette silently sliced through the Strait of Malacca between Sumatra and the Malay Peninsula. Midway was making dark and quiet to confound a trailing Russian spy ship. Running EMCON, no sounds or lights emanated from the 65,000-ton behemoth more than three football fields long. It was a hole in the night. Midway's escorting destroyers ran their deception lighting designed to make them look like nonmilitary freighters in the black night of July 29, 1980.

Gunner's mate technician Brian Pellar was clowning around with a camera and some buddies in their berthing compartment. Slight and inquisitive, Pellar enlisted in the Navy to escape Sierra Madre, a city smothered by smog blown east from Los Angeles and trapped against the San Gabriel Mountains. Pellar, who had no interest in high school, dropped out, and bolted from home as soon as he could. The first stop was nuclear weapons handling school where Pellar shocked himself by finishing first in his class. That brought an immediate promotion and his choice of assignments. He chose Midway to see the world. On the hangar deck, Pellar's division mate, Gary Dunbar, also was thinking about photography as he showed off a new expensive camera he had just bought for his father-in-law.

Kittilson was worn out. He had finished another long stretch of electronics warfare duty, and was relaxing in an electronic countermeasures room near the angle deck. John Morris had worries of his own. The ordnanceman sat talking to a shipmate about how to deal with the "East Coast spit 'n polish boys" aboard Midway.

Not far away a freighter named the *Cactus* sailed on a parallel course to Midway through the narrow strait. At about 2000, Midway's collision alarm jolted Pellar, Dunbar, Kittilson, Morris, and thousands of others. As it blared, Midway lifted out of the water and listed to starboard, as if stretching unseen legs from below. The carrier paused as eyes widened and faces paled. A deep, grinding, thunderous growl rolled through the ship, up through bulkheads, along passageways, and across steel decks. Crewmen looked at each other in bewildered horror. Then Midway settled back down in the water and leveled. Quiet and stillness returned.

"Battle Stations! Battle Stations! Man your battle stations—set condition Zebra!!!" blared a trembling voice from every speaker on the ship. With no clue to what had happened, thousands of sailors mobilized, some scrambling to put on clothes before racing to their battle stations. Kittilson picked himself up after being thrown across his compartment and ran to an outside catwalk just below the flight deck on his way to CIC. The catwalk was gone. Stunned, he reversed course and headed toward the hangar deck. Not far away, John Morris grabbed his float coat, cranial headgear, and climbed toward the flight deck, certain that carnage and death awaited him.

Meanwhile both Pellar and Dunbar headed to the top-secret magazines and assembly areas where Midway's nuclear weapons were stored.

For more than 25 years Midway had carried nuclear weapons. Although stable, certain conditions could spark a low-yield detonation on the carrier. The entry point to Midway's nuclear stockpile and other secret compartments was an odd-looking door with a one-way mirror and an armed Marine guard just inside. An aluminum tray in the door enabled security-cleared crewmen to pass their ID through to the guard before entering the outer door to pick up their department ID badge. More locked doors separated them from their duty stations.

It was almost impossible to hide the nuclear weapons from curious eyes when they were offloaded prior to an inport overhaul or drydock repairs. Armed Marine guards menacingly screamed at any lingering crewman who gazed too long at the odd-looking red-tipped, white and silver bombs on the hangar deck destined for a secure facility ashore or another ship. Noncleared crewmen didn't know it at the time, but they likely were looking at B61, B57, or B43 tactical nuclear weapons. Ranging from 500 to 2,000 pounds in size, the smallest bomb's blast yield was about half that of the bomb dropped on Hiroshima. The largest, the B43s, were more than 50 times as powerful as the Hiroshima detonation. Not knowing what had happened to Midway, both those inside and outside the nuclear weapons compartments were worried. Worry exploded into fear when the call came to abandon the forward section of the carrier.

The Panamanian freighter had changed its course and rammed Midway on its port side, directly across from the island. Three F-4 Phantoms parked at deck's edge were destroyed when the superstructure of the Cactus collided just under the angle deck, lifting Midway out of the water. Midway's liquid oxygen plant (LOX) took the brunt of the blow as the Cactus tore three, 10-foot holes in the side of the carrier, ripped away the catwalk, and jammed the nearby aircraft elevator. The oxygen plant was knocked off its foundation and its piping torn apart. Highly flammable JP-5 jet fuel flowed from the damaged aircraft over the side of Midway. Just below, the liquid oxygen was escaping in a compartment surrounded by a maze of JP-5 fuel pipes. Whip antennas, a satellite-receiving antenna, and the ship's missile defense system antenna disappeared in the collision.

With Midway's load of fuel and ordnance aboard, men cringed at the possibility of a catastrophic explosion.

Kittilson knew none of this as he raced to CIC. The call to "secure for abandon ship" brought him up short. "Jesus, this is serious," thought Kittilson as he and others frantically threw reams of top-secret intelligence, codes, manuals, and other documents into a safe to ensure they went to the bottom if Midway sank. Finished, he headed for the hangar deck. Meanwhile as Gary Dunbar ran to one of the weapons magazines, the carrier's chaplain recited a prayer on the ship-wide public-address system, adding as much worry as comfort to the situation. One of the youngsters in Dunbar's charge, usually a slacker, ran ahead of Dunbar to one of his magazines. He yelled at the Marines guarding the space that men were trapped in an adjacent compartment. Just as Dunbar's men began ratcheting the 60 nuts off a scuttle hatch, a rescue party broke through from the other side. Dunbar and his young hero then headed for the hangar deck and found more than 1,000 terrified shipmates standing, waiting, and wondering whether Midway was about to detonate.

Rumors were instantaneous. One man said he heard an Iranian missile had hit Midway as it transited the Strait of Malacca, a "choke point" only 30 miles wide between the South China Sea and Indian Ocean. Another said the hole in Midway was so large a plane could fly through it. A third opined it had been some kind of terrorist attack by the freighter, probably guided by a nearby Russian submarine.

Brian Pellar had more than rumors on his mind. At the sound of the alarm, Pellar and three others sprinted down passageways and leaped over knee knockers toward the nuclear weapons' storage area. Their mission was to ensure the compartments were still watertight. They peered through the gloom. The compartment, with its cleaning bench, neatly arranged assembly station nearby, and stacks of nuclear weapons was dry. Nearly 30 feet below the waterline, Midway wasn't taking on water.

When the order came to move all crew aft, Pellar joined other nuclear-weapon technicians near the aft weapons storage area. The stench of sweat grew after the ventilation systems were shut down. Fire posed the ship's biggest threat and no one wanted the ship's vent system acting as a fireplace flue spreading heat and flame. More than an hour had passed since the bone-jarring grind of steel and most crewmen still didn't know what had happened. They sat, waited, and wondered if orders would come to abandon ship in the middle of the night. They wondered whether the massive crew could get off Midway before it blew up or sank, whether it had been an accident or something worse, whether those who actually had a job to do in the emergency were getting it under control. John Morris was doing exactly that.

Pandemonium met ordnanceman Morris when he reached Midway's flight deck. The three aircraft hit by the freighter sat at odd angles. Leaking jet fuel glistened on the black asphalt of the flight deck. Fog hung low, mixed with the spray from fire crews and the shouts of damage control parties as they tied down the damaged planes to keep them from falling over the side. The heavily damaged jets were fueled, armed with Sidewinder and Sparrow missiles, and had become a direct threat to Midway's safety.

Missing the rear portion of its fuselage, one of the Phantoms looked like it was ready to fall over the side at any moment. Its wheels knocked askew, it rested on a crushed fuel tank and a port wing pylon, trapping a Sparrow missile. Wedged between the wing and the steel deck, the missile had to be removed. The slightest misstep might touch off a horrific explosion on a flight deck covered with jet fuel and directly over a compartment that leaked liquid oxygen. Morris and two others didn't hesitate. They raced to the wreckage and threw themselves onto the deck. Lying on their backs in a pool of biting jet fuel, they held their breaths as they dismantled the 500-pound missile and then carefully pulled it from the twisted carnage. As others stabilized the leaking fuel, the biggest threat to Midway's safety had been eliminated. (A year later, Morris received the Navy Commendation Medal for his bravery and skill that night. When awarding the medal Captain D. N. Hagen told Morris, "Some never get the chance, others do and fail. My sincere congratulations that you are in the third category: tried and true.")

Nearly five hours after the collision, safety and order returned to Midway once the oxygen plant was secured and leaking fuel plugged. Crewmen staggered to their berthing compartments, some exhausted from fighting the emergency, others equally drained from standing, waiting and worrying. Two petty officers didn't return to their compartments that night. Daniel Macey and Christian Belgum were killed instantly in the liquid oxygen plant compartment. Kittilson, in the compartment directly above, barely escaped with his life, perhaps only because the fully loaded freighter rode lower in the water so its superstructure hit Midway at the liquid oxygen plant level.

July 29 was a night of fear, loss and heroism. It also was the 13th anniversary of the infamous fire and explosion on the flight deck of the carrier Forrestal off Vietnam that killed 134 men. Danger always loomed on Midway's horizon as it remained on alert steaming into the 1980s as the Cold War ebbed in the face of new threats in an emerging theater of conflict.

G RIGIORIY, A FISHERMAN, walked down to the wobbly pier on Zeleny Island. Part of an archipelago near the Kamchatka Peninsula, Zeleny protected Pacific access for Russian naval bases at Vladivostok and Sovetzkaya. Grigioriy heard the jets from deep within the broken clouds before he saw them. Thunder rolled across the island as fighters from Midway and the carrier Enterprise buzzed Zeleny, low enough that the fisherman unconsciously ducked as they streaked overhead. After they had disappeared back into the cloud cover, he wondered why American fighter jets were brazenly flying in Russian airspace that late spring day in 1983.

Three American carrier battle groups comprised of 40 ships had assembled over the horizon near his fishing grounds. It was the largest collection of American warships in the Pacific since World War II. A massive exercise had been designed to hone the combat readiness of American battle groups and to evaluate Russian capabilities and reaction patterns. It showcased Navy Secretary John Lehman's "forward strategy" that tested battle groups in high-threat areas near Russian bases.

American strategists had hoped Midway's provocative flights would evoke a Russian response that included its newly deployed Backfire bomber. The Americans were anxious for a close look at the Backfire. Although the Soviet Air Defense Force in the Far East was placed on alert for several weeks and Russian diplomats later protested the overflights, the exercise prompted little direct response by the Russians.

It wasn't the first time a muted Russian response had baffled American battle group commanders. At the same time, the Russians often seemed to anticipate Midway's moves. Russian ship movement sometimes confounded Tom Brown, captain of Midway in 1978–80 who returned later as the commander of Carrier Task Force 77 with Midway as his flagship. "Midway would be in the Philippine Islands and begin heading north toward Okinawa. At almost the same time, a Russian spy ship off Guam got under way and laid in a perfect course to intercept us just as we were arriving at our destination. Even when we lost those 'tattle tales' sometimes they seemed to appear out of nowhere."

Two years later, the Navy discovered a major reason why the Russians were hard to provoke and seemingly prescient. The Russians were reading Midway's mail and often knew exactly what to expect. For more than 15 years, John Walker, who was not on Midway, had fed the Russians the cryptographic information they needed to read the Navy's coded communications. Navy officials estimated more than one million coded messages had been compromised.

Spies always worried the Navy. Spies on Midway—the only carrier homeported in a foreign country—could be especially damaging. The Naval Intelligence Service (NIS) maintained a regional office in Midway's home port of Yokosuka. Much of the NIS counterespionage activities focused on spies on the ground in Japan, since Midway was at sea frequently and for extended periods of time. However, when Midway pulled out of Yokosuka there almost always was at least one NIS agent aboard. Usually a junior NIS agent saddled with ship duty, he wasn't hard to spot. NIS "doggies afloat" wore civilian clothes. Veteran sailors even learned to spot NIS agents by the type of pen they used.

Ken Lord was one of those agents afloat, a man who spoke with a sharp, purpose-filled voice. One of his assignments aboard Midway was to solve crimes. Some crimes were deceptively destructive. Midway once suffered a series of locker break-ins. Sailors stealing from shipmates devastated crew morale. Lord had little to go on, so he threw some fingerprint powder around at one theft scene in front of some onlookers, and muttered aloud how he planned to solve the crime in a day or two. Sure enough, word spread, and a young man stepped into his office a few hours later to confess. Case closed.

Ship security sometimes followed members of Midway's crew after discharge. Security agents arrested a former Midway sailor, Henry Otto Spade, in Mountain Home, Arkansas, for unauthorized possession of a cryptographic key card. He had been a radio operator aboard Midway and was discharged only months before he was arrested. Facing up to 10 years in prison, Spade received probation. Others on Midway plotted more nefarious schemes.

A KGB operative offered James Wilmoth money for Midway secrets. But a food service worker wasn't privy to classified information. So he recruited third class petty officer Russell Paul Brown who had access to Midway's burn bag in the electronic warfare center. Brown could collect sensitive materials that Wilmoth would sell to Russia. Both were arrested for attempted sale of classified information to a Russian spy. Two months after his arrest Wilmoth was court-martialed and convicted of attempted espionage, failure to report contact by a Soviet Union citizen, conspiracy to transfer classified material, and possession and distribution of hashish. He was sentenced to 35 years at hard labor, later reduced to 15 years and a dishonorable discharge. Brown fared little better. A military judge sentenced him to 10 years in prison, a dishonorable discharge, and forfeiture of all pay and allowances.

Wilmoth had bragged about selling materials to the Russians and his Japanese girlfriend had sent postcards to Wilmoth's Midway friends from Moscow while the two were on vacation. None of their Midway shipmates reported the braggadocio or the postcards to authorities.

Spies inside and outside the Navy made the job of one "senior warlord" in the Pacific more difficult.

Admiral Ace Lyons commanded the Pacific Fleet. A barrel-chested, short man usually with bags under his eyes, when Lyons put his hands on hips, dropped his nose, and locked on with his eyes, most men blinked first. Lyons was renowned for aggressive tactics that left his officers rolling their eyes in his wake. Earlier in his career he had commanded a battle group that successfully ambushed the Russians in a mock attack on the northern edge of the Kola Peninsula. He fooled the Russians by taping the sounds of a battle group and sending a destroyer off in the wrong direction playing the tape.

Admiral Paul F. McCarthy commanded the Seventh Fleet, a twin-tipped force that included two battle groups (Midway in Japan and another battle group homeported on the American west coast). A former captain of the carrier Constellation, McCarthy was no stranger to the nuances of carrier strategy. As a "three star," he was no stranger to the politics of the Navy.

It fell to McCarthy to lead the Seventh Fleet at the behest of Lyons. McCarthy had Midway in his hip pocket as a forward-deployed carrier, but for all the aura of Midway's ability to meet its mission and stay on line longer than most carriers, Midway's limitations played into McCarthy's tactical decisions. The tip of the Seventh Fleet's sword, Midway offered rapid deployment but limited air wing capability, air operations made vulnerable by only two catapults, and a stability problem that limited heavy weather operations. Midway's limitations in heavy weather never affected McCarthy's deployment decisions, when Midway headed toward a trouble spot, McCarthy always knew how long it would take to get a "big deck" carrier into the area for expanded air operations. Although Midway lacked the firepower and versatility of the Navy's newer carriers, the carrier and its crew were ready, quick, and dedicated.

That made "off duty" an oxymoron for a commanding officer of Midway. Some captains struggled to meet the dual mission of military vigilance and the operation of a floating city. The risk inherent in every deployment drove some captains nearly into seclusion. Others thrived as they embraced the burden of command. The reputations of a handful of Midway captains reached near-legend proportions among the men who served under them, even with the shipmates who rarely saw their skipper. Two of those captains were aboard Midway in the 1980s. One was Chuck McGrail who had headed for the Naval Academy after he graduated from Central Catholic High School in Chicago. The other was Riley Mixson, a Georgia boy whose path toward sea had begun at Vanderbilt. More than 20 years later, their paths nearly crossed aboard Midway in the western Pacific.

Chuck McGrail was a horse of a man. Large-featured and a bit sensitive about a receding hairline, he filled every space he entered after taking command of Midway in 1982. Known as a gym rat, McGrail liked to lift weights with the youngsters from Springfield, Dayton, and Orlando. When the weather and command conditions were right, he sat in a lounge chair on the flight deck soaking up some sun, his Marine guard nearby at parade rest. He was renowned for his sense of humor. Midway was abuzz for weeks after the day McGrail settled into his elevated captain's chair on the bridge wearing a Darth Vader helmet and barking orders. His ability to make men laugh was one cornerstone of his leadership acumen.

Another was his accessibility. He became famous for his "green flashes." When the weather conditions are right, the sun setting on the ocean spawns a flash of light that is almost emerald green. When the "weather guessers" told McGrail prospects were good for a green flash, he invited off-duty personnel onto the flight deck. McGrail and green flashes became so synonymous that one day the crew decided to pull a fast one on their skipper. As McGrail answered questions on "Captain's Call," a show he hosted on Midway's TV channel, a crewman sprinted across the set in full view of the camera wearing only a green ski mask. It was the crew's version of a green flash for their captain who usually had the Russians on his mind.

Détente of the 1970s had given way to bellicose bluster in the early 1980s. President Reagan called Russia "the focus of evil in the world," as an invigorated Navy conducted exercises that tweaked and tested the Russians. American and Russian naval sparring intensified on McGrail's watch. Much of it took place in the Sea of Japan and the northern Pacific.

Russian frigates often attached themselves to Midway's battle group. Surveillance was a primary objective. The Russians even picked up Midway's garbage when hundreds of bags were thrown over the side. However, their mission when Midway went to sea often was more than shadow. One day as Midway turned into the wind to launch jets, a Russian destroyer changed course off the carrier's bow, forcing Midway away from the prevailing wind. An irritated McGrail decided to use a little backyard basketball strategy on the Russians that overcast day. McGrail ordered all ahead full and soon Midway's massive turbines powered Midway through the sea at more than 30 knots, opening a distance of nearly 10 miles between the carrier and the Russian destroyer. As the separation lengthened, Midway's plane guard destroyer slipped in between the two, setting itself up as a "pick" to block the destroyer from Midway's course as McGrail again turned into the wind. Two F-4 Phantoms immediately took to the air. Right after, a helicopter lifted from Midway's deck and skimmed the waves straight toward the Russians. Now Midway was running its own pick and roll.

The helicopter drew up and hovered near the Russian warship almost at bridge level as a decoy. After a few minutes, the helicopter banked hard and departed just as the two Phantoms completed their dive at the Russian destroyer from 20,000 feet. The sonic booms that exploded directly over the Russians startled the Americans nearly 10 miles off in the distance. They could only imagine how the acoustic explosions rattled the fillings of the Russian sailors. For the rest of the day, Midway air operations continued without interference. But McGrail knew that before long the jousting between the American and Russian navies would resume. He also knew gamesmanship at sea carried a very real risk of becoming brinkmanship.

McGrail often worked to infuse Midway's purpose with perspective in the minds of his young crew. McGrail had a gift for slogans. Buttons were printed that read "I'd Rather Kill Commies" and "Kill a Commie for Mommy." His favorite verbal period to most conversations was "Press on!"

Crew support for McGrail bordered on worship. He was a man "who never bullshit the troops. They would recognize a phony across the room. He knew that," said a superior officer who also called him a natural and a superstar. "He had an outstanding understanding of operations and tactics. His instincts were as good as I had ever seen. His credibility and believability was extraordinary."

Captain Riley Mixson had caught a bad break. Assignment as commanding officer of a carrier was the capstone of any Navy officer's career. But when Mixson received orders for Midway, he learned his job would be to skipper it into drydock for at least half a year. Mixson took command of a Midway in 1985 that needed stability in both its seakeeping characteristics and its crew. The previous captain had started his career in the Air Force and it seemed to the crew he was more interested acting as the air boss than captain of the carrier. Mixson was handed a crew he felt had become lazy and an air wing that was rusty as Midway headed into port for a major six-month repair project.

A man of average height and heavy-lidded, Mixson's velvet Georgia drawl drew men close and within range of an officer intensely focused on the job of being captain. He trusted his instincts. Experience taught him to "notice when the hair on the back of my neck stood up when something didn't sound right." Instincts borne from more than 25 years as a Navy officer were fueled by an intensity few captains matched.

Midway sailors said Mixson proved a man could be captain of an aircraft carrier for no more than 22 months because that's how long Mixson stayed awake on Midway. His cramped at-sea living quarters were just off the bridge, a drab space six feet by 10 feet. A narrow bed pulled down out of the wall on top of a vinyl blue couch. Next to the couch a small table could be pulled up from the wall and snapped into place—but only if the dark blue entry door was closed. In a space the size of a small closet, a 30-inch-square shower was separated from the toilet by two wall-mounted phones. It was cramped, spartan, and functional. Three hours of sleep was a blessing in Mixson's world.

Mixson's 22 months as commanding officer of Midway was the longest of any Midway captain to that time. Only Mixson's successor, R. A. Wilson, was captain longer, by 25 days. Mixson had flown more than 250 combat missions in Vietnam. He had piloted more than 30 types of aircraft, trapped aboard carriers more than 900 times, and had flown more than 5,000 accident-free hours. Yet he wasn't an air boss in captain's clothing. He became noted for wandering through Midway at 0100, stopping in a fire room for a cup of coffee with the enlisted men on duty. He also liked to walk around the ship with a camera to videotape stand-up crew interviews for broadcast on the ship's television station. He started each day on the 1MC with a "Good morning, Midway." Before long his crew anticipated the greeting, looked up at the nearest speaker, and responded, "Good morning, sir!"

Mixson was the head coach on Midway. He relied on a cadre of department heads to execute game plans, and teach fundamentals. None were more important than his commander of the air wing and Mixson's executive officer. Together, the captain, CAG, and XO were the triumvirate that was ultimately responsible for Midway's ability to meet its missions. It was crucial they work well together. Sometimes that in itself was a daunting mission.

A man couldn't hide on the bridge, a narrow strip of space that wrapped around the pilothouse at the front of the island. Its pastel blue walls contrasted with brightly polished brass telephones and wall-mounted green, red, and yellow alarm trigger boxes labeled "Chemical," "General Alarm" and "Collision Alarm." On the flight deck side of the bridge the captain sat tall in an elevated seat that resembled an upholstered (blue) barber's chair. He had a commanding view of the flight deck and watched over the navigator, officer of the deck, and others from behind. Near his thigh on a marbled blue linoleum counter sat a phone that automatically connected to 32 departments, ranging from CHENG (chief engineer) to PAO (public affairs officer) to AIMD (aircraft intermediate maintenance department).

The bridge filled with tension anytime Mixson and his air wing commander, Tim Beard, were there together. The two most senior officers aboard Midway simply didn't get along the entire 10 months that Beard's tenure overlapped Mixson's command. Sparks between Mixson and Beard flew often. The air wing's performance frequently riled Mixson. From his perch in the island, when Mixson saw a landing or other pilot maneuver he didn't like, he didn't hesitate in ordering his air boss to send the offending aviator up to the bridge as soon as his engines spun down. After slamming down on the fight deck and coming to a stop, the last words a pilot wanted to hear from plane handlers were "Congratulations, sir. You have valet parking today so that you may immediately report to the bridge." They were words that drained the color from most aviators' faces. They knew they were about to come face to face with an angry captain who took no lip and commanded from the strength of thousands of hours of combat and carrier flight experience.

When Beard left Midway on his birthday, he thought he was glad to be rid of his skipper. Beard's wife insisted he call Mixson to say goodbye. Reluctantly, Beard dialed Mixson's number and ultimately came to treasure the call. They set aside the personal and talked of purpose and perspective. As two senior officers. Man to man. "It was like a dam had broken. We talked and talked and I came away realizing how much I had learned. Captain Mixson taught me how to be a captain when my opportunity came with the carrier JFK," recalled Beard.

Below deck, the words "head row" haunted Mike Nordeen. As Mixson's executive officer, he was responsible for ship's operation from the mast down to the keel. Endless "heads and beds" details consumed the XO's day: planning the next underway replenishment, screening cases for captain's mast, and even making sure clogged toilets were repaired.

"Blindfold me and lead me through Midway. I'll tell you when we reach second deck, starboard side." Head Row was infamous for the string of perennially clogged toilets due to a plumbing design flaw in the Midway class.

Nordeen—a former A-7 pilot from the northern reaches of Wisconsin—took a pragmatic approach to learning how to work with the demanding captain of Midway who always seemed to be on the bridge. "Number one, make sure the commanding officer is a success. Number two, make it so that the captain doesn't have to worry about the details. And number three, learn how to read the skipper's writing [intent]."

The XO organized the hearings called captain's masts when sailors ran afoul of regulations and appeared before Mixson for judgment and immediate punishment. Nordeen sometimes worked to influence the course of Midway justice. When it came time to mete out punishment, Mixson generally averted fines, especially for married sailors. A favorite alternative was a suspended fine pending good behavior. An option was up to three days in the brig on bread and water. Many sailors preferred a stay in the brig to a reduction in grade or restriction to the ship for up to 60 days. Nordeen thought Mixson in his early days as captain was a pussy-cat, so "Nordo" tried to irritate Mixson just before the hearings. Captain's mast became an experience most men dreaded. By the time he left Midway the soft-spoken captain from Georgia who had grown up grind-ing optical lenses for his father was widely known as "Bread and Water Mixson."

McGrail's and Mixson's natural camaraderie with their crew set them apart from most Midway captains. Both exuded an easy-going, likeable nature and both made a constant effort to be as accessible to their crew as possible. That interaction became the first step toward the crew's belief that both captains had their welfare at heart. From there it was a short step to complete faith and trust in their skippers. McGrail and Mixson also continued a Midway tradition that had begun in 1977 when Crystal Gale's *We Must Believe in Magic* album went platinum. The album's title song became the unofficial song of Midway. When Midway left or arrived in port, "We Must Believe in Magic" filled the carrier. Gale's words reverberated down passageways and floated across the flight deck.

Mad is the captain of Alpha Centauri
We must be out of our minds
Still we are shipmates bound for tomorrow
And everyone here's flying blind.

Oh, we must believe in magic
We must believe in the guiding hand
If you believe in magic
You'll have the universe at your command

Mad is the crew bound for Alpha Centauri
Dreamers and poets and clowns
Bold is the ship bound for Alpha Centauri
Nothing can turn it around

Oh, we must believe in magic
We must believe in the guiding hand
If you believe in magic
You'll have the universe at your command

It was a hit with the crew that was also played every three days or so
when Midway completed an underway replenishment. UNREPs were vital
to Midway's frequent and marathon deployments in the Indian Ocean, a
duty that placed the carrier at the end of a supply line that stretched
halfway around the world. One link in that chain was a studious-looking
young man with the innocuous name of Bob Jones. Thousands of Bob
Joneses formed the supply lines that fed Midway twice a week when at sea.
They were responsible for the unending underway replenishments of fuel,
oil, fruit, medical supplies, flour, rockets, wrenches, detergent, and even
Christmas trees.

Stationed for a time at NAS Cubi Point in the Philippine Islands,
Jones, the son of a navy family, greatly influenced the quality of life as well
as the operational readiness aboard Midway as it steamed in the Indian
Ocean 7,000 miles away. Jones received SITREPS (situational reports)
from the air wings that listed the top 10 and the top 50 most-needed items.
After a while, he saw the same items on the reports. Jones noticed the air
wing on Midway was frequently short of certain brake and electronics sys-

tems components. So he watched for those items and expedited them as "hot cargo" to Midway whether the air wing was asking for them on a given day or not.

Supply officers like Jones also dealt with the egos of the Navy's 250-member admiral community. One time an admiral sent Jones a message demanding that his baseball caps be made of khaki in size 7-7/8 inches, an enormous hat size. To the keep the admiral happy, Jones commissioned a Philippine seamstress to custom make the hats. Six days later, the admiral's caps were aboard his battle group's flagship.

Produce from the States was barely edible by the time it reached the Philippines and often rotted by the time it reached Midway's battle group. Some spaces and passageways on Midway routinely reeked of rotten food. Jones and his compatriots solved the problem by buying directly from Philippine and Guam growers. On other occasions, Midway's crew lambasted the Navy's supply chain when both necessities and niceties didn't arrive as requested. One time Jones shipped two 20-foot containers of ice cream to Diego Garcia, en route to Midway's battle group. The ground crew wasn't informed the two containers were refrigerated and needed auxiliary power. Within hours the ice cream melted on a Diego Garcia tarmac.

Ice cream was a big deal to the Midway crew when it spent as much as 111 days "on the line" away from its homeport. Marathon deployments were separated sometimes by only a few weeks home in Yokosuka. Over time, they took a toll on both morale and operational readiness. They also made liberty all the more cherished by the thousands of young men aboard Midway. One of their favorite liberty ports was Subic Bay in the Philippines. It was a kind of liberty that rarely was discussed with wives or girlfriends when sailors returned home. The Philippines were a sexual wonderland.

Felisa Regner had a perfectly round face. Barely five feet tall, her dark Philippina skin contrasted with blue eyes aflame with opal brilliance. Her eyes always quickly sizied up each sailor who walked into any of the three bars she managed in Olongapo City, just across "shit river" from the Philippines' Subic Naval Base where Midway moored. Only about 12 blocks long, Olongapo City's bar district was legendary. Regner managed the Pussycat Mojo Club, the Tom-Tom Club, and the FTN Mojo Club.

They competed for sailors' patronage with the likes of Pauline's, Marmont 3, Willows, Marilyn's Super Inn, Cherry Club, and Muff Divers Club.

Mere mention of liberty in Olongapo City gave sailors "channel fever." It was a condition suffered by many on their first extended deployment. Anticipation of storied liberty in Olongapo became so intense it interfered with sleep. So chiefs frequently pulled a time-honored prank, telling first-timers channel fever was a real malady caused by being at sea too long and that a shot administered in sickbay could restore a normal sleep pattern. When they reported to sick bay, the co-conspiring orderlies waved a giant syringe in front of the "patients," told them to drop their pants, and after a poignant pause . . . squirted a massive injection of ice water on their back-sides. The prank paled in comparison to what lay in store in Olongapo City.

It was Regner's job to manage the bars for the Chinese owner and to see to it sailors enjoyed themselves without getting into too much trouble. Virtually everything was available from the 14- to 18-year-old girls recruited from wretchedly poor rural families to work the bars as "hostitutes." As many as 200 worked in some bars. Regner kept the San Miguel beer flowing, her girls healthy, and Midway sailors happy.

That meant keeping a stash of XXXX condoms in her purse behind the bar, reminding her girls to shower the day before Midway arrived, and making sure they went to the Navy clinic for the required pap smear every two weeks. Midway's weekly newsletter published a list of the bars that maintained perfect compliance with local "social hygiene" programs. One 4 D Road, Crazy Horse, Freaks, and AC-DC Disco were among those with laudable track records.

Venereal disease was rampant in the Philippines and on Midway. As much as 18 percent of Midway's crew visited onboard VD clinics after departing Subic Bay. Sailors came aboard with a variety of newly acquired ailments, including gonorrhea of the throat, genital herpes, venereal warts, and gonorrhea of the eyes. After one in-port stay, two Midway sailors each carried six different sexually transmitted diseases.

No Midway sailor wanted to come home with VD. So a standard was established. Since most cases of venereal disease took 30 days to treat, the PCOD ("pussy cut-off date") was published aboard Midway 31 days prior to arrival back in Yokosuka.

Since some sailors didn't want a case of "clap" on their record, Regner helped many sailors get treated for VD outside Navy channels. She sent them to a physician friend who prescribed the necessary medications for $100. Several strains of herpes and gonorrhea had become resistant to penicillin so Trobicin was the medication of choice. Some Olongapo "drip clinics" were run by scam artists. Dipping a penis in salt water and injecting vinegar up the urethra tube were "prescribed" and useless.

It was far more expensive to treat a case of the clap than to get it. Beer usually cost 25¢ (depending upon the exchange rate) and the cost of a girl for the night rarely exceeded $20. Frequently, though, the girls serviced their customers in the bar by slipping under the table for oral sex. If a group of buddies was being tended to at once, there usually was a bet on the table. He who smiled last, won. Entertainment came in many forms. Some bars were famous for their nude dancers' ability to perform cigarette tricks.

While drunken binges were rampant, violence was rare in the bars. The prostitutes threatened a "Philippine haircut" (slit throat) if a customer got out of hand, and Regner knew to let two brawling sailors slug it out so that neither could claim he was pick-pocketed by the locals who broke up the fight. When it came time to return to Midway, drunken sailors staggered across a bridge that spanned a canal filled with putrid sewage on its way to the bay. Children as young as eight, nine, and 10 years of age floated in bonka boats on the sewage and yelled up to sailors on the bridge to throw them a Philippine peso which usually was worth only a few cents. Young girls in bonka boats sometimes dressed in long skirts and bared their breasts for a peso flipped from the bridge. A youngster who missed a tossed coin thought nothing of diving into the sewage to retrieve it. More than one drunken sailor reported back aboard Midway rattled by the sight of children swimming in sewage for a few cents.

A few days in Olongapo City often made for lifetime memories shared only in hushed tones at reunions. Port calls from Kenya to Kirachi to Hong Kong were far tamer. Generally it was even more sedate when Midway returned to Yokosuka. Usually Midway stayed there only four to six weeks before heading back out to sea. But in 1986, Midway put in to Yokosuka for six months for repairs and experimental modifications intended to correct 41 years of instability in even moderate sea conditions. The Great Blister Experiment was intended to improve Midway's instability by attaching 32-ton steel compartments called blisters to the carrier's hull, thus keeping Midway operational until 1997 when the nuclear-powered John C. Stennis aircraft carrier replaced it.

High above in the island as Midway transited the mouth of the bay, Captain Riley Mixson felt antsy. He had taken command of Midway just in time to sail into Yokosuka for the extended repair. Now he was anxious to do some real navy work. Something felt different when Midway eased out into tame three- to four-foot seas. Mixson's hair on the back of his neck sounded an alarm as he felt the surge of Midway's turbines as the carrier started to move under its own power. A few minutes later, Midway rolled to one side, then the other. "Do you remember sitting this high and rolling like this?" Mixson asked his air wing commander, Tom Bowman. The CAG shook his head and rolled his eyes.

After more than a half year in the yard, the "USS Rock & Roll" was alive and well. Three officers aboard Midway weren't particularly surprised. Long before Midway left the shipyard, they had learned the Great Blister Experiment might produce some surprises.

Bill Center had one of the most demanding jobs aboard Midway. As chief engineer, every gasket, valve, pump, circuit, and connection was his responsibility. He had reported aboard Midway with unmatched credentials. He had graduated from the Naval Academy with four majors (political science, naval engineering, economics, and history) and had already commanded two ships. As CHENG, no one understood the guts of Midway better than Bill Center.

More than 40 years old, Midway had needed a lot of work beyond its stability problems. Center knew Midway had been dangerously overweight. Naval engineers worried its hull girders couldn't continue to support the topside weight. If they failed, cracks in the hull might develop. Excess weight had to be removed and the hull strengthened. In addition, flight deck and hangar bay work was necessary to accommodate the imminent arrival of F/A-18 Hornets aboard Midway. Another issue had been a three-foot trim by the stern. The carrier's flight deck sloped uphill, stern to bow. F-4 Phantoms did not react well to landing against the side of a hill. The stern sat so low in the water the Navy was worried whether Midway could survive an aft torpedo hit. Still another problem was reduced freeboard. The top-heavy Midway rode too low in the water. Moderate sea conditions sent water crashing over the deck, creating a host of operational, safety, and maintenance problems.

Improving seakeeping stability had been almost an afterthought. When the suggestion of adding the blisters to the work list was made, Midway's senior officers took a calculated risk and acquiesced, believing it was likely impossible to complete in the allotted six months. However, one obstacle after another fell away and within a few months Sumitomo Shipbuilding was installing blisters it fabricated from American-made steel.

Some Midway officers worried that the Navy had rushed the design and inadequately tested the blisters in light of Secretary of the Navy John Lehman's high-profile campaign for a 600-ship, 15-battle-group Navy. Lehman claimed the Russian Navy possessed 1,700 ships as he pushed for his 600-ship naval force. Midway's orders were to upgrade for F/A-18 capability, lose weight, install the blisters, and get Midway back into the deployment rotation of a Pacific Fleet responsible for patrolling more than 100 million square miles of ocean.

Workers pulled more than 56 miles of unused cable from overhead spaces, lightening Midway by 48 tons. They shaved another 300 tons by reducing armor plating around the aftersteering gearbox from six to three inches. Sumitomo built special rails in the bottom of its dry dock, lowered the massive blisters onto the rails, and moved the units into place, usually to within a half inch of a perfect fit. Each blister was blessed at a Shinto shrine in the bottom of the dry dock. When Midway conducted "wet checks" after the final installation, only two areas needed additional attention. It was a remarkable and an oft-repeated measure of the quality of ship maintenance performed by Japanese shipyard workers on Midway throughout its 18 years in Yokosuka.

One day a Sumitomo official was asked what he thought of the blister project. He sucked air through clenched teeth creating an inverted sssssss sound, a mannerism some Japanese used to connote concern. Sumitomo didn't think the huge, eight-foot-wide blisters (the standard was four feet) would solve the stability problems. Just as the last blister was being welded to Midway's hull, the blisters' designers paid a visit to Captain Mixson, CHENG Center, and XO Nordeen. They confirmed Sumitomo's concerns.

The blisters had been rushed through design and testing, admitted the designers. Now, as the blisters' installation neared completion, the final test results indicated that perhaps they would make Midway too stable in some respects. They did. In subsequent sea trials, Midway "snapped back" to level quickly and sometimes dangerously if air operations were under way. When Midway sailed in seas of 13-second wavelengths, the carrier began to "rock and roll" even in practically calm water. Wavelength, not height, excited Midway's rolling propensity.

The 92 blisters also increased Midway's badly needed reserve buoyancy, boosted the carrier's hull strength, enhanced Midway's survivability, and improved turning stability to such an extent that Midway could turn inside 1,500 yards. That agility would prove to be extremely useful five years later in combat.

Mixson and his crew learned to live with Midway's continued instability and developed operational procedures to minimize its effect. Changes in course sometimes minimized the rolling, other times the crew laid low and hung on. Mixson's rule of thumb allowed pilots to land during five- to six-degree rolls but once they got to eight degrees, pilots were waved off. Even eight-degree rolls, though, were tame to what Midway sometimes experienced.

Less than a year after the blisters were installed, Midway crossed paths with four typhoons in a single deployment, producing tales of legendary heavy-sea rolling. But it was a typhoon in 1989 that yielded the king of Midway rolls. The carrier steamed off the coast of Luzon as a typhoon bore down on the carrier. For more than 24 hours, Midway rode it out, seas lashing the ship and gale winds screaming across its deck. The crew leaned into each roll. First one side, then the other, for hours. Many stayed in their bunks, alternately green and pale. Others remained at their duty stations for lack of anything else to do.

Brian Olson idled away the time by sitting in his maintenance shop, watching the PLAT, the automated camera on the flight deck that recorded aircraft landings. Midway began to lean to port. It kept leaning. Steeper. Steeper, as equipment slid across the compartment. Amazed, Olson watched the television monitor as the sea engulfed the angle deck. The jolt of the deck hitting the water pulsed through the ship. Finally Midway paused and began to right itself. Then the starboard side plunged deep into a trough before the carrier finally settled.

Clammy faces were white with fear. Antennas along the flight deck had been ripped off by the waves. Seawater rushed into the hangar bays before receding. Armored plating along the ship-edge sponson deck had warped under the pressure. The fueling station at the bow was in shambles. It was hours more before Midway broke free of the storm. As the carrier pressed ahead, word spread through the ship. Midway had survived a 24-degree roll, eclipsing the legendary roles of past deployments.

Days later when Midway put in for repairs, patches marking the occasion appeared on crew uniforms. Two of the most popular were "She Could Do No More Than 24" and "I Survived the 24 Degree Roll." The crew joked that during the next inport stay, a periscope would be installed on Midway's keel so when the carrier finally "turned turtle," it could find its way home. It was one overhaul that CHENG Bill Center did not have to oversee. Center received command of another ship, a guided-missile cruiser named Reeves. He didn't know that in that capacity he would come within three days of being "attacked" by a fighter jet from Midway.

After leaving Midway, Center had become known on the Reeves as a skipper who didn't have much use for rules that made little sense to him. The prescribed uniform when underway seemed silly to a "shorts and T-shirt kind of guy." Renowned as a "crew's captain," he enjoyed liberty in Subic Bay alongside his crew. Having watched Riley Mixson inspire near-worship by his Midway crew, Center took a number of leadership lessons with him to Reeves. He fostered the same kind of "can do, against all odds" spirit that defined the attitude he witnessed on Midway.

Reeves slowly patrolled a patch of Indian Ocean. The men on the bridge stared at a solitary white light five miles off toward the horizon, expecting it to disappear in a massive explosion. They barely registered the sudden whine overhead before the windows on the bridge exploded, glass and metal shards slicing through them. At the sound of General Quarters, Reeves' damage control parties raced forward to the smoking rubble at the bow. A 500-pound bomb had dropped out of the night sky, ripping through the forward deck of the Reeves and into its line locker, disintegrating one of Reeves' two anchor chains as its detonation lifted the Reeves up onto the ocean's surface.

At the most unexpected times, a ship's crew faced danger and potential disaster as one deployment blurred with the next. Often tragedy and loss became the defining characteristic that separated one from another. The Reeves crew was both lucky and disciplined. Within a few minutes of the explosion, damage control parties had secured the bow and those injured on the bridge were being treated. The crew had reacted with the precision its captain, "Wild Bill" Center, had developed, even though Center had transferred off the ship only three days earlier. Center's standard of teamwork, discipline, and confidence stood the Reeves' crew well that night when a Midway aviator mistook the Reeves' white bridge light for the landmark light on the bombing target barge, five miles away.

The wounded cruiser limped to Diego Garcia for repairs. Most important to the crew, it continued on to a scheduled liberty call in Australia. When Reeves tied up, a pallet of beer waited on the pier for the crew, along with an apology from Midway's pilot. Officers ordered the crew not to talk about the incident and confiscated photos they had taken of the damage.

Throughout the fall of 1987 Iran had threatened to sink reflagged Kuwaiti oil tankers transiting the Strait of Hormuz. It was Midway's mission to project American power and peacekeeping purpose. About an hour after sunset on November 19, Ironclaw squadron Commander David Greene, J. C. Carter, Doug Hora, and "Hoot" Gibson shot off Midway southeast of India on a 70-minute reconnaissance mission. Midway was running EMCON to keep its position undetected. No radar emanated from the ship. Midway aircraft on patrol were on their own. An hour and a half passed. Alarm grew when the Prowler failed to return or contact Midway's traffic control. Soon the intelligence center grew crowded as Captain Rich Wilson and other officers arrived, looking for answers and finding none.

Ironclaw's aviators in the squadron ready room grew silent. Stillness deepened into worry as time passed. A cake sat in front of the squadron skipper's chair. It had been baked in anticipation of David Greene's 1,000th trap aboard a carrier. Greene was regarded as one of the most easy-going aviators aboard Midway. Very little seemed to bother him. Devoutly superstitious, he always wore his lucky socks when he flew. He once said he avoided reading books to preserve his vision. He simply loved to fly. Canadian born, Greene didn't share the arrogance of most pilots, many of whom were full of themselves in the aftermath of the movie Top Gun and its lingering popularity.

Greene's milestone never came. A massive search by aircraft from Midway, Diego Garcia, and other ships found no trace of the aircraft or sur-

Another Midway fighter jet is launched off the USS Midway in 1965, one of nearly 12,000 combat sorties against North Vietnam that year. Thirteen Midway pilots were killed, four more listed as missing in action.
(NATIONAL ARCHIVES)

Thousands of USS Midway sailors worked so hundreds could fly. Firemen apprentices Jim Glasker, Sam Davis, and Jack Adhearn scrape the rust off the inside of one of Midway's boilers.
(NATIONAL ARCHIVES)

Back aboard Midway, Lt. Michael Weakley stood up through wing damage inflicted by the enemy on September 24, 1965. (NATIONAL ARCHIVES)

Lt. Charles Hartman and Lt. Cdr. Edwin Greathouse explain how their prop-driven Skyraider shot down a MiG-17 fighter jet over North Vietnam on June 20, 1965.

(NATIONAL ARCHIVES)

Daily Air Plans were accompanied by satirical cartoons in 1965, including one revealing what Midway's crew thought of actress Jane Fonda visiting North Vietnam. The cartoon was sent to Secretary of Defense Melvin Laird.

(WALLY GIRARD)

A sailor is dwarfed by Midway in a San Francisco shipyard in 1971.   (U.S. Navy)

The "worlds' greatest fighter pilot," Mugs McKeown, and Jack Ensch fly inverted back to Midway a few days after they had shot down two enemy MiGs only minutes apart. (U.S. Navy)

More than 3,000 South Vietnamese refugees were ferried aboard Midway on what became known as the "Night of the Helicopters."

(LARRY GRIMES)

A Russian Badger bomber is escorted by Midway aircraft as it approaches Midway.
(U.S. NAVY)

Midway was infamous for its marathon deployments. A handful of family photos were all that linked young sailors in cramped berths with their families as Midway patrolled at the tip of the sword half a world away. (Discovered aboard USS Midway in 2003.)

The 'pickle' in their hands, two landing signal officers bring home another aircraft. More than 100,000 pilots trusted LSOs as they landed aboard Midway. (CURLY CULP)

Air operations aboard Midway went around the clock, whether it was combat operations or night qualifications. Military studies showed night landings aboard carriers were more stressful that combat. (CURLY CULP)

vivors. Ironclaw's skipper and three bright, young aviators had disappeared without a trace.

Five days later the memorial service would be held on Midway. Shock would still numb many as the colors would be posted, then a flag presented for each lost aviator. Three men would stand in front of their shipmates in a ceremony they dreaded. The pressure to measure up would be enormous. One of the three wandered through Midway in search of refuge to think. Another stared into a Bible. A third reviewed the finer points of Navy protocol for the time when Midway would slow, work would stop, and men would look to them for meaning and perspective.

It fell to Kyle Hancock to present his dead skipper's flag. Prayers, a responsive reading, and then Bill Mysinger read Job 14, passages about the brevity of life, and certainty of death. Dan Shanower, a man widely admired for being able to find humor in nearly every situation, stood and spoke from his heart, memorializing fellow aviator Doug Hora who once called El Dorado, Arkansas, home. A benediction, rifle salute, Taps, the retirement of the colors, and it was over.

Midway remained on station, patrolling the Sea of Japan, Indian Ocean, and points in between, a city at sea where numbing routine always carried risk. Mysinger, Hancock, and Shanower knew they soon would be in the air again, fulfilling electronic countermeasure missions as Midway's deployment continued. It was one of 20 Midway deployments between 1981 and 1989. The Cold War had began to thaw and Middle Eastern radicalism broached national borders to become international terrorism. For some on Midway, these dynamics defined their Navy career in the 1980s and beyond.

Dan Shanower spent most of the next 14 years as a Navy intelligence officer. His Navy career ended on September 11, 2001, when a hijacked commercial airliner slammed into the Pentagon, killing him. A year later, civic leaders in his hometown of Naperville, Illinois, memorialized Shanower's legacy. They planted a riverside garden to honor the former aviator who 15 years earlier stood tall on Midway paying tribute to fallen aviators in another era of international uncertainty.

Jets thundered onto Midway's flight deck as the carrier plowed through the northern Pacific, 125 miles northeast of Tokyo on the morning of June 20, 1990. Routine flight operations continued as the day turned to afternoon. A damage control storeroom full of pipes, three decks below the No. 1 elevator, began to fill with smoke. As it grew thicker, Midway's Flying Squad—a hand-selected team of 30 damage control specialists— was summoned. Flying Squad Investigators were the first responders to almost every potential emergency. As often as 150 times a year, the carrier's Flying Squad was summoned to handle noxious fumes, toxic substance spills, small fires, and false alarms. The Flying Squad was the first-line fire department on Midway. If they deemed a given situation serious, the rescue and assistance team was called as reinforcement.

Jeffrey Vierra was a part of the Flying Squad. An office clerk in the repair division, he volunteered for the assignment after a hull technician, Joe Stalaboin declined. Stalaboin instead became a member of the rescue and assistance team. Stalaboin didn't think much of the initial alarm that mobilized Vierra. Then Stalaboin's R&A team was summoned. Maybe it was serious.

Stalaboin raced to the forward galley as Vierra and others reached the smoldering storeroom. When they opened the hatch to the storeroom, an explosion ripped through the men, slamming them against each other and into steel bulkheads in the confined passageway. The explosion blew the door on the far side of the nearby galley off its hinges. As the smoke and heat thinned, blackened sailors writhed on the deck.

Stalaboin stopped to help an injured shipmate and then half-carried him back to the main galley that had been designated a triage area. It seemed to take forever, dragging the injured man to the galley. When he arrived, Stalaboin choked at the scene. Human forms vaguely resembled men from his department. Men who had shared his berthing compartment, had eaten meals with him, and who had stood his watch. Men were so badly burned he recognized them only by the shape of their torsos, confirmed by the seared clothing that shook on quivering bodies. Burned flesh and melted hair mixed with the smells of asphalt, oil, smoke and steel.

Forty-five minutes later after the fire crews had regrouped to attack the fire, a second explosion roared through Midway. More injuries. At that point, emergency crews, most of them from the damage control department, grew more cautious. Their mandate always was "don't let the cancer spread." They retreated to set fire boundaries in surrounding compartments while others carried more wounded to the emergency triage area. Soon word passed to Yokosuka that there were serious injuries too numerous for Midway to handle. Within an hour, the critically injured were moved to the flight deck for airborne evacuation.

Meanwhile, fire crews continued to fight the fire, using the ship's ventilation system to flood the surrounding compartments with foam. As the sun set on Midway, four helicopters landed with 10 corpsmen from a medical clinic in Atsugi to help Midway's medical department treat the injured. Flooding continued almost until midnight as the fire control battle turned into a marathon. Volunteers stepped forward to take the place of exhausted fire control sailors, some of whom were carried by Midway's Marine detachment to the forward mess where they could peel off singed clothing and breathe safely.

Finally, in the early hours of June 21, the crews beat the fire. Those who relieved them began draining the flooded compartments. At 0840, emergency crews entered the compartment where the first explosion had occurred and found two bodies. Five hours later the bodies of Jeffrey Vierra and Ulric Johnson came ashore. Nine others, seriously burned, had already been flown off the carrier.

In an instant, routine, risk, and death had become one. It was a confluence that frequently scarred duty aboard Midway. As the tides of détente and dispute ebbed and flowed through the end of the 1980s, Midway's life was drawing to a close. Four months before the fire, the Navy had announced Midway would be decommissioned the following year. Despite the long-anticipated decision, flight operations continued, young men trained, and sailors responded when alarms sounded. Soon Midway would be handed two last missions. One would be to attack, the other to save lives.

CHAPTER 13

MISSION ACCOMPLISHED

MIDWAY'S OMNIPRESENT HUM settled in the soles of air boss Terry Pudas. He looked down through the hazy red glow that enveloped the flight deck. Knots of helmeted men looking alien in the night ops glow dotted the flight deck. Reflective jersey tape and muted flashlights floated like leisurely fireflies. Pudas imagined the clank of tie-down chains being dragged across the deck and the combustive pulse of the tractors' engines. The white helmets of tense pilots barely moved inside their cockpits as they, too, waited. Pudas knew the night air below carried a blend of exhaust and jet fuel fumes that coated jackets and skin.

Pudas' breathing was shallow, his pulse staccato. His men stood poised to launch the first strike of Desert Storm. A Midway A-6 Intruder would be among the first to go "feet dry" from the Persian Gulf, leading air attacks against both the aircraft and suspected chemical weapons of Saddam Hussein.

Not far away, the chilled blue eyes of Captain Art Cebrowski narrowed as he counted the real and theoretical threats that surrounded Midway. He reviewed the endless training that had preceded the dawn of Desert Storm. The former Vietnam pilot was regarded as one of the most cerebral officers the Navy had produced in recent years. As a boy growing up in Connecticut, he had repeatedly watched Don Ameche in a WWII movie, *A Wing and a Prayer*, about a U.S. carrier used to decoy the Japanese. At Villanova University, he had turned down an invitation from Admiral Hyman Rickover to interview for the Navy's nuclear program. Arthur Karl Cebrowski's mission had been to become a naval aviator. Now he commanded the vanguard of Desert Storm aboard Midway.

For five months he had been planning the moment when his fighters and bombers would attack Iraq. It had started within minutes of learning on August 2, 1990, that Saddam Hussein had invaded Kuwait. Cebrowski asked "Gator" (Midway's navigator) for maps of the Persian Gulf. Calculating eyes scanned for only a few seconds before Cebrowski planted a finger just north of Qatar in the Persian Gulf. "No way," the navigator said. "The Navy doesn't allow carriers in the Persian Gulf." But Cebrowski rarely thought like the Navy. Often the Navy played catch-up to Cebrowski's thinking. He knew that at a particular point in the Gulf, key targets would be in range (including the critical "loiter time" needed over targets) of Midway's Hornets and Intruders. He knew the prevailing wind there would add a knot or two to Midway's speed. And he knew Midway's recently installed blisters made it the stiffest carrier in the Navy and gave it the turning capability it needed to maneuver in the confines of the Persian Gulf. Three months later Midway arrived on station in the Persian Gulf, precisely where Cebrowski had predicted.

As he waited for the first launch, Cebrowski knew Midway was structurally up to the demands of Desert Storm. He couldn't be as sure about his crew, despite rigorous drills as Midway transited the Indian Ocean. Cebrowski's demanding expectations of Midway had fellow carrier captains hooting in derision. At an early Desert Storm war-planning meeting, the captains had been asked how many sorties they could mount in a 12-hour period. Most said their crews could mount 30, maybe 35 sorties. Cebrowski said Midway could put 70 sorties into the air. No one at the table believed him. But the meticulous Cebrowski had researched Midway's record in Vietnam and learned the carrier had reached that level of efficiency on several occasions. He knew it could be done, and staked both his claim and belief in Midway, accordingly.

It was up to Midway's crew to deliver on Cebrowski's promise. One day he told Midway's weapons officer he wanted to conduct a drill that was the equivalent of loading and launching 35 sorties. Midway's crew delivered only half that many. Not good enough. Cebrowski ran the drill again. This time, 35 sorties were ready to go. Still not good enough. Cebrowski told his senior officers the real objective was to train for 75 sorties in a 12-hour period. They had kept practicing as they approached the Persian Gulf.

"Jim, I want to run a drill at 0100," Cebrowski told his air wing commander, Jim Burin, one day. "Create a worst-case scenario. We've got to know if we're ready." Burin paused only briefly before agreeing. The hollow voice echoed through Midway a short time later in the middle of the night. "This is an immediate drill! Assume inbound attack. Launch the air wing NOW." Thousands of men scrambled to their duty stations. Tractors on the flight deck rumbled as yellow shirts raced across the deck, nearly colliding with pilots sprinting toward their planes. Jet-starting huffers fired up as shooters got organized at the catapults and others began directing aircraft forward. As Midway turned into the wind, the first aircraft was ready to launch—in less than six minutes. Cebrowski had wanted to see if his crew was primed. They were. Equally important, he wanted his crew to know they were ready for war. Most were men who had never experienced combat.

Worry lines plowed across Burin's brow. The CAG was responsible for Midway's 56-aircraft air wing. A demanding set of missions spanning the first few days of the air war had been in place for weeks. His aviators had practiced them in what were called "mirror images" over the Gulf of Oman. It had been Burin's job to blend Midway's air wing of Hornets, Intruders, and Prowlers into an efficient attacking force capable of flying missions 15 to 18 hours a day for weeks at a time from the deck of the oldest, smallest, and most difficult-to-land aircraft carrier in the Navy.

It was one thing to practice in a tranquil Indian Ocean sky. Burin knew very few of his aviators had faced enemy fire. Few had been asked to review their personal security folders prior to a mission so that if they were shot down in enemy territory, search-and-rescue personnel could verify their identity. Few had zippered a "blood chit" written in the language of the enemy offering a $1,500 reward for their safe return. Burin was commanding a peacetime air wing on the edge of war.

Nerves knotted Mike Shutt's stomach in the first black hour of January 17, 1991, as he sat in his Hornet on Alert 5. As Midway prepared to launch its first strike at 0100, Shutt was ready to launch within five minutes if called upon. Shutt watched the pantomime gestures of shooters, plane captains, and aircraft handlers that directed one Midway Intruder after another to a catapult. The carrier's Intruders had the lead on night missions with the Hornets in support. During the day, the Hornets took primary attack responsibility with the others in support. Shutt's canopy shuddered as one Midway jet after another thundered toward the bow. Soon their lights mixed with the stars and quiet returned to the flight deck. Fluorescent catapult steam drifted off the deck into the night as men looked at each other, their hearts pounding. Desert Storm had begun as Midway's jets streaked toward two targets. One was an airfield near Basra in Iraq, the other a bunker in Kuwait suspected of containing chemical weapons.

A few hours after the first launch, Shutt's pulse quickened as all 24 of Midway's Hornets prepared to attack the enemy at first light on January 17. They were to coordinate their inbound flight over Iraq with a group of 12 Marine Corps aircraft. The Marines' assignment was to fire high-speed antiradiation missiles (HARM) at air-defense installations every 30 seconds for 12 of the 15 minutes Midway's aircraft were "feet dry." Shutt approached the Iraqi coast almost at Mach 1. Shortly after crossing the beach, contrails (condensation trails) ribboned the sky.

"My God," Shutt thought, assuming the contrails were from surface-to-air missiles, reminiscent of those he had evaded while flying more than 100 missions over Vietnam. "This is going to be a long war." Shutt was wrong. The Marines had fired all 24 HARMs almost as soon as they entered Iraqi airspace. Midway pilots pressed ahead, delivered their ordnance, and returned safely to Midway.

By the fourth day, American jets had obliterated most Iraqi SAM sites, in part through the use of tactical air-launched decoys that both confused and exposed Iraqi air defense systems. Once the SAM sites were destroyed, Midway jets could fly above the antiaircraft fire with relative impunity. Once the first few days' preplanned missions had been completed, each day's target assignments (called air tasking orders, or ATOs) arrived on Midway by helicopter about 2300 the night before. The short notice and lack of flexibility in the ATOs irked Midway's air wing officers. It was symptomatic of the command-and-communication issues between the Air Force and Navy that became a hallmark of Desert Storm.

Midway targets evolved as Desert Storm moved through the war planners' four phases. The first stage had destroyed Hussein's command and communications infrastructure, "decapitating" his forces. The second had achieved air superiority over the Kuwaiti theater of operations. The third phase prepared the battlefield for the ground invasion. The fourth would support the ground assault.

Some missions produced unexpected results. Midway's jets sometimes attacked ships in the northern Persian Gulf as well as targets in southern Iraq. On one occasion, Midway pilots flew over a commercial oil tanker high up in the Gulf, a region most commercial ships had vacated weeks earlier. Its presence was mystifying. A few days later, it was spotted again, this time with its stern open to the sea. Inside was a hovercraft. Midway pilots received authorization to bomb the tanker, and, in doing so, inadvertently created a significant oil slick.

On another occasion, an S-3 Viking sidled into Midway's landing pattern. Midway didn't have any Vikings in its air wing but because Midway was running EMCON, the mysterious pilot couldn't be contacted. Pudas called Captain Cebrowski. "Go ahead and recover," he ordered. The S-3 lined up on Midway and landed, but its tailhook skipped over the arresting wires, forcing the pilot to go full throttle, pull up, and come around again. Who was that guy? Then Pudas had an idea. He dialed into the frequency used by a nearby carrier with its pilots. The conversation chilled him. "Where are you?" "I'm 180 degrees to the ship." "What? Where are you?" "Now I'm in the groove, ship dead ahead, I'm . . ." "WAVE OFF! WAVE OFF!" The only ship dead ahead of the plane was Midway. If the pilot thought he was about to land, the communications officer on the other ship knew the pilot was lining up on the wrong ship.

The pilot, likely exhausted, had been trying to land on the wrong ship. He failed to notice Midway's smoke stack that was an obvious clue the carrier wasn't the pilot's nuclear-powered carrier. He failed to recognize Midway's unique set of arresting wires and a much smaller landing area. Mind-numbing exhaustion had become the Desert Storm enemy that threatened American lives.

Air boss Pudas' eyes burned. He had rarely slept more than 15 minutes at a stretch in the early weeks of Desert Storm as Midway's jets thundered toward the enemy day and night. A typical strike package numbered 25 aircraft including the bombers, escorts, command-and-control aircraft, and tankers. With only two catapults ("really, one catapult and a spare"), one of Pudas' nightmares was an equipment breakdown that delayed a launch. Even a small leak in a jet blast deflector system could take a catapult down. At one point in Desert Storm, Midway met its day's missions with only one operational catapult. Jets roared down one catapult while a repair crew frantically worked on the other, only a few yards away.

After three weeks of nonstop operations, part of Midway's flight deck glistened in the Gulf sun. Much of the nonskid coating on the port side had been worn off. Midway's deck became so slippery that Pudas watched in horror as a stationary A-6 Intruder slid across the deck during a relatively benign Midway roll. On occasion Midway's rolling became so severe that Pudas called out the swells' degrees to the plane handlers on the flight deck so they could time their relocation of aircraft to the passing crests and avoid losing an aircraft over the side. It was necessary choreography unique to Midway, made worse by the worn nonskid surface.

Pudas and Captain Cebrowski faced a critical decision: replace the nonskid at sea so Midway would be operational for the imminent ground war or take a chance and stay on the line flying combat missions under dangerous conditions. As the air resource coordinator for the Persian Gulf, Cebrowski knew the Navy's carriers had been "under tasked" by the Air Force war planners. So Cebrowski took a calculated risk. Confident the other carriers could shoulder the Navy's load, he took Midway off the line. Exhausted crews could enjoy a brief respite as others scrambled to apply new nonskid so Midway would be ready when the ground assault came.

Pudas called other carriers to find surplus nonskid as the flight deck's chiefs got to work, figuring out how to prepare the deck in the middle of the ocean. Helicopters soon appeared inbound from the horizon, delivering cans of the thick nonskid liquid asphalt to be applied to the steel deck. It took only six days before Midway was ready to rejoin Desert Storm. A maintenance operation that normally took a month or more in port was accomplished in less than a week at sea. No one could remember an instance where a carrier had successfully installed nonskid in combat.

As Midway reentered the war, air boss Pudas still worried about a variety of complications that could produce a "locked deck" preventing the recovery of aircraft when they returned to Midway. Backup plans always churned in Pudas's mind. If a helicopter's fold-up blades locked in the down position, he was prepared to amputate a blade or even push the helo over the side if safe recovery of aircraft required it. At night, he worried about exhausted young men walking into propellers or tumbling down the deck in the wash of a jet's exhaust. Midway's rigid nonskid flight deck surface was notorious for ripping skin and tearing muscle from bone. It was Pudas' job to keep that from happening. He converted a small workspace near Pri-Fly into sleeping quarters and outfitted it with a monitor so periodically he could close his eyes for 15 minutes while staying connected to the flight deck and the war over the horizon. For many on Midway, Desert Storm was an intense marathon. For the air boss of Midway, it was an unending series of split-second decisions driven by timing and anticipation. If any were wrong, men could die.

Exhaustion threatened the lives of men on the flight deck as well, including aviation electrician's mate Shane Dulansky. Only 18, he was less than half the age of Midway. For as long as he could remember, Dulansky had wanted to follow in the footsteps of his grandfather who had been in the Navy from the 1920s into World War II and an uncle who had served as a Navy aviation mechanic.

Slight and with intense dark eyes, his transition to shipboard life had been a rocky one. Dulansky had joined the air wing in the Philippines in early 1989. Within two hours of reporting at NAS Cubi Point, Dulansky had watched a bomber-navigator burn to death in a flight line fueling accident. The bright, gleaming jets Dulansky had admired in movies were nowhere to be found. Instead, he was assigned to real-world carrier aircraft that were smeared greasy and primer gray. Dulansky wondered what he had gotten himself into. His initial doubts grew into outright consternation on Midway.

The two communities that coexisted on the flight deck of Midway sometimes clashed in the heat of battle. The squadrons of pilots and aircraft maintenance personnel intermingled with the flight deck personnel that fueled, armed, troubleshot, and prepared aircraft for launch. The squadrons' maintenance crews generally looked down on the flight deck crew, believing they didn't have what it took to qualify for a squadron assignment. It sometimes made for tense and occasionally combative confrontations.

Often Dulansky found himself on the flight deck, head inside a plane, frantically repairing a malfunctioning electrical circuit as its pilot grew anxious to launch. On occasion Dulansky perched on the jet's tail or rear portion of the fuselage out over the water as the plane sat at flight deck's edge. Worried about being knocked into water 50 feet below and being sucked under the carrier to a near-certain death, he usually had only minutes to remedy a problem or face the wrath of a pilot for a "downed" plane.

Meanwhile others were being ordered by flight deck control to move aircraft in a tightly timed ballet to keep planes launching and to clear the deck in time for recovery. The needs of traffic control were sometimes counter to the priorities of squadron maintenance. It wasn't uncommon to see a squadron aviation electrician scooting under the belly of an aircraft, head and arms unseen inside the fuselage, as an aircraft handler directed it toward a catapult. Fistfights sometimes broke out between air wing mechanics and the flight deck crew, each answering to their master.

Those conflicts took place in a brutal desert environment. JP-5 jet fuel burned eyes despite goggle protection. Flight deck crews often walked with a hand on a moving aircraft's drop tank, their head down so that the grains of flight deck nonskid coating blasted into the air by jet exhaust bounced off their cranials instead of burrowing into their unprotected faces. Greenhorns quickly learned to listen to the word of the all-knowing—the air boss—especially on Midway. A sharply rolling deck could flip a man into the sea or push him into a jet's searing exhaust blast before he could react. Midway's flight deck crew knew to practically stop in their tracks when they heard the air boss say "ship to port, heel to starboard" in their headsets. They knew to instantly "get planted" on the deck as Midway turned across seas that could send men flying and aircraft skidding toward the six-inch-square berm at the edge of the flight deck.

After six weeks of Desert Storm air assaults, more than 1,700 tanks, nearly 1,000 armored personnel carriers, and almost 1,500 artillery pieces had been destroyed. Desert Storm's final phase depended upon deception. The ground offensive included a fake amphibious assault. Midway supported the feint, navigating through more than 1,000 enemy mines laid in two broad belts off southeastern Iraq. The day before the bogus invasion from the sea might begin, Midway pilots pounded coastal and nearby island targets close to where the amphibious landings were to take place. The strategy was so effective that 11 Iraqi divisions comprised of nearly 80,000 men dug in to repel the phantom landings. Nearly half of Iraq's artillery pointed toward the coast, away from the actual American assault.

On February 24, a gruesome end to Desert Storm appeared in the crosshairs of Midway fighters as they streaked through a hazy night sky. They peered through gooey smoke rising above burning oil fields to find the string of headlights of retreating Iraqis heading north. Six weeks earlier, Midway pilots had bombed communication towers, bunkers, and aircraft. Now they bombed men walking home through the desert. Time and again Midway pilots lined up on "the road of death" that led toward Basra, Iraq, obliterating a beaten army.

At 0430 on February 27, sweat and exhaustion caked BK #10, generally considered the most decrepit of Midway's WWII-era bunkrooms. It was carpeted with remnants of long-forgotten origins and the overhead was crammed with cables, wires, and piping. It looked more like the inside of a boiler than a place to live. Junior officers trudged out of BK#10 on their way to another flight brief. As they turned from the harshly lit passageway into their ready room, their eyes widened and then locked onto the closed-circuit television. "REJOICE, WE ARE VICTORIOUS."

Desert Storm was over. Peace closed Midway's final combat chapter, one in which the 46-year-old carrier had set a new standard in naval aviation. The Navy's smallest and oldest carrier, Midway was the only one of the six American aircraft carriers in Desert Storm not to lose an aircraft. Midway had flown more sorties per aircraft per day than any other Navy carrier— despite being limited by having only two catapults. Midway aviators flew 3,019 sorties and had dropped more than four million pounds of ordnance in the air campaign. Day in and day out, Midway had met its mission, just as it had 25 years earlier off the coast of Vietnam. Midway's crew had made good on Cebrowski's promise to Desert Storm's skeptical carrier captains.

As Midway passed the Hormuz Strait on its way home to Yokosuka, all 12 boilers were on line. Midway steamed at 30 knots, nearly the same speed its boilers produced almost 50 years earlier. Soon Midway's fighters and ordnance would be replaced with refugees, diapers, and pet food.

Ed Lawton, an investigator with the Office of Special Investigations, arrived at Clark Air Base in the Philippines as spring warmed to summer in early June 1991. The father of three tried to focus on his caseload of unsolved crimes and counterespionage operations. He had undergone surgery and six months of aggressive radiation treatments, and was making an arduous recovery.

Only eight miles away, Mt. Pinatubo was awakening from more than 600 years' dormancy. Steam had been billowing from new vents since April. On June 9, a low-level eruption powered a column of ash into the sky. The next morning, Lawton turned on his television to learn "it was the real deal, the evacuation was on." He and 16,000 others must evacuate. Now. Everyone was limited to one suitcase each. Pets must be left behind, although evacuees were told they probably could return to Clark Air Base in three days once Mt. Pinatubo settled.

Those with cars drove to the flight line where caravans formed to make the run to Naval Air Station Cubi Point near Subic Bay Naval Base, three hours away. As the sun rose on the 10th, hundreds of vehicles snaked their way out of Clark onto the McArthur Highway for the 40-mile trek to Olongapo City and the adjacent Navy base. The rough road jarred nerves and the switchbacks near Olongapo taxed engines and patience.

As the evacuee families settled in at NAS Cubi Point, a sense of calm returned. Perhaps they could return to Clark sooner than expected. Only three days later, Mt. Pinatubo shattered. More than 1,000 feet of the 5,725-foot volcano disappeared in a massive explosion that left a half-mile-wide crater. Lava and ash rocketed into the upper atmosphere, ultimately reaching 22 miles above and around the earth. Only hours after the eruption, typhoon Yunya passed within 30 miles of the billowing cloud of ash and lava. Tropical moisture mixed with volcanic ash to create an airborne cement that crushed virtually everything it touched.

The earth shook for eight hours as panicked Olongapo residents fled and the Air Force evacuees at NAS Cubi Point huddled in uncertainty. An unnatural cloud of ash spread over the nearly abandoned Clark Air Base and then NAS Cubi Point on what became known as "Black Saturday." Within hours the roofs of nearly 60 Navy buildings collapsed. A gray, ashen snowfall deepened to a foot on aircraft, turning the Navy base into a dusty moonscape. Electrical lines snapped and palm fronds slumped under the pressure of liquid ash. An eerie, dusky light enveloped the frightened refugees. The Navy base was no longer safe.

While the evacuees sought refuge from the suffocating ash, in Japan Midway's department heads were summoned to a meeting by a commanding officer most had barely met. Only three days earlier, a West Virginian who had seen air combat in Vietnam became the 40th and last captain of Midway. As Art Cebrowski's replacement, Larry Ernst possessed the same penetrating blue eyes, solid jaw, and strong, confident nose. Long and lean, he was demanding yet gregarious. He had a reputation as a fighter pilot's fighter pilot. He was an aircraft carrier captain from central casting.

Ernst grew up worshipping fighter ace and legendary test pilot Chuck Yeager. After his father died when Ernst was nine, his mother raised three children in the hilly coal mining country of southern West Virginia. As high school graduation neared, Ernst faced the prospect of joining thousands of other West Virginia hillbillies who counted only two options in life: go to work in nearby coal mining camps, or head northwest to Ohio to find work in a foundry or manufacturing plant. But a high school counselor set Ernst on a life path that led to Midway. He enrolled the youngster in a Navy ROTC program. Outstanding test scores led to a scholarship at a college of Ernst's choosing. Not having given college much thought, he turned to a friend for ideas. He suggested Ohio State University because the school had a good football team led by a cantankerous coach named Woody Hayes. That was good enough for Ernst who later earned his wings in 1967.

It was his mission over the ensuing 10 months to prepare Midway for decommissioning and for transfer to the Navy's Ready Reserve Fleet in the backwaters of Bremerton, Washington. Those plans, though, soon veered south.

Shortly after the change of command ceremony, Ernst assembled his senior officers to discuss the possibility of a rescue mission to the Philippines. Could Midway respond quickly enough? Ernst was taken aback at the response. Department heads immediately began planning a rescue mission in the absence of orders. It wasn't a question of "if" but "how." Supply chiefs scoured Yokosuka for cots, diapers, extra food, medical supplies, linen, and even pet food. Ernst's XO, John Schork, plotted how to accommodate possibly thousands of evacuee families on the hangar deck. The medical department identified five specialists at Yokosuka Naval Hospital who could be assigned to Midway if needed. Midway Magic, decades in the making, had created a perpetual energy that transcended changes of command.

Only three days after assuming command, Ernst was ordered to take Midway to the Philippines. American lives were at risk. Through the night of June 16, Midway loaded enough emergency supplies to accommodate 5,000 refugees for up to two weeks. Hundreds of sailors passed more than

1,000 cots, baby diapers, pet food, and personal items aboard only hours before Midway headed south. By the time Midway left Yokosuka the following morning, more than 200,000 people had been forced from their homes in the Philippines. Midway and 22 other ships, including the Navy's newest carrier, the Abraham Lincoln, steamed toward rescue.

By that time, Ed Lawton was living in desolation at NAS Cubi Point. Aircraft on the flight line sat low in the rear, blanketed by hundreds of pounds of wet ash, their noses up in the air. Barges in the bay had sunk under tons of raining ash. Since his arrival from Clark Air Base, Lawton had helped Navy criminal investigators burn classified documents inside a toppled 12-foot gray metal locker in preparation for a second evacuation in less than a week. It was nearly soundless outside. Birds had disappeared. The coating of wet ash deadened life's cacophony of wildlife, vehicles, people, and work. Every few minutes a slow crackling sound cut through the dead air when a palm tree imploded under the pressure of the raining ash.

As the Navy's relief force arrived off the coast on June 21, Lawton and thousands of others picked up their suitcases and climbed onto a bus headed for the pier. Lawton didn't know his destination was Midway. Choking on the ash, he stood alone waiting to board the next bus for the pier. Earlier his family had been ordered to the docks for immediate evacuation aboard the Abraham Lincoln. He would have find and catch up to them later.

When Lawton arrived at the dock, Midway stood ready. A suffocating heat draped the bay and floating ash caught in the back of throats as the line of evacuees crawled forward onto Midway's hangar deck. Most evacuees were dressed only in a T-shirt, shorts, and sandals, one suitcase in tow. As Lawton and others stepped onto Midway, they were flabbergasted by what they saw. Midway sailors sat at rows of tables ready to process each refugee. The exhaustion that had creased their faces melted into surprise, relief, and then gratitude.

After each evacuee was processed, a Midway sailor escorted him or her to anything they needed. An observant Midway crewman noticed Lawton walking gingerly. When he learned of Lawton's ongoing recovery, arrangements were immediately made for him to bunk down in officers' country. Many refugees were hungry. Anticipating that, one end of the hangar bay had been converted into "Ernst's Eatery" where steak dinners awaited them. Some asked to send messages home to loved ones and then were escorted back to a hangar bay awash in groups of cots that stretched the length of two football fields. Near the middle, an oversized American flag hung from the ceiling, gently rocking above the heads of exhausted evacuees as they collapsed onto empty cots and pulled up clean blankets.

More than 1,820 evacuees slept aboard Midway that night. Many thought pets had been banned but had smuggled them to the pier in hopes of talking their way on board. Midway's officers had anticipated pets. As a result, 23 cats, 68 dogs, and one lizard accompanied their owners onto the carrier. For the only time in 46 years, yaps, yelps, and meows could be heard aboard Midway.

The next day Midway left Subic Bay for Cebu Island. The evacuees slept, oblivious to the drama that unfolded up on the bridge as Midway ferried them out of danger. Ernst had slept for only a few minutes at a time since Midway headed south on its rescue mission. Like every captain before him, he had learned to take 10-minute naps while sitting in the captain's chair on the bridge. As Midway steamed full speed toward Cebu in anticipation of returning for another load of evacuees, the carrier was forced to slalom through dozens of small native fishing boats as it wove through the narrow passages of the Philippine archipelago. Most bonka boats refused to get out of Midway's path so Ernst and the navigator used the carrier's bow wave to gently push them aside as Midway steamed toward Cebu Island.

Upright in his chair, Ernst had closed his eyes. Within minutes, the hair on the back of his neck rose. Ernst awoke to see a cruiser's red mast lights emerge from behind a massive rock outcropping. It was on a collision course with Midway. "Hard right rudder!" yelled Ernst. "Belay that order," countered the navigator without looking up, confident in his charts, calculations, and heading. "THIS IS THE CAPTAIN, HARD RIGHT RUDDER NOW!!!"

Ernst was relying on his instincts as a fighter pilot. His training had honed an ability to instantly assess the relative motion of independent objects, an essential skill for survival in the cockpit of a supersonic jet fighter. Ernst didn't need to look at charts or check a course. He had opened his eyes and instantly knew his aircraft carrier was in imminent danger of collision. Midway heeled hard as it turned, the cruiser's mast nearly grazing the edge of Midway's flight deck as it passed into the night. The evacuees below never knew how close they came to a collision at sea after fleeing a volcano's eruption.

Arrangements were made to fly the evacuees from Cebu Island to Guam and on to the United States. Ed Lawton made his way to Fairchild Air Force Base in Washington, and finally his father's house in Santa Monica, California. Ironically, his Philippine-born wife and children had not left Cebu Island for the United States as Lawton assumed they would in his race to catch up to them. It was two months before the Lawton family was reunited.

The impact of Midway on those evacuees would last a lifetime. Captain Ernst received a letter from one evacuee who had finally made it home to Universal City, Texas. Air Force Sergeant Thomas J. Schatz wrote:

> ". . . what I witnessed (aboard Midway) in my humble opinion, was above the extraordinary. Not only were normal shipboard duties taken care of, so were all our needs. When asked for information, it was explained clearly and when asked for assistance, it was executed into action immediately even though fatigue could be seen (in your crew's) minds and bodies . . . Let them know that because of their example, if I ever encounter a U.S. sailor in need of any sort of assistance, no matter how inconvenient it might be for me to render it, I will do it gladly and without hesitation. God bless and Godspeed USS Midway . . ."

Midway both saved and changed lives.

Two months later a white banner in Yokosuka stretched nearly the length of the officers' brow from the ship to the deck of Pier 12. Bright blue letters read "Sayonara Japan." After nearly 18 years as America's only carrier homeported in a foreign country, Midway pulled out of Yokosuka for the last time on August 10, 1991.

Midway had become an institution in the Japanese culture. Thousands of shipyard workers had spent their entire careers maintaining and overhauling the aircraft carrier. Midway's performance was considered a direct reflection of their devotion to duty and craftsmanship. Japanese fathers had taught sons how to maintain the increasingly sophisticated equipment aboard Midway. They had taught them how to get onto the ship even before the crew disembarked to take advantage of every inport minute before Midway pulled out of Yokosuka and back into a Tokyo Bay channel that was usually as congested as a Los Angeles freeway.

As the helicopters followed Midway out of Yokosuka the last time, Ernst and his crew had planned one last tribute to their gracious hosts. Nearly 400 Midway sailors in dress whites assembled on Midway's flight deck in a tight, block formation. Like a Big 10 college marching band, standing shoulder to shoulder they spelled "SAYONARA" for the news crews that hovered above. The final image on Japanese television that night was of hundreds of Midway sailors, many of them teenagers, paying their respects to a people some of their fathers had fought to the death little more than a generation earlier.

Most sailors had been dragged kicking and screaming to Midway in Japan, unhappy at being forward deployed far from home, and doomed to one of the oldest carriers in the fleet. More often than not, when it came time to rotate off Midway, they were dragged kicking and screaming after succumbing to both the special relationship Midway had forged with Japan and to the daring role Midway had played at the "tip of the sword" in the Pacific. In six of Midway's last 10 years in Japan, it posted the highest reenlistment rate of any carrier in the fleet.

But Midway's time had passed. The U.S. Navy faced the prospect of reducing its carrier fleet from 14 to 12. The future lay in nuclear carriers. Midway had become a relic that no longer was cost-effective for a Navy fighting for every Congressional appropriation dollar. Naval aviation technology had bypassed Midway as well. Hugely expensive modernizations had enabled the carrier to keep pace with advances in technology for nearly five decades. They extended the carrier's life to 47 years, well beyond the most ambitious predictions of the planners who had designed the Midway class in the early days of World War II. Its two sister carriers, the Coral Sea and Franklin D. Roosevelt, had been scrapped years earlier. The costly modernizations of Midway had proven to be too expensive and thus doomed them to the scrap yard in 1990 and 1977, respectively. It was time for Midway to come home and step aside.

The old man shuffled toward two Midway sailors. He barely had enough strength to make it up the brow from the Seattle waterfront onto Midway. They stepped forward and each took an elbow to help him aboard. A stained and ragged 1955 Midway cruisebook was pinched under his arm, its bamboo cover design worn nearly bare. He was visiting his old ship for the first time in nearly 40 years. He was crying.

Shortly before midnight on September 4, 1991, Midway had entered Puget Sound. Midway's navigator carefully positioned the carrier at the mouth of the 120-mile-long Strait of Juan de Fuca that ended at Elliott Bay and Seattle. Midway had made its way at 16 knots through a passage renowned for its congested fishing nets and ground fog. Out ahead, a helicopter scouted for fishing boats as the sky awakened in the east. A sight emerged that brought conversations short. A flawless sunrise revealed a majestic Mt. Rainer, dead ahead. The crew silently stared. They were home. Midway soon would tie up for a six-day liberty visit and a three-day open house.

Midway was destined for a dingy, industrial area of Seattle. Rusty, ocean-going containers littered the waterfront, far from the brightly polished Seattle emmbarcadero that greeted gleaming white cruise ships and tourists. Midway officers wondered aloud who would go out of their way to see an old aircraft carrier destined for the scrap heap. The old man and more than 50,000 other Pacific Northwest residents did. Lines on the waterfront stretched inland between grim buildings as the locals waited patiently to come aboard.

After Desert Storm, most American carriers had returned home to an enormous outpouring of American public support and appreciation. Only Midway had left the combat theater destined for a foreign country. Upon arrival in Japan, the carrier had been met by families and the usual handful of diehard Japanese protesters. In Seattle, tens of thousands walked aboard and gazed across the massive hangar deck. They stood on the worn, rippled flight deck and thought back to the television news reports broadcast from Persian Gulf carriers that prompted some Air Force officers to call CNN the Carrier News Network. Several stopped the first Midway sailor they saw and simply said "thank you." Some were overwhelmed with memories from another lifetime when they had discovered manhood aboard Midway. As old Midway sailors left the carrier for the last time, young men 50 years their junior prepared to take Midway to its funeral.

On September 14 Midway turned to the east and entered San Diego Bay. Off to port were restricted Navy facilities perched on the side of the Pt. Loma peninsula. At water's edge the ominous black nuclear submarine silhouettes floated motionless in their pens. Off to starboard, jets thundered back toward the west, taking off from NAS North Island out over the Pacific and within sight of Mexico, only a few miles away. Midway stayed centered in the narrow deep-draft channel, passing large concrete blocks that rose out of the water. Crusty from neglect, they had been built in the shock-filled days following Pearl Harbor so San Diego's massive Navy fleet could be moored at the mouth of the harbor and flee to open water if Japan attacked San Diego. Midway would be retired in a city fiercely proud of its Navy heritage.

Exactly 46 years and four days from the moment Midway joined the Navy fleet as the world's largest and most powerful warship, it completed its last major mission. As it settled alongside a NAS North Island pier, the time neared for a final inspection, mummification, and removal from active duty.

It was Captain Ernst's job to gut Midway. Together with Executive Officer John Schork, he would lead the six-month process that would end with Midway's decommissioning. It was a massive job and one that Schork, the son of a Navy captain and who had been born in Yokosuka, found bittersweet. Trained as an A-6 Intruder pilot, he and Ernst earlier served aboard one of Midway's sister ships, the Coral Sea.

But before work began in earnest, Midway went to sea one last time on September 24. The Navy wanted a precise reading of the old carrier's capabilities before it was prepared for retirement. So Midway's boilers were lit once more as the crew and 100 inspectors readied themselves for two days of drills off San Diego, not far from Mexico's Coronado Islands. The tests were brutal. Inspectors ordered flank speed for hours at a stretch and then an emergency stop. Just as Midway's power plant had performed in the aftermath of World War II, it shot a bone-jarring shudder through the ship as Midway bit into the water and its wake boiled white. Every piston, circuit, and pump on board measured up to the seagoing demands of the inspectors.

By the end of the day, the inspection team was overwhelmed. Though Midway's fate was certain, the inspectors found Midway ready and capable of continued service. On the bridge, an inspection admiral turned to Ernst. "We have two-year-old nuclear carriers that can't do all that Midway did today. Be proud."

"Does that complete the inspection, sir?" asked Ernst. It did. Midway completed a two-day inspection in one glorious, late-summer day off San Diego. Ernst ordered flank speed. Midway's boilers bulled the carrier through the water one last time at the same 33 knots they had first achieved on Midway's shakedown cruise five decades earlier. Rear Admiral Joseph Prueher, the last flag officer aboard Midway, was moved, noting that after more than 47 years, "Midway sprinted across the finish line."

The sun had set behind Midway, pink spilling across the horizon as Midway plowed toward San Diego's skyline, barely visible through the deepening near-violet marine haze. The Indian summer wind that swept Midway's deck softened as the carrier slowed to enter San Diego Bay the last time. As Midway passed the Pt. Loma Lighthouse and once again approached the submarine pens, hundreds of Midway's loudspeakers erupted with Aaron Copland's haunting and majestic "Fanfare for the Common Man," composed in the dark days of World War II. It had become Midway's official UNREP song. It would play one last time the following spring.

When Ernst and Schork first saw the plans to prepare Midway for decommissioning, they were surprised to see the work assigned to civilian contractors while nearly 2,000 Midway sailors, intimately familiar with every hatch, space, and bulkhead, were being rotated off the ship or dumped into the domestic job market. Ernst devised a plan that staggered the reassignment of Midway sailors, enabling many to complete various aspects of the shutdown process and thereby save taxpayers an estimated $10 million. Plan approved.

Ernst moved quickly to implement it. He was a demanding skipper, believing he set a high standard of performance by "getting what you inspect, not what you expect." Yet he necessarily leaned heavily on his department heads as the process to hermetically seal Midway from the outside world got under way. Each of the 2,000 compartments was systematically stripped bare. Large "tri-walls," four-foot-by-four-foot boxes on the hangar deck, were filled with tens of thousands of items. Electronic gear was pulled from its brackets, some of it destined for the next new Navy carrier, the George Washington, scheduled for commissioning on July 4, 1992. Galleys that had produced 13,000 meals a day grew hollow as countless pieces of cooking equipment were hauled away. The massive catapult system was pulled out of the ship's chest, dismantled, and stacked on the hangar deck. Literally tons of books, manuals, and documents were sorted, cataloged, packed, or destroyed.

Crews started aft and forward, high in the island and at the keel, and worked toward the center of the ship. As each compartment, repair shop, ready room, and berthing space was cleaned out, both a Navy and civilian inspector had to sign off before that space was sealed. Sometimes letters to sons and pictures of wives were discovered tucked into berthing space crevices, dusty and worn reminders of how Midway stretched families across generations and half the world:

> *Hi Son,*
> *We love you and miss you a lot. It was sure nice talking to you. It was sure hot here today. It was real hot here yesterday. It has cooled down quite a bit since a couple of days ago. It won't be long before school starts. Dad goes on nights starting Monday, Aug. 31.*
> *How come you will be out at sea only a few weeks? That seems like a short time. You sure are seeing the world. We got your letter and postcard today. It sure is pretty. How far are you from Tokyo? Have you ever rode the bullet train? Bet it would be fun to ride.*
> *Our garden is just about all gone now. A few tomatoes left, but not many. Well, I will close for now and write when you have some time. We love and miss you a lot. Thank you for all the postcards. It is sure nice that you can send some home to let us see what it is like over there. Bye for now.*
> *Love you very much and miss you,*
> *Dad & Mom*

Meanwhile other crews sucked standing water out of the ship and sealed valves and pumps. Some dressed Midway with a final coat of paint, sealing the rust of age. Others painted a heavy fiberglass mixture called "lagging" onto pipes and ductwork to encase asbestos-laden insulation and to coat areas that had been chipped bare. Desiccant material was installed to pull moisture from the air in Midway. Slowly, inexorably, Midway was being eviscerated, dehydrated, and sealed with the meticulous care of an Egyptian king being prepared for the next life.

At dusk, Schork periodically walked Midway after the decommissioning crew had disembarked. The former aviator sometimes stopped in one of Midway's squadron ready rooms. Decals and stickers were the only remnants of hundreds of highly trained and supremely confident young men who had once sat in easy chairs during briefs and then debriefs after punching holes in the skies over the Mediterranean, Sea of Japan, Vietnam, Indian Ocean, the Arctic, and Iraq. Schork stood quietly, enveloped by the emptiness. He listened to the men who had sailed and flown before him. His skin tingled at the intimacy and history that no coat of paint could hide, no desiccant could suck into arid stillness.

An eerie, vapid hollowness spread as compartment after compartment was sealed and with it the souls, dreams, and life's memories of the young men who had occupied each. Spaces once filled with voices were draped in a silence sometimes fractured by a creak or groan, the death rattles of Midway. As the scope of work shrank, so, too, did Midway's crew. Each week, fewer men hiked across the brow to work inside a ship that grew more solemn with each passing day. As each sailor left Midway the last time, another slice of the carrier's soul went with him.

As the work progressed, Hangar Bay One received special treatment. XO Schork wanted it museum quality. He ordered the chief responsible for the area to make absolutely sure every fitting was polished, every surface painted. Hangar Bay One—the front door for most visitors who came aboard Midway—was to sparkle for years to come. In fact, before Midway was decommissioned, its senior officers speculated that perhaps someday it would become a museum or at least be open to the public. Ernst and Schork made sure much of Midway's memorabilia was transferred to warehouses at the nearby Naval Training Center for possible display in the future.

December 24, 1991 was a silent night aboard Midway. Only a year earlier Midway and its crew had stood a post in the middle of the Persian Gulf, nerves made ragged by the din of imminent war. After leading naval aviation's charge in Desert Storm, Midway had raced to the rescue of thousands of Americans fleeing one of the largest volcanic eruptions of the twentieth century. The carrier had then returned home to be stripped and preserved in case another mission summoned her. Now Midway sat silent. All that remained was the final goodbye.

A PUFFY GRAY SKY HUNG OVER Coronado Island early on the morning of April 11, 1992, the last day Midway would be an operating warship of the U.S. Navy. Connnected to San Diego by a sweeping bridge, Coronado was home to Naval Air Station North Island. There, Midway rested.

NAS North Island had a long-standing claim, albeit disputed by some Norfolk boosters, to being the birthplace of naval aviation. The first military flight school had been established there in 1911. To prepare naval aviators for the advent of carriers, a wooden deck the size of an early carrier was built on the ground to provide realistic training for pilots in biplanes. It wasn't long before North Island regularly posted naval aviation firsts that included the first seaplane flight, night flight, midair refueling between two planes, amphibian flight, and the first use of a radio in an aircraft. It was a fitting location to decommission what was once the nation's most pioneering sophisticated carrier.

As the sky lightened, a heavy, reflective sadness awaited thousands prepared to make the short pilgrimage to the pier where patriotic bunting along Midway's rails sagged in the salty morning air. The red, white, and blue trim was reminiscent of a similar backdrop 47 years and one month earlier when Midway had been christened.

Among them, four pilots who collectively bracketed Midway's history braced themselves for the mission to say a proper goodbye. Admiral Riley

Mixson who lorded over Midway's blister experiment in the mid-1980s would pay his last respects. The soft-spoken Georgian had commanded a carrier group in the Red Sea during Desert Storm little more than a year earlier. One of Midway's most renowned 1970s Vietnam combat pilots, Mugs McKeown, would soon take his seat in the audience. The former commander of Top Gun, infamous among friends for his ability to make up jokes, was even more widely recognized for a quote attributed to him: *"Beware the lessons of a fighter pilot who would rather fly a slide rule than kick your ass."* Dick Parker lived less than two miles from Midway's berth. The lanky aviator who first flew aboard Midway on Halloween Day 1945 in time for Operation Frostbite was among the 5,200 people who had been invited to the decommissioning. The fourth was a man who had awkwardly shared the christening podium deep under Midway's bow, George Gay. The famed survivor from the Battle of Midway would make one of his last public appearances. He would sit on display in front of more than 3,000 spectators that included dignitaries from Japan. Their presence made Gay and some of the other World War II veterans uncomfortable. Battle scars stretched across the decades.

The men who first nurtured Midway's soul in an era of Helldivers and the sons who flew Midway's supersonic Hornets dressed with care to reflect, say goodbye, and forever close a life's chapter.

Meanwhile, several hundred Midway sailors—most of them less than half the average age of the audience—donned dress blues and white hats before the short walk to Midway. Many would be manning the rail of Midway. Tall, erect, and motionless, most would stand precisely arm's length apart, high above the pier on the flight deck and outside passageways. NAS North Island personnel mobilized to direct the imminent crush of thousands of civilian vehicles.

By midmorning, the overcast yielded to a bright San Diego spring sun. The daily Pacific breeze that swept across the Navy base began to build, breathing life into the bunting, pennants, and flags that surrounded Midway. The sun sparkled on the line of cars leaving San Diego, rising up onto the sky-blue bridge and then gently descending in a sweeping arc to starboard, on final approach to Coronado Island's tollbooths. Bumper to bumper, they taxied down Third Street and jogged half a block to the main gate of NAS North Island. Those with their invitation in hand were met with a snap salute and instructions to drive from one uniformed sailor to the next, leading to the parking area. The sun warmed as the parking area filled and people in hushed tones walked toward a silent Midway.

More than 30 rows of seats, each nearly the length of Midway's 1,000-foot flight deck, awaited them on the pier. Some were reserved for dignitaries and special guests. Every living former skipper of Midway except one had confirmed plans to attend. A special area had been reserved for a remarkable group of men. Some arrived alone. Most were escorted by younger family members who slowed their pace to stay even. The old men were original "plankowners" of Midway, sailors who had been part of the 1945 commissioning crew. They were young men who had taken Midway above the Arctic Circle in winter to test planes in ice and snow. Men who months later shuddered when a captured German V-2 rocket rumbled off the stern, unsure if Midway would withstand its massive thrust. They had stood at the dawn of naval missile warfare. Some had reached manhood aboard Midway. Others had already learned life in the stench of war. Many had left Midway to return to their boyhood neighborhood to live the next 40 years carving out careers as private investigators, power plant operators, and insurance brokers.

More than 46 years later, nearly 50 of them had made a personal pilgrimage to San Diego. From Rochester and Savannah, from Missoula and Flagstaff. Some were in wheelchairs. Many sat listing to one side, favoring one painful hip or the other. Their jackets draped spare frames, a Windsor knot at their Adam's apple, and an ill-fitting virgin USS Midway ball cap slightly askew.

Near the podium, Captain Larry Ernst and his XO, John Schork, scanned the pier as it filled. Above them Midway's skeletonized crew stood the rails near the painted silhouettes of North Vietnamese MiGs shot down by Midway aviators. Navy officials took their seats on one side of the on the dais. George Gay settled into his seat on the other side, nearly alone and hidden behind dark glasses and a Midway hat pulled low on his brow. The decommissioning ceremony was about to take on a life of its own. The weeks of drills were over and if there were to be any glitches, the point of anticipating and avoiding them had long passed.

Captain Ernst took a deep breath to calm the butterflies in his stomach as he stepped up to the microphone. Confident in front of his men, he had never faced a more intimidating public speaking task. He was about to reenact a ceremony that dated back to the 1600s when a British admiral first hoisted a horsewhip as a threatening gesture against the Dutch, an act that gave rise to a ship's commissioning pennant as its symbolic heartbeat. The crowd gazed up at Ernst and behind him, at a towering Midway as the sun bounced off the bay and danced on its hull.

In his most commanding voice, he welcomed dignitaries and announced the lineup of speakers. Midway took on a human personality as Ernst and subsequent speakers spoke of its history. Crew and ship became one. Mission and mantra blended into a single persona called "Midway Magic." It became she.

"Born in war, she is retiring in peace," said Admiral Robert Kelly, commander of the Navy's Pacific Fleet. "That is an enviable accomplishment for any warship. While peace is closer than ever in our lifetime, the battle is not won," he said, noting the threat of global war had been replaced by regional hostility. The Secretary of the Navy, H. Lawrence Garrett, said much the same, "offering an emotional farewell. Midway has done her part. She is ready to stand down and retire. The Midway legend will be remembered years from now by the American Navy."

Time and again, speakers' comments turned to people. Captain Ernst talked of Midway's origins as a battle carrier, born at a time when the enemy was pummeling the American Navy. He turned to George Gay, asked him to stand and be acknowledged for his heroism in the Battle of Midway "that brought the fighter cover down to the deck and allowed unopposed American dive bombers to set three Japanese carriers ablaze in less than five minutes." As Gay stood, a breeze played with his tie. He nodded at the ripple of polite applause before sitting down.

Ernst concluded with a personal reflection about Midway's final mission, one that rescued the evacuees from the Mt. Pinatubo volcanic eruption in the Philippines less than a year earlier. "When the refugees walked on board and into the bright lights of Midway, they were treated to a steak dinner and a cheery smile from Midway sailors. I've never been prouder of men under my command. I learned 'Midway Magic' is not an empty catch phrase. Midway Magic is an amazing ability to excel. No matter what the odds, or how great the opposition, or how difficult the task. Midway Magic is real and I'm grateful for having had the opportunity to share in it."

With nothing left to say, no chronicle of Midway left to relive, it was time to decommission the 41st aircraft carrier of the U.S. Navy. It was time to draw 47 years of service to a close. Ernst's voice began to soften as he ordered his executive officer to execute the act of decommissioning, "Executive

Officer, take charge. March off the crew, haul down the pennants and the colors, secure the watch." His voice had waned to little more than whisper.

"Midway, atte-e-e-n-hut! Inboard face. March off!" Hundreds of sailors turned on their heel as the Navy band's horn section and kettle-drums struck the majestic "Fanfare for the Common Man" one last time. Young men, ramrod erect, eyes ahead, followed each other down the fore and aft gangways onto the pier. In perfect precision they marched into a block formation near the crowd, their eyes never wavering from dead ahead. As they stood at attention, three World War II–era SNJ Texan train-ers split the sky overhead, a haunting reminder of the era in which Midway's keel first touched salt water. Soon two 1942 F4F Wildcats passed overhead. For a few moments, Midway bathed in the sounds of a war it had missed by one week. As they disappeared into the marine haze, "Fanfare" crested into a crescendo and then settled into silence.

Unnoticed by most, Ernst had left the podium. He reappeared up on Midway, frozen in salute, looking almost straight up as two crewmen low-ered Midway's commissioning pennant, the National Ensign and Union Jack. As they descended the main, a bugler aft on Midway began playing the chilling 24 notes of Taps. A half-beat later, a lone bugler on the bow began. The "Echo Taps" thudded into hearts on the pier below. Old men stiffly reached for handkerchiefs as Midway ceased being an American Navy warship. Midway sailors, still in formation with their backs to the ship, looked into the wizened, sorrowful eyes of men nearly four times their age. Some lowered their eyes in a wash of memories. Sadness and reflection turned the pier into a mosaic of individual solitude.

Captain Ernst slowly walked down the gangway, cradling the commis-sioning pennant. He paused before stepping onto the pier. Behind him, a thunder began to roll out of the east over San Diego's skyline. It developed into an powerful, almost invigorating roar as four F/A-18 Hornets of the VF-151 Vigilantes, one of Midway's Desert Storm squadrons, passed only a few hundred feet overhead, down the length of Midway's now-deserted flight deck and out over the Pacific.

At precisely 1200 on April 11, 1992, Midway Magic rested.

Several weeks passed before Midway was ready to be towed up the West Coast to Bremerton, Washington. After sailing across every ocean on the globe, standing marathon posts in harm's way, and steaming at flank speed on humanitarian missions, giant lines tethered the powerless carrier to a seagoing tug.

On the morning of departure Executive Officer John Schork was still at NAS North Island. As Midway was pulled from the pier, he jumped in his car and drove around the air station's perimeter road so he could watch his carrier greet the Pacific one last time. He sat for a long time and watched as Midway's carcass moved under another ship's power.

Yet Midway's spirit lingered. As the carrier was pulled slowly north along the Southern California coast, its rudders locked in place, the small armada passed Catalina Island. As it did, Midway began to drift to the left of center, a seemingly impossible feat for a ship with no power and no steering. It appeared to be drifting *into the prevailing current*, toward deeper water and, ultimately Japan. The crew on the seagoing tug was at a loss to explain it. Alarmed, they slowed and then resumed power, watching carefully. After several minutes Midway settled back in behind the tug, yielding to destiny.

The 47-year odyssey had come to an end. In its wake, the world politic had forever changed; the lives of 200,000 Americans had been influenced in ways others couldn't begin to fathom; and a Navy standard of reliability and accomplishment had been permanently forged as the yardstick to measure others.

After more than 17,000 editions of the "Plan of the Day," Midway's final POD reflected that measure of excellence:

> *Today we say goodbye to a proud warrior. As we leave, each of us will take our memories of Midway with us. I will remember the "Magic." For years I had heard of it, but never really understood. Having been on other carriers whose attitude was "We can't do that," when I got here in January 1991 the real spirit of Midway hit me: "What can we do to make it work?" It was pervasive—everyone's attitude was—work together and we can do anything. In the last 16 months, we fought a war, conducted a major evacuation, changed homeports, "aced" an INSURV, and smoothly decommissioned the ship. We did it safely and professionally. Yes, I will remember the "Magic"—you guys were the "Magic." It was a privilege to sail with you, best of luck in the future.*
>
> *—John Schork*
> *Executive Officer*
> *Midway*

AN EPILOGUE
OF REBIRTH

M ORE THAN A DECADE LATER, Midway sat quiet, tied to a crusted berth
at Puget Navy Shipyard in Bremerton, Washington. Rust had streaked
and paint had peeled. The heavy salt air had separated patches of nonskid
flight deck coating from the steel plating below. The island's gray paint had
paled over time. The coveted best-carrier "E" and silhouettes of MiGs shot
down over Vietnam had become ghostly images, like hieroglyphics from
another age. The larger ex–USS Independence and Ranger carriers on
either side dwarfed Midway as it lifted and sank with the passing tides.

Below deck, Midway was a honeycombed cave, the air heavy with the
smell of oily rubber and hydraulic fluid. Massive blue air tubes snaked
through compartments, up ladders and outside, sucking salty must from
Midway's innards. Regardless, mold in the heads had spread across shower
stalls and sinks. In hundreds of workspaces, countless pieces of electronic
equipment had been removed, leaving gaping holes in consoles with electrical entrails coiled on counters. Dust had caked in the long-vacated crew
berths, coating worn letters and creased photos left on the deck by sailors
and overlooked by the decommissioning crew.

Hi son,
We love you and miss you a lot. It sure was nice talking to you. It
was sure hot here today. It was real hot here yesterday. It has

cooled down quite a bit since a couple of days ago. It won't be long until school starts. Dad goes on nights starting Mon. Aug. 31.

How come you will be out at sea only a week? That seems like a short time. You sure are seeing the world. We got your letter and postcard today. It sure is pretty. How far are you from Tokyo? Have you ever rode the bullet train? Bet it would be fun to ride.

Our garden is just about all done now. A few tomatoes left, but not many. Well, I will close for now, and write when you have some time. We love and miss you a lot. Thank you for all of the postcards. It sure is nice that you can send some home to let us see what it is like over there. Bye for now.

Love you very much and miss you,
Dad & Mom

The 1987 letter was found by a visitor aboard Midway 15 years later. Mom still lived on the same street in a northern California town, and still grew her backyard tomatoes that she shared with her unemployed truck-driver son who had once experienced the world as Midway patrolled at the tip of the sword.

Some men never came home. More than 175 had died on Midway. Young men with names like Donahue, Hofman, and DuCros. The sons and brothers of the Medford, Belle Glade, and Columbus families. Others who were "snipes," "grapes," and "shooters" had come of age aboard, leaving their childhood behind in engineering spaces, galleys, and gun tubs as Midway set new standards of diligence, accomplishment, and perseverance. (When the carrier Abraham Lincoln made headlines in 2003 for being at sea 282 days, it was noted that the deployment was the longest since 1973 when a carrier named Midway had spent a marathon 327 days at sea.)

Then they had moved on, forever changed after closing a life's chapter aboard Midway. Yet the magic remained part of their lives. It took Ed Lawton, one of the thousands of Mt. Pinatubo refugees rescued by Midway in 1992, more than 10 years to track down the carrier's captain, Larry "Pappy" Ernst, in Arizona so Lawton could pay his respects and say thank you.

While Midway rested, Milt Pertl worked tirelessly in Pennsylvania to help two Vietnamese he had befriended. They were among the thousands rescued by Midway during the "Night of the Helicopters" when South

Vietnam fell in 1975. He made it his mission to find the helicopter crew that had ferried them to safety so they, too, could express their appreciation of a second chance at life.

Others stayed in the Navy, sometimes under extraordinary circumstances. Jack Ensch, the backseater for "the world's greatest aviator," Mugs McKeown, flew off Midway one day in 1972 and hours later found himself a prisoner of war. While spending months in captivity, his mangled thumb was amputated without anesthetic shortly before a Vietnamese "doctor" realigned both dislocated elbows by yanking on each arm. Ensch survived, served with honor, and was awarded the Navy Cross, Legion of Merit, Bronze Star (two awards), Purple Heart (two awards), Meritorious Service Medal (three awards), Air Medal (eighteen awards), Navy Commendation Medal (three awards), and Prisoner of War Medal, among others.

The courageous Vietnamese pilot who had dared land his Cessna "Bird Dog" on Midway in 1975 with his wife and five children crammed into the fuselage built a new life in America. He waited tables at Disneyworld 22 years later, his children having been educated and now settled in new lives. His daring trust in Midway Magic had been rewarded many times over.

Meanwhile, an invisible Midway network grew across the country and across generations. A decade passed before Midway's final captain, Larry Ernst, reconnected with his executive officer, John Schork. More than 22 years after serving together on Midway, a couple of weapons specialists, Gary Dunbar and Brian Pellar, learned of each other's whereabouts. Both had survived Midway's collision with the Panamanian freighter one night in 1980. Almost 30 years had passed since two doctors aboard Midway mended bodies ripped in combat. They discovered both were still practicing medicine, one in San Diego and the other about 90 miles away in Los Angeles. When they met over lunch, it had been almost 50 years since photographer's mate Bob Haskins had seen Jim Braden. It was nearly 57 years since Eugene Scott had stood in the snow on Midway's flight deck during Operation Frostbite, taking orders from his squadron's skipper, Dick Parker. He found Parker quietly living in retirement in Coronado, California. nearly three generations later.

Meanwhile by 2000, Midway's future in the Navy's mothball fleet was growing short, its destiny uncertain. Older sister ships that hadn't been sold to foreign countries had become razor blades and ocean reefs. After 47 years of service and eight years of quiet, Midway's end was near.

Only a few months after decommissioning in 1992, a group of San Diego leaders had begun to develop a vision of Midway as a naval aviation museum. Their goal was to work with the Navy, take custody of the carrier, and assign Midway a final mission, one of becoming the American flagship of naval aviation museums in the cradle of naval aviation, San Diego.

By 2003, hundreds of volunteers had joined the campaign. More than two dozen permits and approvals had been secured as a prelude to providing the Navy with more than 2,200 pages of application documentation on everything from earthquake proofing to hull maintenance to a detailed business plan. Thousands from across the country had contributed financially to the effort that required nearly $2 million in engineering, administrative, and other costs *before* the Navy would make the ultimate decision on Midway's fate.

The campaign crested midsummer while Midway veterans across the country went on with their lives. Most were unaware of the effort to save Midway. Weapons specialist Brian Pellar had become an artist in nearby Orange County and frequently visited friends in San Diego. Pellar made a point to visit San Diego's Navy Pier 11A, the proposed site for the Midway museum. The pier was a historical landmark. Countless Navy warships had tied to it, including the Navy's first carrier, the USS Langley (CV-1). Pellar was crestfallen when a guard told him that perhaps the Secretary of the Navy wouldn't award Midway to San Diego because it would be another terrorist target in a bay filled with dozens of active-duty Navy ships, an air station, and secret installations.

Bob Haskins was spending his summer in the Berkshires of western Massachusetts, not far from Savoy where he had grown up before becoming a Midway photographer's mate in 1953. He was establishing a trailer as a vacation home on a forested acre he had owned for years, a project that delighted his three-and-a-half year-old granddaughter.

Retired and now a golfer, gunner's mate John Clancy still missed his long talks with John Hipp in Midway's gun tubs on the blackest nights when the Milky Way split the sky in two as the two men shared life tens of thousands of miles from home. It broke Clancy's heart when he later learned Hipp had died while still a young man.

Then, on August 29, 2003, Acting Secretary of the Navy Hansford

T. Johnson awarded Midway to the nonprofit San Diego Aircraft Carrier Museum. Midway would be towed from Bremerton to Oakland and then to San Diego, arriving in San Diego Bay just after sunset on January 6, 2004. Within six months Midway—once the largest ship in the world—would open as the world's largest floating museum.

After nearly 12 years of rest, Midway Magic was rekindled in 2004. A magic still burning in the hearts and souls of those who had walked her decks, fired the boilers, and endured marathon sea deployments of draining boredom punctured by terror on a floating island of America, thousands of miles from home.

Midway has embarked on a new mission. A mission of tribute, respect, preservation, and education as naval aviation undergoes a twenty-first-century transformation. Yet for all the changes that lie ahead, naval aviation's soul will remain in the hearts of the 18-, 19- and 20-year-olds who shoulder the load and meet each day's mission. In Midway's case, it was magic.

ACKNOWLEDGMENTS

MIDWAY MAGIC IS CONTAGIOUS. It seeps into the skin and colors the world with attitude, confidence, and grit. It infects all who come in contact with it. The magic struck me in 1995. I had volunteered to assist a group of visionaries who had a crazy idea that they could transform the Navy's most accomplished aircraft carrier—then in mothballs—into the American flagship of naval aviation museums. The notion was to establish, in the cradle of naval aviation, San Diego, California, a museum, tribute, educational center, and cultural heritage attraction. It would be located only a few miles from where wooden platforms, each about the size of a basketball court, had been built on dirt nearly a century earlier so that pilots in biplanes could learn to land at sea.

My condition became chronic when I peeled back Midway's history as I talked with hundreds of the 200,000 Americans who had served aboard the carrier. The result is this chronicle, one based largely on their stories, personal histories, ship's documentation, and official Navy records. Their respect for Midway was both heartfelt and profound. When inevitable discrepancies developed, the author made judgment calls that often tilted toward those who had walked the flight deck, mended the broken bodies, scraped the boilers, and flown among the gods.

Like Midway, this book is possible only because of the people who gave it life. The leaders of the San Diego Aircraft Carrier Museum—Alan

Uke, Admiral. Riley Mixson, John DeBlanc, Patti Roscoe, David Flohr, Chuck Nichols, Pete Litrenta, Ed Fike, John Hawkins, and Reint Reinders, to name a few—were extraordinarily supportive and encouraging to the development of the first chronicle of Midway's odyssey. Dozens more played key support roles.

Hundreds of Midway sailors were generous with both their time and cherished Midway collections. Men like Vern Jumper welcomed me into their homes time and again for interviews. Others, like Maddie Register and Bob Haskins, made enormous contributions by sharing their personal Midway historical collections, which ultimately found a permanent home in Midway's museum archives. Still others, like Buzz Nau, kindly read over my shoulder to help ensure Navy nomenclature and nuance accuracy.

Officials at the Naval Historical Center and at the National Archives and Records Administration were patient and professional in helping an apprentice navigate the maze of our nation's archive collections in search of the tiny sliver centered on Midway.

My agent, B. J. Robbins, was the rudder that kept *Midway Magic* true to course, steering me clear of the research-rapture shoals that threatened to ground the project. Her professional counsel was unerring, even when I was sure the backstory of one of Midway's 40 commanding officers or the 1943 engineering considerations was both fascinating and inescapable to a narrative that spanned 47 years. Together with the very professional publishing team at CDS, *Midway Magic* stayed on course and on mission.

Very special friends demonstrated marathon patience and asked about the project, even as its development stretched to two years. They always remained interested, even in the face of glacial progress. Across the Saturday night dinner table or over lunch, their sincere interest was both heartwarming and inspiring. I couldn't let them down. I had the bug.

And through it all, two people gave me my bearing and a sense of mission every single day. Their uncompromising optimism—before reading a single word—steeled my resolve when interviews dragged and searches proved fruitless. My wife, Marjorie, and our son, Garrett, frame my life with meaning and purpose. They are my magic.

APPENDICES

STATISTICS –
GENERAL FACTS

Keel Laid	October 27, 1943	Commissioning	September 10, 1945
Propulsion	Conventional	Horsepower	200,000 shaft plus
Speed	30 plus knots (35 mph)	Length overall	1001' 6"
Extreme width	258"	Displacement (full)	70,000 tons
Height (total	222' 3"	Area of flight deck	4.02 acres
Number of propellers	4	Weight per propeller	22 tons
Height of propellers	18 ft.	Number of catapults	2
Aircraft elevators	3	Telephones	1,500 plus
Crew	4,500 plus	Boilers	12
Aircraft	up to 80	Compartments	over 2,000
Electric Motors	over 2,000	Miles of piping	about 200
Miles of copper conductors	3,000	Miles of fire hose	4.5
Ship fuel capacity	2.23 million gallons	Jet fuel capacity	1,241,534 gallons

Population electrical power could serve:
   1 million

Homes fuel supply could heat
   in 1 year   3,000

Monthly payroll   1,200,000

Ship's stores   6

Daily food requirements:

Bread	1,000 loaves
Vegetables	5,000 lbs.
Meat	4,5000 lbs.
Dry provisions	20,000 lbs.
Potatoes	3,000 lbs.

Generated power equivalent
   in locomotives   140

Monthly business in ship's
   stores $1 million

Fresh water produced daily
          240,000 gallons

Meals served daily   13,000

Ship's capacity of consumable goods:

Dry provisions	1,500,300 lbs.
Vegetables	205,000 lbs.
Meat	240,000 lbs.
Dairy	66,3000 lbs.

SOURCE: USS Midway Decommissioning Ceremony, 1992

USS MIDWAY
AN ABBREVIATED
CHRONOLOGY

October 27, 1943	Midway's keel is laid. Midway, built on a Montana-class battleship hull, becomes the most sophisticated carrier in the world.
March 20, 1945	Launched and christened.
September 10, 1945	Commissioned, weighing 45,000 tons. First ship too large for the Panama Canal; largest ship for the next ten years. Missed World War II by one week.
March 1946	Operation Frostbite pushes the envelope of sub-Arctic naval air operations. Midway teaches the U.S. Navy how to fly among the icebergs.
September 6, 1947	Midway successfully launches a captured German V-2 rocket in Operation Sandy: the dawn of naval missile warfare.
Oct. 1947–Mar. 1948	First deployment to Mediterranean; mistral off France capsizes launch, drowning eight crewmen.
October 5, 1949	Commander Ashworth flies P2V-3 Neptune from Midway off Virginia to the Panama Canal and then San Diego, 4,800 miles nonstop in 25 hours, 40 minutes.
Jan.–May 1952	Fifth deployment to Mediterranean during which craps game robbery produces worldwide headlines.

December 1954	Departs for world cruise, reassigned to Pacific Fleet where the "Midway Magic" reputation takes hold.
October 1955	Decommissioned at Puget Sound Naval Shipyard for modernization that includes adding an angled flight deck, three catapults, and other improvements that enable simultaneous launch and recovery operations.
September 1957	Recommissioned, now 62,000 tons.
June 13, 1963	A pilot lands aboard a carrier for the first time without control of his aircraft. The fully automatic landing system tested on Midway proves a technology vital to the establishment of the space program.
August 1965	First combat deployment to Vietnam. Midway aviators shoot down the first MiG of the war. Two more are shot down three days later.
February 1966	Decommissioned for four-year overhaul: flight deck grows from 2.82 to 4.02 acres. Delays ultimately produce a $202 million price tag that sparks national controversy and scuttles overhaul plans for the other two Midway-class carriers.
October 1973	First carrier homeported abroad, in Yokosuka, Japan.
April 1975	Conducts Operation Frequent Wind (fall of Saigon), taking aboard 3,073 refugees.
Mar.–Nov. 1986	The Great Blister Experiment in Yokosuka to improve stability and reduce legendary rolling.
January 1991	The oldest and smallest carrier in the fleet, Midway is the flagship of Persian Gulf operations in Desert Storm. Outperforms all other carriers in the war.
June 1991	In Operation Fiery Vigil in the Philippines, Midway takes aboard Air Force evacuees from the Mt. Pinatubo eruption.
April 11, 1992	Decommissioned at North Island NAS (San Diego).
January 6, 2004	Returns to San Diego after a 13-day tow from Bremerton, Washington, and becomes a naval aviation museum.
June 7, 2004	Opens as the San Diego Aircraft Carrier Museum.

SOURCES AND
BIBLIOGRAPHY

EXTENDED CREW INTERVIEWS/EXTENDED EMAIL CORRESPONDENCE

Bazinet, Gerald

Beard, Tim

Beddoe, Allen

Bell, Jim

Bowman, Mike

Brown, Tom

Burin, Jim

Calderone, Anthony

Carmack, Aaron

Carmody, Dale

Carver, "Gun Boss"
    (Aboard USS Enterprise)

Casey, Neal

Cebrowksi, Art

Center, Bill

Cherenson, Ed

Clancy, John

Clayton, Pete

Cobb, Mike

Coblenz, Don

Cochran, Barney

Conroy, Phil

Corsi, Joe

Coulter, Gene

Crane, Doug

Cvitkovich, Larry

Dall, Raymond

Davis, James

Dennig, Tony

Deel, Charles

Delaney, Joe

Derby, Francis

Dickensheet, Don

Doremus, Robert

Dresser, Bob

Dulansky, Shane

Dunbar, Gary

Eld, Dale

Spearly, Ed

Prendergast, Tim

Saucier, Steve

Schork, John

Stalaboin, Joe

Stark, Jon

Stock, Monty

Struchen, Don

Sullivan, Ken

Swift, Doug

Triola, Dominick

Turner, Tom

Uke, Alan

Utterback, Tom

Van Cleef, Jacque

Vance, Donald

Vandiver, Gordon

Vinezeano, Tony

Virag, Larry

Wanish, George

Wells, Jim

Wood, Victor

Zingheim, Karl

Zullo, William

Books

Baldwin, Sherman. *Iron Claw.* New York: William Morrow & Co., 1996

Blair, Col. Arthur H. *At War in the Gulf: A Chronology.* College Station, TX: Texas A&M University, 1992.

Brown, Charles H. *Dark Sky, Black Sea.* Annapolis: Naval Institute Press, 1999

Clancey, Tom. *Carrier.* New York: Berkley Books, 1999

Coletta, Paolo E. *American Secretaries of the Navy.* Annapolis, MD: Naval Institute Press, 1980

Davis, Martin. *Traditions and Tales of the Navy.* Missoula, MT: Pictorial Histories Publishing Co., 2001

Drendel, Lou. *And Kills MiG.* Warren, MI: Squadron/Signal Publications, Inc., 1974

Fahey, John A. *Wasn't I the Lucky One.* Virginia Beach VA: B&J Books, 2000

Francillon, Rene. *Vietnam: The War in the Air.* London: Aerospace Publishing, 1987

Francillon, Rene J. *Tonkin Gulf Yacht Club.* Annapolis, MD: Naval Institute Press, 1988

Freeman, Gregory A. *Sailors to the End.* New York: Harper Collins, 2002

Friedman, Norman. *U.S. Aircraft Carriers.* Annapolis, MD: U.S. Naval Institute, 1983

Gaddis, John Lewis. *We Now Know. Rethinking Cold War History.* Oxford: Oxford University Press. 1997

Gardner, Lloyd C. & Gittinger, Ted. *Vietnam The Early Decisions.* University of Texas Press, Austin, TX. 1997

Goodspeed, M. Hill. *U.S. Naval Aviation.* Pensacola, FL: Hugh Lauter Associates, 2001

Gordon, Michael R. and Trainor, Gen. Bernard E. *The General's War.* New York: Little Brown & Co, 1995

Green, Michael. *Aircraft Carriers.* New York, NY: MetroBooks, 1999

Hallion, Richard P. *Storm Over Iraq.* Washington, DC: Smithsonian Institution Press, 1992

Hersh, Seymour M. *The Target Is Destroyed.* New York, NY: Random House, 1986

Holland Jr., Admiral W. J. *The Navy.* Washington, DC: Lauter Levin Assoc., 2000

Ireland, Bernard. *The Aircraft Carrier: An Illustrated History.* Seacaucus, NJ: Chartwell Books, 1979

Issacs, Jeremy. *Cold War, An Illustrated History, 1945–1991.* New York: Little, Brown & Co., 1998

Lawson, Robert. *Carrier Air War.* China: Barnes & Noble Books, 1999

Levinson, Jeffrey L. *Alpha Strike Vietnam.* Navato, CA: Presidio Press, 1989

Long, Art. *Tail-End Charlie.* Internet-published: 1stBooks, Inc., Date unknown

Love, Robert W., Jr. *History of the U.S. Navy, 1942–1991.* Harris, PA: Stackpole Books, 1992

Marolda, Edward J. *Carrier Operations: The Vietnam War.* New York, NY: Bantam Books. 1987

Marolda, Edward J., and Oscar Fitzgerald. *The United States Navy and the Vietnam Conflict, Volume II.* Washington, DC: Naval Historical Center, 1986

Marolda, Edward J., and Robert J. Schneller Jr. *Shield & Sword.* Annapolis, MD: Naval Institute Press, 1998.

McCauley, Martin. *Russia, America & The Cold War 1949–1991.* England: Pearson Education Ltd., 1998

Merskey, Peter B., and Norman Polmar. *The Naval Air War in Vietnam.* Annapolis, MD: Nautica & Aviation Publishing, Co., 1981

Morrison, Wilbur H. *Pilots, Man Your Planes.* Central Point, OR: Hellgate Press. 1999

Musciano, Water A. *Warbirds of the Seas.* Atglen, PA: Schiffer Publishing, 1994

Nelson, Derek and Parsons, Dave. *Life and Death Stories from the U.S. Navy's Approach Magazine.* Motorbooks, Intl. Osceola, WI, 1991

Nichols, John, and Barrett Tillman. *On Yankee Station.* Bluejacket Books, 1987

Polmar, Norman. *Aircraft Carriers.* New York: Doubleday & Co., 1969

Polmar, Norman. *Chronology of the Cold War at Sea 1945–1991.* Annapolis: Naval Institute Press, 1998

Pawlowski, Gareth L., *Flat-Tops and Fledglings.* London: A.S. Barnes & Co., 1971

Raven, Alan. *U.S. Battleships.* Annapolis, MD: U.S. Naval Institute, 1985

Stine, G. Harry. *ICBM,* New York: Orion Books, 1991

Unknown. *The Cook Book of the U.S. Navy.* U.S. Government Printing Office, 1945

Vistica, Gregory L. *Fall from Glory. The Men Who Sank the U.S. Navy.* New York: Simon & Schuster, 1995.

Walker, Martin. *The Cold War.* New York: Henry Holt & Co., 1993

Wragg, David. *Carrier Combat.* Annapolis, MD: Naval Institute Press, 1997

Historical Records

Auer, James. (political advisor to the Commander of U.S. Naval Forces, Japan) Oral History Interview by Koji Murata, March, 1996

All Hands, April 1966

The Bluejackets' Manual, U.S. Naval Institute, 1951

"Blister Letter," from Capt. J. H. Cooper, USN, to Senator Phil Gramm, February 9, 1988

Captain James O'Brien's letter to Midway families/dependents, August 1, 1965

Compass, The. United States Naval Training Center, Bainbridge, MD, 1952

"Cold Weather Operations" Attire rules for pilots on Operation Frostbite, 1946

Command History by Capt. R. D. Mixson, 1986

Commissioning Ceremony Program

"Conduct of the Persian Gulf War," by the United States Navy, 1992

Correspondence regarding Mt. Pinatubo evacuation by Battle Group Foxtrot flag officer RADM Tim Wright, June 1991

Cruise Book of USS Midway, 1947–48

Cruise Book of USS Midway, 1950

Cruise Book of USS Midway, 1952

Cruise Book of USS Midway, 1953

Cruise Book of USS Midway, 1954

Cruise Book of USS Midway, 1954–55

Cruise Book of USS Midway, 1958–59

Cruise Book of USS Midway, 1959–60

Cruise Book of USS Midway, 1963–64

Cruise Book of USS Midway, 1965

Cruise Book of USS Midway, 1971

Cruise Book of USS Midway, 1972

Cruise Book of USS Midway, 1973

Cruise Book of USS Midway, 1974

Cruise Book of USS Midway, 1976

Cruise Book of USS Midway, 1978–79

Cruise Book of USS Midway, 1979–80

Cruise Book of USS Midway, 1984–85

Cruise Book of USS Midway, 1985–87

Cruise Book of USS Midway, 1990–91

Cruise Report, September 3, 1952

Deck Log, January 12, 1973

Deck Log, May 11, 1972

Deck Log, May 18, 1972

Deck Log, May 23, 1972

Deck Log, April 11, 1992

Deck Logs, September 2–5, 1947

Decommissioning ceremony video, April 11, 1992

Decommissioning correspondence, 1992

    President George Bush

    Secretary of Defense Dick Cheney

    Secretary of the Navy H. Lawrence Garrett III

    Chief of Naval Operations Frank B. Kelso II

    Commander in Chief, Pacific Fleet Admiral R. J. Kelly

    COMNAVAIRPAC Vice Admiral Edwin R. Kohn

Decommissioning publication of the USS Midway (CV-41) San Diego, CA, April 11, 1992

Dispatches: Trading Movies, May 18, 1946

EISRA-86, Report of the USS Midway, 1986

"Farewell to Midway" (decommissioning poem by Commander Gary N. Cook, USN, retired)

Forum 41 newsletter, June 1971

Gay, Lt. George, Biography in 1992 CV-41 Decommission Information Kit

Grapevine Drydocker newsletter, February 18, 1966

Hanish, Land G., *1965 USS Midway Cruise Book*. Marceline, MO: Walsworth, 1966

Hull Department Bills, USS Midway (CVB-51), Register No. 1 (Restricted), 1950

Lest We Forget, April 10, 1972–3, March 1973

Medical Cruise Report, WESTPAC, 1972–73

Memorandum by State Department Policy Planner Gerard C. Smith on Quemoy/Matsu Crisis. August 13, 1958

Midway Newsletters:

Midway Current, April 26, 1947

Midway Current, June 7, 1947

Midway Current, June 18, 1948

Midway Current, February 25, 1949

Midway Current, April 1, 1949

Midway Current, January 29, 1950

Midway Current, February 5, 1950

Midway Current, February 12, 1950

Midway Current, February 19, 1950

Midway Current, February 10, 1955

Midway Current, July 1955

Midway Missile, January 1959

Midway Missile, March 1959

Midway News, October 27, 1945

Midway News, December 11, 1945

Midway News, February 28, 1946

Midway News, March 7, 1946

Midway News, March 14, 1946

Midway News, May 12, 1946

Midway News, June 5, 1991

Midway News, June 18, 1991

Midway Spectrum, May, 1975

Midway Spectrum, September–December 1977

Midway West, November 29, 1963

National Intelligence Estimate 11-4-82: "The Soviet Challenge to U.S. Security Interests."

Navy Times article, October 26, 1981

"Navy Unit Citation," issued by the Secretary of the Navy. November 22, 1965

"Nick Danger, Third Eye," (collected adventures) by J. R. Reddig (1979–80)

Operation Frostbite Cruise Report, 1946

Operation Sandy booklet given to crew aboard the USS Midway, September 6, 1947

Personal information booklet, *This is the USS Midway (CVB-41)*, September 1, 1945

Plank Owner Certificate, September 10, 1945

"Plan of the Day for USS Midway," March 28, 1946

"Plan of the Day for USS Midway," April 11, 1992

"Report of USS Midway CV-41 EISRA-86," by R. D. Mixson. February 19, 1987

Roster of Officers, June 1, 1946

Shakedown Cruise Report, November 26, 1945

Ship's Aviation Summary, 1959

Ship's History, 1946

Ship's History, 1955

Ship's History, 1957

Ship's History, 1962

Ship's History, 1970

Ship's History, 1992

Ship's Service Restaurant Menu, Naval Station Guantanamo Bay, Cuba, circa 1950

Shipyard Bulletin, *Newport News Shipbuilding and Dry Dock Co.*, September 1945

Snoopy cartoon series, April 18, 1972–January 9, 1973, USS Midway Air Wing.

Thanksgiving Dinner Menu (on board), November 22, 1945

Underway Training Report, November 29, 1949

United States Congress Biographical Directory: Clare Booth Luce http://bioguide.congress.gov/scrips/biodisplay.pl?index=L000497

U.S. Navy news release, July 7, 1974

U.S. Navy news release, June 14, 1963

US Navy video of the crash of LCDR George Duncan, July 1951

US Navy video of UNREP, date unknown

US Navy video of USS Midway Commissioning, September 1945

Welcome Aboard booklet by Capt. Blackburn, date unknown

Miscellaneous

CNN Special Cold War Episode transcript: "Excerpts from Kennan's Long Telegram" www.cnn.com/SPECIALS/cold.war/episodes/02/documents /kennan/

http://midwayjoesnavy.myqth.com/2_USS_Midway_C.html

Howard, Lt. Col. William L., *"Operation Paperclip."* U.S. Army Ordnance Corps website www.goordnance.apg.army.mil/oppaperclip.htm

Letter from A. J. Booth, Deputy Director of Naval History to McLean Johnson, May 31, 1989

Letter to Captain Larry Ernst, CV-41 from Mt. Pinatubo evacuee, June 28, 1991

Letter to James H. Kelly from U.S. Navy, February 1, 1987

Letter to Senator Phil Gramm from U.S. Navy, February 9, 1988

Neidermair, John C., Naval Architect Reminesences, 1978

Neptune Papers III, Naval Nuclear Accidents at Sea, Greenpeace International (www.lostsubs.com/neptune_papers_3.pdf)

Online Dictionary of American Naval Fighting Ships, USS Natoma Bay

Online Hazegray Organization: "Death and Rebirth of the Supercarrier," www.hazegray.org/navhist/carriers/supercar.htm

USS Constellation Overnight Stay Notes, March 22–23, 2002, www.globalsecurity.org/military/systems/ship/cv-41.htm

www.chinfo.navy.mil/navpalib/ships/carriers/histories/cv41-midway/cv41 -midway.html

Articles, other publications

"2 killed, 16 injured in carrier Midway fire," *Navy Times.* July 2, 1990

"2 MIGs Shot Down 50 Miles From Hanoi," *Washington Star.* June 17, 1965

"12100 Navy Planes Give Show Today," *New York Times.* October 27, 1945

"A Balanced and Lethal Force," by Vice Adm. John B. Nathman, *Sea Power.* June 2001

"A Milestone in Our Naval History, A History of USS Midway," *Naval Aviation News.* July–August 1992

"A Word With You," *Midway Multiplex.* 1987

"Aircraft Carrier MIDWAY," *Shipyard Bulletin.* Newport News Shipbuilding. March 1945

"Aircraft Carriers of the US Navy," Mayflower Books, NYC. Date unknown.

"All-Weather Carrier Landing System," *U.S. Naval Institute Proceedings.* July 1965

"America Pays Honor to Its Heroic Navy," "Keep Fleet Strong Navy Chiefs Urge," "Truman To Review Fleet Here Today," *New York Times,* October 27, 1945

"Appendicitis Victim Taken from Labrador Cutter," *Boston Globe.* March 12, 1946

"Arctic Battleground," *Time* magazine. March, 1946

"Armed with memories, sailor returns to Midway," *Rochester Times-Union.* March 1992

"Being Toss Off Carrier Thrills Our 300-Pounder," *Boston Globe.* March 5, 1946

"Big Gray Ships Move Into Line for Grand Review by President," unidentified New York newspaper, October 25, 1945

"Carrier Midway Back From Arctic Finds Navy Effective in Frigid Zone," *The Christian Science Monitor.* March 30, 1946

"Carrier Midway Damaged in Storm off Greenland," *Unidentified Newspaper.* March 9, 1946

"Carrier Midway is retired—again," *San Diego Union-Tribune.* April 12, 1992

"Carrier Midway Pilot Lost Attempting Landing at Sea," *Boston Herald.* 1946

"Carriers Could Launch A-Bombs From Arctic," *Boston Herald.* March 9, 1946

"Cost-Effectiveness of Conventionally and Nuclear-Powered Aircraft Carriers," Report by the General Account Office. August 1998

"Crash on Carrier Off Vietnam Kills 4," *Washington Post.* October 25, 1972

"CVB Shakedown," *Naval Aviation News.* February 1946

"CVB's: The Battle Carriers." *Naval Aviation News.* January 1963

"Crew of IRONCLAW 606 Remembered." *Flagship Flyer.* November 27, 1987

"Desert Storm at Sea." *Proceedings Naval Review 1991*

"Espionage Against the United States by American Citizens," *Defense Personnel Security Research Center.* July 2002

Excerpt from *Midway Multiplex.* January 25, 1987

"F-4 Phantom: End of an Era," USS Midway publication. April 1986

"Farwell, Midway Magic," *Naval Aviation News.* July–August, 1992

"Fleet Maneuvers in Arctic Serve Warning on Reds," *Lubbock Evening Journal.* September 5, 1952

"Flyers Press Their Attack in N. Viet Nam," *Washington Star.* June 21, 1965

"Fond Farewell to the USS Midway," *Sea Classics.* May 1992

"Gale Makes Ship 'Loop'," *Daily Record.* Circa March 12, 1946.

"Giant Carrier Heads North to Test Arctic Equipment," *Boston Globe.* March 2, 1946

"Giant Carrier Midway Ends Arctic Workout," *Boston Globe.* March 28, 1946

"History of Ships Named Midway," Office of the Chief of Naval Operations. July 19, 1968

"History of the Attack Aircraft Carrier, CVA-41," US Navy Public Information Office. June 13, 1960

"History of the USS Midway," Office of Naval Records and History. 1947 (est.)

"History of the USS Midway," Office of the Chief of Naval Operations. 1960 (est.)

"Home-Porting, Midway Style." *Naval Aviation News.* March 1980

"How Warships Will Line Up in the Hudson River," *New York Sun."* October 25, 1945

"In gulf, fears of war in season of peace," *Philadelphia Enquirer.* December 20, 1990

"In Memoriam," *USS Midway*. June 25, 1990

"In Memoriam," *USS Midway CV-41*. November 24, 1987

"Japan: The Meaning of the Flap," *Friday Morning*. June 5, 1981

"Japanese Protestors Await Midway," *Friday Morning*. June 5, 1981

"Jet Plane Tested Aboard Flattop in New Technique," *Boston Globe*. March 11, 1946

"Know-how Paid Off!" *Approach* magazine. May 1973

"Ky Decorates 4 U.S. Pilots," *Washington Star*. June 22, 1965

"Launch." *The Hook*. Summer 1978

"Life at Sea, U.S. Marine Corps," (recruiting brochure for sea duty). Circa 1950

"Mediterranean: New Focus for East-West Showdown," *U.S. News-World Report*. January 16, 1948

"Midsea Transfer Seen in Bleak North Atlantic," *The Commercial Appeal*. March 16, 1946

"Midway, Ace in the Hole," *Naval Aviation News*. August 1981

"Midway called the 'finest' by her crew," *Navy Times*. September 23, 1991

"Midway Claims Constant Speed Record," *Naval Aviation News*. September 1956

"Midway Due for Overhaul," *Naval Aviation News*. March 1966

"Midway Ends 'Disaster' Cruise." *San Francisco Examiner*. March 26, 1960

"Midway Finds Snow Biggest Foe on its Cruise to Arctic," *Naval Aviation News*. October 1946

"Midway Firing of V-2 Heralds New Weapon, "*Naval Aviation News*. November 1947

"Midway Home from Vietnam Conflict," *Naval Aviation News*. January 1966

"Midway Magicgram," *USS Midway*. Fall 1990

"MIDWAY receives a special present!" *Bluewater Family Bulletin*. December 31, 1987

"Midway Returns from Artic Test," *New York Times*. March 29, 1946

"Midway Task Force 77," *Washington Star*. Date unknown.

"Midway's Back from Operation Frostbite," *Boston American*. March 29, 1946

"Milton Pilot Pioneering Flattop Helicopter Rescues," *Boston Globe.* March 6, 1946

Mixson, Riley. Biography in USS Midway booklet. Date unknown.

"Modernization of the Midway," *U.S. Naval Institute Proceedings.* February 1971

Monitor newspaper article, Boston, MA. January 1970

"Mothballing the Midway," *The San Diego Union-Tribune.* March 1, 1992

"Navy Pilot Lost in Landing Crash on USS Midway," *Boston Globe.* March 2, 1946

"New Carrier Commissioned," *Portsmouth Star.* September 11, 1945

"Now What, Navy?" *Proceedings Naval Review 1992.*

"Of National Defense," *Parade* magazine. December 15, 1957

"Operation Frostbite," *Life* magazine." 1946

"Operation Frostbite," *Midway News* Rotogavure Suplement. March 28, 1946

"Operation Frostbite," *The Bee-Hive.* United Aircraft Corporation. Spring 1946

"Operation Iceberg Battles the Arctic," *Philadelphia Inquirer.* March 31, 1946

"Operations (Shakedown)," *Time* magazine. December 3, 1946

"Powerful Gray Diplomats," *Naval Aviation News.* May 1953

"Recon Marines Volunteer to Jump Out of an A-3," *Whale Watcher.* June 2002

"Retrospective: The Midway Class," *Proceedings.* 1986

"Saigon, The Final 10 Days," *Time* magazine. April 24, 1995

"Sailors Still Throwing Plastic Overboard," *Bluewater Bulletin.* June 19, 1990

"Seeing Earth from 80 Miles Up" *National Geographic,* Vol. XCVIII, No. 4, October 1950, pgs. 511–428

"Seamen Lost When Launch Overturns," *Associated Press.* February 17, 1948

"Spun-Glass Pants Prove Good Foul-Weather Garb," *Boston Globe.* March 7, 1946

"Taking Stock: Worldwide Nuclear Deployments 1998," *Natural Resources Defense Council.* March 1998

"The Jumbo Flattop," *Shipmate.* June 1946

"The Turbulent Post-War Years; Evolution of Aircraft Carriers," *Naval Aviation News.* October 1963

"Two 'Dead" S.D. Fliers Are Vietnam POWs," *San Diego Union*. February 4, 1967

"U.S. Airmen, Civilians Aboard USS Midway Flee Volcano," *United Press International*. June 22, 1991

"U.S. Carrier Midway Is Steaming Into Yokosuka and Bringing With It Host of U.S.-Japan Woes," *Wall Street Journal*. October 4, 1973

"U.S. Marines Said Ordered to Europe Diplomatic Move," *Lubbock Avalanche-Journal*. January 4, 1948

"USS Pueblo: A MIDWAY Warrant Officer Remembers," *Bluewater Bulletin*. October 31, 1990

"USS Midway. First of a Kind, One of a Kind," *The Hook*. Vol. 6, No. 2, pgs. 16–27 Bonita, CA: Tailhook Association. Summer 1978

"USS Midway 41: Welcome." *Circa* 1990.

"USS Midway: 'Sayonara Japan!" *Seahawk* (Commander Fleet Activities, Vol. XXII No. 31). August 9, 1991

USS Midway–themed edition, *The Salute,* Puget Sound Naval Shipyard. November 26, 1957

Various Vietnam War newspaper articles, 1965–72

"Vern Miller Looking for Cold Weather," *Boston Globe*. March 1, 1946

"Welcome Aboard USS Midway CVA-41." *Circa* 1960

"When the Rubber Meets the Road," *Flagship Flyer.* September 9, 1990

"Where They Were," by Robert S. Norris, William M. Arkin, William Burr, *The Bulletin of the Atomic Scientists*. Nov./Dec. 1999

MIDWAY AWARDS
AND CITATIONS

American Campaign Medal	November 1945 – March 1946
World War II Victory Medal	September 1945 – December 1946
China Service Medal	February 1954 – May 1954
National Defense Service Medal	June 1950 – July 1954
Navy Occupation Service Medal	December 1947 – October 1954
Armed Forces Expeditionary Medal	September 1958 – December 1959
Armed Forces Expeditionary Medal	March 1961 – April 1961
Armed Forces Expeditionary Medal	April 1965 – June 1965
Vietnam Service Medal	July 1965 – November 1965
Vietnam Service Medal	May 1971 – June 1971
Vietnam Service Medal	June 1971 – October 1971
Meritorius Unit Commendation	May 1971 – October 1971
Armed Forces Expeditionary Medal	October 1971
Vietnam Service Medal	May 1972 – November 1972
Presidential Unit Citation	April 1972 – February 1973
Vietnam Service Medal	January 1973 – February 1973
National Defense Service Medal	December 1960 – August 1974
Navy Unit Commendation	April 1965 – November 1975
Navy Unit Commendation	April 1975
Armed Forces Expeditionary Medal	April 1975
Humanitarian Service Medal	April 1975
Battle Efficiency Award	January 1976 – June 1977
Battle Efficiency Award	July 1977 – December 1978
Navy Unit Commendation	January 1978 – June 1979
Navy Expeditionary Medal	April 1979 – June 1979
Meritorious Unit Commendation	November 1979 – February 1980
Navy Expeditionary Medal	November 1979 – February 1980
Navy Expeditionary Medal	August 1980 - November 1980
Battle Efficiency Award	July 1980 – December 1981

 IN MEMORIAM

TOO OFTEN, MIDWAY SAILORS NEVER COME HOME. Nearly two hundred made the ultimate sacrifice, sometimes in combat, often by accident, and always tragic. Most were memorialized in the cruise books (some with notations as listed below), published at the conclusion of each deployment or posted on a wooden plaque aboard the carrier. Others were eulogized in the carrier's newspaper. Each sailor should never be forgotten.

As you recall through word and picture
The wanderings of Midway,
Remember too,
Those whose journeys ended here.

For them life's voyage moved
From the ocean of the present
To a sea of experience
We have yet to sail.

For more than forty-five years
Midway has steamed,
Returning to safe harbor—
Mission following mission.

Amid the pulsation of four shafts
And the throb of jets at military power,
The true beat of her heart
Depends on the courageous—

Those who tread the decks,
Populate the compartments,
Operate the machinery,
Serve in harmony.

Remember the faithful
Whose final service
Was given in full measure
On this Gray Lady.

Recall them as part and parcel
Of our life at sea.
Strands of the fabric
Of our being.

In these pages they remain
One with us—
    Our mission,
    Our memory—
    Midway Magic.

—excerpt from the 1989–90 Cruise Book

1940s

Glenn P. Butler
Harry Duane Campbell
William Anton Conrad Jr.
Laird B. Darling
Hershel Harold Donahue
William Louis DuCros
Albert Daniel Fisher
Philip Schubert Hofmann
Jack Jeter
James W. Lamm
Harry Andrew March Jr.
Vincent Geza Nemeth
Raymond Julius Poncel
James Monroe Story
Chester Victor Truchel
Harold Oakley Williams
James Russell Williams

1950s

Charles Roger Babcock
LTJG A. G. Bergevin
LTJG Doulas A. Blank
LTJG J. Brender
John A. Brown
Bradford R. Darling
LTJG A. J. Delano Jr.
ENS William R. Dinsmore
LT James W. Ferguson
Norman C. Fox

LT John J. Hale
LTJG Hugh C. Hayworth
CDR W. H. Heider Jr.
Joe H. Ingram
LTJG R. T. Johnston
G. L. Leland
LTJG William J. Leonard
J. J. Mazy
G. H. Pearce
LTJG J. D. Rivers
LTJG George M. Sostarich
LTJG Noel J. Stace
LTJG Guy T. Thrower
Frank J. Vallone
LTJG James R. Ward
Karl George Wenzel
LTJG T. L. Williams

1960s

Amspacher, ATR3	KIA
LT Jerome S. Andre	
Joseph Edward Armstrong	
John R. Brown	
LTJG Brown	KIA
LTJG Brunhaver	MIA
LT Butler	POW
LTJG Christian	KIA
ENS Joe Eddie Crosswhite Jr.	
Clyde Eugene Davis Jr.	
LCDR Doremus	MIA

LTJG Doughtie	KIA	LTJG Robert A. Clark	MIA
LTJG Reay Gordon English		Bobby Don Cobb	Died
CDR Franke	MIA	Roger Cook	
LT Gollahon	KIA	LCDR William A. Counts	
LCDR Gray	KIA	John Albert Cournoyer	
CDR Charles Edward Guthrie		Charlie Curry	
Maurice Eugene Hanson		Jimmy Lee Davis	
LTJG Robert J. Hendershott		LT Raymond P. Donnelly	Died
LTJG Richard Lee Karns		LCDR Michael W. Doyle	MIA
CDR La Haye	KIA	LT Paul V. Duncan	
CDR Lynn	KIA	LT John C. Ensch	POW
LT Charles R. Mandly		LT Jot Eve	
Russell Marshall Jr.		LTJG David A. Everett	POW
LT McKamey	MIA	John Aboud Faries	
LTJG McMican	KIA	LT James L. Feeney	
LTJG Murray	KIA	Stephen A. Felix	
Plants, ATR3	KIA	Bruce Flanary	
LTJG Romano	KIA	LCDR Donald A. Gerstel	MIA
LT Ronald Samuel Sterret		LTJG Everett E. Goodrow	
CDR Richard McKenzie Tucker		Robert Haakenson Jr.	Died
CDR George Morwood Veling		Richard H. Hall	
		Jeffrey L. Hawley	
		Andrew A. Hill Jr.	

1970s

		Joe Stanley Jones	
LCDR James L. Anderson	Lost at Sea	SGT Roy Frank Kinzalow	
Andrew K. Ball		R. C. Knox	
CDR Charles Barnett	MIA	LCDR George R. Kroyer	
John Bates		Enrique Lazarte	
LTJG William J. Bates		Daniel J. Lefevre	
Christian John Belgum		John Lindahl	Lost at Sea
LTJG Michael S. Bixel	Lost at Sea	Daniel Francis Macey	
Randy A. Blake		Mark H. Maciecki	
Clayton Blankenship	Died	LT Michael T. McCormick	MIA
Troa Bleuins		Edward P. McDonald	Died
Ronald R. Cawein		Joseph McGibbon Jr.	
Daniel Cherry	Died	William McIntosh	
Thomas A. Cipriani		LCDR Henry Benjamin Meyers Jr.	

LT David L. Moody

LT Julian L. Moon III

Edgar S. Moore Jr.

Lee Hampton Moore Jr.

Pedro L. Morales

Gary L. Morgan

Lawrence Winston Morris

Lannie Moss

John Muirhead

LT Aubrey A. Nichols   POW

LCDR Gordon C. Paige   POW

LT E. B. Pearlman

LTJG Michael G. Penn   POW

LT Richard L. Pierson

AT2 Roger Poe

LCDR K. L. Ramussen

Feliciano Reyes

LT Charles R. Rhodes

Plummer Lee Rhodes

LTJG Gary L. Shank   MIA

Johnny A. Stefano

William S. Stringham   Lost at Sea

Leslie Cardell Taylor

LCDR Clarence O. Tolbert   MIA

LCDR Theodore W. Triebel   POW

LT N. J. Tucker

LT D. H. Vonpritchyns

James Watts

CDR Dennis C. Weeks

LTJG George A. Wildridge

Robert Yankoski

Richard J. Zerbe

David James Zuidema

1980s

John Aguirre

John Becerra

Romeo F. Cabrera

LT John Hatcher Carter

LTJG Jay Cook

Joseph H. Courtney

LT Thomas R. Doyle

Enrique Escasa

Candelario Fuentes Jr.

LT David A. Gibson

Leslie Glenn

CDR Justin Noel Greene

Christopher Hayes

LT Douglas A. Hora

Curtis Jones

Michael Knaus

LT Kevin R. Kuhnigk

LTJG R.J. MacFarlane Jr.

LTJG Mark Martone

ENS Christopher Mims

LCDR Timothy K. Murphy

Leo D. Ortiz

John Peyton

Joseph S. Pfleghaar

William A. Phillips Jr.

Steven E. Seitz

Robert Shaffer

LTJG David M. Sperling

Johnny L. Steel

Mark E. Todd

1990s

Kevin J. Hills

Ulrich P. Johnson

Robert S. Kilgore

Anthony Terry

Jeffery A. Vierra

Brian P. Weaver

In addition, hundreds of volunteers worked on the 12-year campaign to bring the decommissioned Midway to San Diego as the future flagship of floating naval aviation museums. Among those who did not live to see Midway arrive in San Diego but will forever remain part of the Midway family are:

Dick Burt
Robert Dose
John Iarrobino
Jim Marvin